Lecture Notes
in Control and Information Sciences 174

Editors: M. Thoma and W. Wyner

IFIP

A.J.M. Beulens, H.-J. Sebastian (Eds.)

Optimization-Based Computer-Aided Modelling and Design

Proceedings of the First Working Conference
of the IFIP TC 7.6 Working Group
The Hague, The Netherlands, 1991

Springer-Verlag
Berlin Heidelberg New York
London Paris Tokyo
Hong Kong Barcelona Budapest

Editors

Adriaan Jacobus Maria Beulens
Haagse Hogeschool Faculty of Informatics
P.O. Box 85862
2508 CN The Hague
The Netherlands

Hans-Jürgen Sebastian
Universität Oldenburg
Fachbereich Informatik
Postfach 2503
W-2900 Oldenburg
Germany

ISBN 3-540-55135-2 Springer-Verlag Berlin Heidelberg New York
ISBN 0-387-55135-2 Springer-Verlag New York Berlin Heidelberg

Printed in Germany

Typesetting: Camera ready by authors
Offsetprinting: Mercedes-Druck, Berlin; Bookbinding: B. Helm, Berlin
60/3020 5 4 3 2 1 0 Printed on acid-free paper

Editorial Preface

The world in which we live and in which organisations function seems to become more and more complex. This increased complexity may be caused by changes of the environment in which organisations and people have to function, changes of the organisations, and of the products and services that they produce. Factors that contribute to this complexity include environmental-, and technological factors.
Environmental complexity may be related to market changes, increased legal constraints for organisations, and social and political developments. Market changes include globalization of markets and changes from a sellers to a buyers market with individual and increasing consumer demands. As a result organisations are confronted with increasing requirements with respect to product specifications and service levels, and shorter product life cycles. Increased legal constraints and obligations may be related to product content, packaging and associated information content, transport and storage constraints, and waste and pollution constraints. Last but not least social and political developments result in changes in our society that may affect the way in which people in organisations are able to cooperate and the way in which these organisations are structured and can be managed.
Technological complexity may be related to the effective and efficient use of new and sophisticated production, product, packaging, storage, transport and information technology. The use of complicated technology must enable organisations to reach and serve their markets in a competitive manner. More and more, information technology (IT) and information are considered to be of strategic importance for organizations, in the sense that IT and information are of vital importance for management, communication and primary processes. As a result the need for information systems (IS) with increased capabilities, improved performance and more "intelligence" has grown rapidly over the last decades and it seems that this need is still growing. This holds in particular for specific types of information systems such as model-based decision support systems (MBDSS) and knowledge based decision support systems (KBDSS). These systems are meant to support decision makers in organizations to perform their tasks efficiently and effectively.
The increased need for more sophisticated systems on one side, and the ever improving price/performance ratio of computer systems and software on the other side, have been providing and continue to provide a challenge for researchers in the areas of computer science, information systems, AI, DSS, operations research, decision making, business management, and cognitive psychology. This challenge is to perform research in the theoretical fields that are pertinent for building effective (KB)DSS and applied research concerned with actually building and implementing DSS.

Researchers have not left this challenge unnoticed during the last two decades. A lot of theoretical and applied research has been performed and has been reported about during conferences and in a variety of scientific papers and books. These developments have also lead to the establishment of several scientific working groups whose members share an interest in a number of topics related to (KB)DSS. The IFIP-TC 7 (System Modelling and Optimization) Working Group 7.6 with the working title "Optimization-Based Computer Aided Modelling and Design" (OCAMD) is one of these working groups. It was founded in 1988 and started its work during the 14'th TC 7 General Conference on System Modelling and Optimization. During this conference some special sessions concerned with the topics of interest for the TC 7.6 working group were held.

The first Working Group Conference "OCAMD" of WG 7.6 was organized by and held at the Faculty of Informatics of the Haagse Hogeschool from April 2-4, 1991, The Hague, The Netherlands.

The working conference dealt with recent developments in the field of modelling and optimization, and with knowledge based decision support systems. This contributed to the realization of the aims of the working group. The aims of the working group 7.6 are:

- to promote theoretical research in the field of optimization including mathematical programming and optimal control;
- to encourage the development of sophisticated knowledge based systems in which refined optimization models and algorithms are used;
- to contribute to the exchange and dissemination of information and collective experience among the interested groups and individuals;
- to support the practical application of such systems in control, engineering, industry, economy etc.

The working conference was attended by about 40 scientists, which originated from Czechoslovakia, France, Germany, Great Britain, Hungary, The Netherlands, Switzerland, and the USA. The papers presented during the conference covered a broad range of topics and applications and comprised mainly:

- Computer Aided Design, Manufacturing and Decision Support Systems that contain optimization models; (CAD, CAM, MRP, DSS - theory and applications).
- Computer Aided Modelling and Design of Information and (Knowledge Based) Decision Support Systems;
- Expert Systems using Optimization Based Reasoning;
- Expert Systems for Optimization or Control Problems.

A selection of papers, accepted by the International Program Committee and presented during the Working Conference, are included into this proceedings volume since:

- they are thought to reflect the current state of research in areas of interest to the field of (KB)DSS, and/or
- they are of value for the dissemination and exchange of information related to research topics of interest, and/or
- they describe relevant practical experiences related to designing, building, implementing and using (KB)DSS.

The International Program Committee and the editors of this volume feel that the first working conference of WG 7.6 contributed to the aims of the working group. Further we feel that the conference contributed to generate new ideas about important research topics for the future. This encompasses research in areas such as improved model management, automatic generation of specific DSS, improved methods to design and implement DSS, and the use of different technologies in DSS. We trust that these proceedings will be of value to both researchers and those interested in building applications in the area of (KB)DSS.

The Editors,

Prof. Adrie J.M. Beulens,
Prof. Hans-Jürgen Sebastian

Contents

A decision support system to determine bankhall concepts

Ing. H.H. Blaauwgeers
Ing. M.T.H. van Hettema
Department of Applied Mathematics
Rabobank Nederland

Abstract:

The Rabobank consists of about 900 local cooperative banks which have in total about 2000 branches. These branches are located in different areas with different types of clients. Therefore the bankhall of a Rabobank is not standardized. A bankhall concept in an agricultural area is not the same as in a suburban area. To assess the functions and the organization of a bankhall the Department of Applied Mathematics has developed a simulation model to support decision making on the various bankhall concepts.

The simulation model has two subsystems. The first subsystem is the dialogue system. This system takes care of the communication with the user and the devices. The second subsystem is the simulation model itself.

Building a decision support system is not a guarantee that it will be used to support decisions. There are several aspects which have to be considered before implementing a decision support system. The (end)users must be convinced that the system is a real help in decision making. The problem of data collection and data handling should not be underestimated. The access to the system has to be simple and flexible. And last but not least, the user has to have the knowledge to interpret the results in the right context.

1. Introduction

The Rabobank organization consists of about 900 local cooperative banks which have about 2000 branches. The 900 local banks have founded the cooperation Rabobank Nederland. Rabobank Nederland supports the local banks and handles all the banking activities which cannot be done by a local bank. Because of the cooperative structure of the Rabobank organization the local banks are responsible for their own business. They have their own interest rates policies, commercial policies, human resource development, allocation policy etcetera.
So each local bank is unique.

To support the local banks, Rabobank Nederland uses some standard characterizations based on client segmentation and product segmentation. All the decision support systems, which have been developed to support local banks and which are dealing with products and clients are based on these segmentation. Although there is a standard characterization each decision support system has to cope with the specific characteristics, behaviour and policies of the local banks.

One of those systems is a bankhall simulation model. This simulation model can be used to solve processing problems in the bankhall and to support decisions concerning the layout of a new bankhall. The decisions are based on workload, number of clients to accommodate and the customer service level.

The bankhall simulation model consists out of two subsystems. The first subsystem is the dialogue system. The dialogue system takes care of the communication between the user and the bankhall simulation model. With this system the user is able to define which data will be used, to modify the data, to define the model, to save data and model and to start the simulation. The second subsystem is the simulation model itself. This model is behind the scene of the user. It is an replicate of the layout of the bankhall under investigation. All the activities, processes, queues etcetera which take place in the bankhall are reproduced within this model.

Implementing a model which is user friendly, can be time consuming. A lot of details have to be taken care of. But implementing a nice system is not a guarantee that it will be used properly by the user or the owner of the system. There are two aspects involved in using the simulation model. In the first place there is a problem of data collection. The systems used at counters nowadays, are not able to present in an adequate way information which is of interest for a simulation model. The other aspect is the user himself. He has to have knowledge of what is going on in the bankhall and how it is simulated.

2. The general bankhall concept

Although each local bank is unique, still there are general aspects in processing clients in a bankhall. By constructing bankhall-elements such as a central cashier, quick cashier, counters, clerks, ATM's, etcetera and by defining standard processes as handling the different types of transactions, it is possible to compose a bankhall.

Each client has at least one transaction and sometimes even more. These transactions can be advice, money transactions, travelling reservations, insurance, etcetera. To handle these transactions a bankhall has to be staffed and equipped with counters, ATM's and computer systems. The transactions can be divided into two groups: the cash transactions and the non-cash transactions. The cash transactions are transactions where value-documents such as money and cheques are involved. These documents are not stored at the counter for security reasons. In general there is a special cash system with a cash-organization somewhere in the building, which is functionally part of the bankhall but physically separated.

There are three main concepts of the cash organization. In the first place there is the clerk's own cash system. This is a special cash system with security provisions and is used only in small bankhalls. A second concept is the central cashier with pipeline connection to the counter. The cashier can sit anywhere in a secured room in the building. The information to and from the cashier is handled by the counter information system and the documents are send via a pipeline. The last concept is a so-called quick cash. The cashier in the quick cash performs the same functions as the central cashier. But also clients with simple withdrawal transactions can be handled.

If a central cash system or a quick cash system is applied, two types of cash-transaction, return and no-return are of interest. The handling of a 'no-return' transaction, for example a deposit, is simple. When the transaction is sent to the cashier, the clerk can proceed with the next transaction or client. A return transaction, for example a withdrawal, implies that a client cannot leave the counter before the clerk gets response from the cashier. During the period that the return transaction is processed by the cashier other transactions of the same client can be handled by the clerk. In case of a clerk's own cash system there is no distinction between return and no-return transaction, for the clerk has to perform all the activities associated with the transaction.

The accommodation at the counter to handle transactions depends on the time it takes to handle the transaction. There exist three types of counter accommodation. In the first place there is the standing accommodation. This accommodation is merely used at counters for transactions with a short processing time, for example deposits and withdrawals. The clerk sits or stands behind the counter and the client stands in front of the counter. Transactions which normally take a longer time are handled in a sitting accommodation, where the employee as well as the client sits. These sitting accommodations are merely used for advice, special and time consuming transactions. There is also a mix of the sitting and standing accommodation, the so called combi-accommodation. This accommodation has a standing accommodation as well as a sitting accommodation.

The staffing of the counters depends on the kind of transactions, which can be handled on the counter. There are three kinds of employees available: the clerk, the first clerk and the consultant. The first clerk can handle all the transactions which can be handled by the clerk and some additional transactions. The consultant can handle all the transactions, assigned to that counter.

Directly related to the bankhall concept is the client's behaviour. The behaviour of the client depends on the type of client and the transactions he has with him. There are two main client types, the private and the business client. In general the business client (the smallest group) is served at a special counter. At this counter, mostly at the far end of the bankhall, private clients cannot be handled. Another aspect of the behaviour of the client is the length of the queue in front of the counter. The client will always choose the counter where he can handle most of his transactions. And if there is an alternative he will choose the one with the smallest queue length. Clients who have only withdrawals are mostly handled by an ATM or a quick cash if available.

The assignment of a clerk to a client is according to the transaction list of the employee and that of the client. In principle a clerk is assigned to handle the client. When there are transactions, which cannot be handled by the clerk, the first clerk comes into action. To handle the most difficult transactions, the consultant serves the client.

3. The model implementation

The users of the simulation model support the consultants of the local banks. They have a very little knowledge of computers and operating systems. Therefore much attention is paid to a user-friendly dialogue system. No special training is needed; on all control levels help is available. The simulation model is implemented on a PC in the process oriented language Simscript. PC-Simscript which is incorporated in the simlab development environment has a lot of facilities available such as mouse-driven pull down-menu's, graphics and animation. These facilities are easy to use when building user friendly dialogue systems.

The nature of the simulation model itself is a queuing system. Therefore the model needs information on the arrival pattern of clients and their transactions and information on processing times of these transactions. For each client type there is an arrival pattern and a transaction distribution. The processing times of the cash transactions depend on the cash organization. For example a withdrawal at the ATM has a shorter processing time than a withdrawal at a money counter with a central cashier. The processing times are split up in logical parts depending on the cash organization. Modification of a component of the organization can easily be adapted.

Before running the simulation model the bankhall and the initial conditions have to be defined. In the first place there are the counters. For each counter the cash organization, the staffing, equipment, type of clients and the transactions which can be handled by the clerks have to be defined. The counters determine which cash system is used. In the second place there are the ATM's. For each ATM the type of ATM, the type of client and the transactions which can be handled have to be known. The initial conditions are the number of simulation runs, the simulation period and the number of clients in front of the door at the beginning of the simulation run. The data concerning arrival patterns and transaction distributions together with model specifications and initial conditions can be saved as model data.

The results to support the decisions are presented for each client type and counter or ATM. The results are queue lengths, waiting time, idle time, workload and utilization. Also some input data such as bankhall layout, arrival patterns and transaction distribution is presented.

4. Working with the simulation model

The first activity before using the simulation model is data collection. During a period of 2 to 4 weeks arrivals and transactions are registered. The registration is done manually. The cash transactions are recorded by the counter system. However this system has a very poor report facility. Therefore the summary of the recordings has to be copied manually. The data collected are processed by a data collection program, which calculates the arrival patterns and transaction distributions for the simulation model.

After the data collection, the arrival patterns and transaction distributions together with some general information are read by the simulation model. At this point the interactive modelling starts. Counters and ATM's are defined by using the dialogue system. To evaluate the model, the current bankhall is simulated. After this evaluation the transaction distributions and arrival patterns are updated to meet future expectations. The bankhall layout is adjusted. After the update and adjustments the simulation model is run. This process goes on and on until an adequate bankhall concept is found.

5. Problems

In this project there are two main problems. One problem is the user of the system and the other one is the performance of the simulation model. The user of the system has a marginal knowledge of simulation and therefore no feeling in what is essential in the simulation model. To cover his lack of knowledge all possible details are requested to add to the simulation model. This turns out to be a tremendous assault on the performance. It appears that the user has no feeling with simulation. Often the user starts for example with an undersized model so the workloads of the employees are approximately 100%. This resulted in very long execution times.

The other problem was the performance. The model has been built on a PC in PC-Simscript. PC-Simscript operates with virtual memory by using a swap file. Simulation of a large bankhall using graphical displays causes a lot of swapping. As time proceeds the swap file grows which leads to performance reduction. This problem can be solved by running the model on a MicroVax and using the human interface on the PC. This requires additional communication software. Of course, sending the model data to and receiving the results from the alternate computer is also time consuming but in relation to the processing time, on the alternate, it can be quite profitable. Performance tests on a MicroVax 2000 resulted in an eight times shorter processing time.

6. Conclusions

If a process oriented language is used the design of a bankhall simulation model is not a very difficult task. To implement the model with a user friendly interface is time consuming although adequate tools are used.

A minor problem is that of the data collection. This can be solved when in the future the counter systems have report facilities for management information.

The user is one of the critical success factors of the system. If the user lacks knowledge of simulation and decision problems it is very hard to make the simulation model successful. The user has to be educated in using simulation models. Training is not sufficient.

Simulation of very large models on a PC leads to strong performance reductions. To cope with the performance problem it is comfortable to have escape routes, for example to migrate the model to a faster machine.

Constraint logic programming as a modeling tool

Johan M. Broek

Rotterdam School of Management, A.I. Lab.,
P.O. Box 1738, 3000 DR Rotterdam,
(johan@ailab.eur.nl).
Also: ITK, Tilburg University.

1 Introduction

Advantages and disadvantages of programming paradigms and languages are not unconditional, but depend heavily on the kind of programming task being performed. Modeling can be regarded as a programming task. Examples of other programming tasks include systems, graphics or user interface programming. Modeling usually consists of three steps: understanding the problem, writing a program that solves the problem, and if necessary optimizing this program. It goes without saying that understanding the problem is often the most difficult step in modeling. Sometimes successive prototypes are developed to be able to understand more about the problem and to sharpen the model specifications. Also, due to uncertainty and lack of data often several program versions and data sets will have to be considered.

The lack of adequate modeling tools makes experimentation and prototyping costly and time consuming. As a consequence useful information is often used too late or not at all. Modeling is a programming task where flexibility and short development times are more important than sheer program execution speed. Also, recent publications on decision support systems and computer assisted decision making stress the need for integration of databases, modeling tools and graphics. Constraint logic programming (CLP) is a relatively new paradigm that presents an overall framework for this integration.

Like Prolog, constraint logic programming languages are highly interactive and enable symbolic computation and stratified design. On top of that they also provide sophisticated and efficient constraint solving techniques and control mechanisms. The constraint solvers are integrated parts of a high-level programming language with deductive capabilities.

It has been shown that decision models can be implemented in CLP languages in an elegant and flexible way [6, 12, 2]. The constraints state relations directly in the intended domain of discourse. The development times and the programs are short, due to the declarative nature of these languages.

Thinking in paradigms may also lead to inefficient use of resources and counter-intuitive or unproductive problem solutions. For instance, the object-oriented programming paradigm dictates that every part of a program is an object. Instead of thinking of adding two numbers in the usual sense, we should think of numbers as objects and the addition operation as a message being sent to one object, where the other object is an argument of the message. Thinking in this way about adding numbers is clearly overdone and unproductive. We argue that programmers should know the limitations of the approach they are using. Like all paradigms, CLP also has some limitations and disadvantages. The theoretical limitations are defined in the CLP *scheme* [10]. In this paper some practical limitations are discussed.

The outline of this paper is as follows. The CLP paradigm is an attempt to remedy some of the deficiencies of Prolog and the logic programming paradigm.[1] In section two we describe these deficiencies. In the third section the principles of constraint logic programming are briefly outlined. A short description of several CLP modeling applications is given. Some advantages and disadvantages of CLP are illustrated by small examples.

2 Logic programming

The combination of relational form, non-deterministic computation and unification in Prolog results in a high-level programming language with solid theoretical foundations, cf. [13]. One of the advocated advantages of Prolog is that it allows a declarative programming style. Roughly, this means that when writing a Prolog program we only need to think about *what* should be accomplished and can leave the *how* part to Prolog. Because most Prolog program clauses have both a procedural and a logical interpretation, Prolog programs are easy to read. That is, we

[1] The terms 'logic programming' and 'Prolog programming' are not equivalent. Prolog is an approximation of the logic programming paradigm. See [5] for a detailed discussion.

can understand the function of a Prolog program without having to simulate a computer in our heads. This is an important advantage because it speeds up program development and makes Prolog programs easy to maintain.

Purely declarative programming has not yet been achieved in Prolog or other current logic programming systems. Shapiro [17], argues that seeking purely declarative languages is like looking for the philosopher's stone. There are many sophisticated algorithms that cannot be expressed simply by imposing sophisticated control over a logic program that defines the solution. For example, no smart control will turn the exponential slowsort program [13] into a quicksort algorithm. Many classes of seemingly simple problems have no general efficient solution.

Prolog is an excellent programming language for writing symbolic computation or natural language programs. However, Prolog should not be considered a general purpose language. For example, in principle one could try to implement, say, an operating system in Prolog. In practice one implements those systems in imperative programming languages like C, Pascal or assembler, as these languages have been designed to exploit conventional hardware. In fact, the core of most Prolog systems is implemented in C or assembler. In this paper the advantages and disadvantages of Prolog as a modeling language are considered.

It has been pointed out before that Prolog can be used as a modeling language. For example, Minch [14] argues that logic programming can be used as paradigm for financial modeling. Minch (unwillingly) also demonstrates that programming in Prolog can be troublesome. Other authors have used Prolog and logic programming in areas such as, database modeling, computer graphics, and even spreadsheet modeling. Despite the high expectations of a number of authors, the number of applications of Prolog in industrial settings has been limited sofar (cf. [8]). Part of the reasons for this disappointing progress should be sought in the language itself.

Attempts to apply the language to 'real life' operations research or financial modeling problems have revealed a number of shortcomings of Prolog. These shortcomings can be summarized as follows. Firstly, Prolog carries out computations in the *Herbrand universe.* Unification is used to solve equations in this universe, i.e., on uninterpreted terms. When modeling a problem, one must use a mapping from the intended domains, such as sets or rational terms, on the Herbrand universe. Secondly, Prolog lacks control facilities.

The first shortcoming of Prolog can be illustrated using simple arithmetic. Some people may be surprised by the answer `No.` to the query,

```
?- 2 = 1 + 1.
```

The answer `No.` is the only correct one as the constant 2 and the compound term `1 + 1` cannot be unified. In Prolog special predicates are used to do arithmetic. These predicates do not fit very well into the logic programming paradigm.

One of the desirable properties of many Prolog programs is what might be called 'reversibility'. For example the `member/2` predicate, which is defined by the following program,

```
member(X,[X|_]).
member(X,[_|Tail]) :-
    member(X,Tail).
```

can be used both as a test and a generator. In practice the reversibility of Prolog programs is limited because extra-logical operations force us to use predicates in one direction only. Still the advantages of reversibility are obvious: it saves both code and programming effort.

As stated before, arithmetic in Prolog is performed using special predicates, such as, `is/2`, `>/2`, `=</2`, etc. These predicates make reversibility troublesome. Moreover, they force us to read the program in a procedural way. Consider the following two queries:

```
?- X = 3, Y is X.

?- Y is X, X = 3.
```

The declarative meaning of these queries is the same, however, the second query will probably cause an error to be signalled as the second argument of the `is/2` predicate is non-ground.

In MU-Prolog this problem can 'solved' by postponing evaluation of certain messy predicates until some preconditions are satisfied using *wait declarations* [15, 16]. This method is called *coroutining* or *lazy evaluation*. It can be seen that lazy evaluation can be used to implement local propagation algorithms. Consider, however, the next simple example:

```
?- X >= 3, X =< 3.
```

Suppose that the predicates `=</2` and `>=/2` are subject to wait declarations and will only be evaluated if both arguments are ground. In the above query the variable `X` is not instantiated and therefore the system won't return the obvious answer `3`. This example clearly illustrates that although we may use lazy evaluation to implement local propagation algorithms, we still have to use a *generate and test* algorithm to find the answers.[2]

[2]The reader is invited to write a program that can handle the query `?- X > 3, X < 3.`

The second shortcoming of Prolog is its lack of control facilities. In Prolog the control part of the algorithms is (almost) fixed. Sometimes we want to be able to influence the control part. For instance, the problem is very complex and a more specialized control is necessary, or we want to make a sound implementation of negation as failure. Combinatorial problems are not as easily solved as they can be stated in Prolog. The 'natural' or 'declarative' way of stating these problems in Prolog results in (usually inefficient) generate and test programs (cf. [21]).

Several extensions to Prolog, such as, functional programming in Prolog, equation solving, meta-rules, coroutining, and intelligent backtracking, have been proposed to remedy the shortcomings of Prolog. One of the most recent extensions is the combination of constraint solving and logic programming.

3 Constraint logic programming

CLP languages try to combine the declarative aspects of logic programming with the efficiency of constraint solving techniques. The basic idea in CLP is that unification can be seen as a kind of constraint solving. Unification can be replaced by the more general concept of constraint solving.

Stating a problem as a set of constraints yields several advantages: the constraints state properties directly in the intended domain of discourse [10]; the constraints have the ability of representing properties implicitly as opposed to having bindings to variables; the constraint solving paradigm enables the use of interesting problem solving techniques like local value propagation, data-driven computation and consistency checking [21].

Constraints state relations between objects directly in the intended domain of discourse. This makes programs relatively easy to read. We do not have to simulate a constraint solver in our heads to understand what is written. The set of constraints that describes the problem is at the same time an implicit representation of the solution. The constraints do not explicitly state how the constraint solver must derive the answer. This makes programs very short.

Examples of CLP languages are CLP($\Re$) [11], and CHIP [6], Prolog III [3]. The CLP *scheme*, defines a class of languages based upon the paradigm of rule-based constraint programming [10]. Each instance of the scheme is a programming language and is obtained by the specification of the domain of computation, which is defined by the basic elements in the domain, e.g., all integers; the allowed operators on the basic elements, e.g., $+$ and $*$; the predicates on terms constructed from basic elements and operators, e.g., $=$, $\neq$ or $\leq$.

A particular instance of the CLP scheme is CLP($\Re$). The domain of computation is the set of real numbers and the constraints solved by the system are linear equations and inequations.

Prolog III, uses a simplex like algorithm to solve linear equations and inequations of rational terms, and provides a saturation method to deal with Boolean terms.

CHIP provides three computation domains: finite domain restricted terms, Boolean terms, and rational terms. For each domain CHIP uses specialized constraint solving techniques: consistency techniques for finite domains (cf. [21]), equation solving in Boolean algebra for Booleans and a symbolic simplex-like algorithm for the rationals.

3.1 Applications

Constraint logic programming languages have been used to solve 'real life' problems occurring in operations research, such as scheduling, warehouse location, and project planning [6, 7].

In [2], the authors describe an asset & liability management (ALM) simulation model implemented in CHIP. Constraints are used to model the behavior of several bank control accounts subject to policy rules, changes in interest rates, and optimization objectives. The program uses a simplex-like algorithm in combination with tree search techniques to find interesting ALM strategies.

LOGISIM [9], is a program for simulating and diagnosing hybrid circuits. These hybrid circuits, which are widely used in the aircraft industry, consist of electromechanical, electro-hydraulical, and hydromechanical components. LOGISIM employs several constraint solvers to validate these hybrid circuits.

Feelders and Daniels [4], report the use of CLP in financial diagnosis. The system uses a combination of quantitative and qualitative information, to identify and explain significant changes in the financial structure of a firm.

In qualitative economics, one tries to model and explain economical systems on the basis of qualitative data. Qualitative constraints are used to state book keeping relations and economic laws [1].

Other applications of CLP languages include modeling electric circuits, computer graphics, and computer-aided design. In the following, advantages and possible disadvantages of the CLP paradigm are illustrated by small examples.

3.2 Two examples

The first example is derived from [3] and illustrates the use of linear rational terms. Consider the following example:

```
payment([],0).
payment([Now|Then],Amount) :-
  payment(Then,Amount * (11/10) - Now).
```

In Prolog III [3], this little program can be used to compute a four year annuity of an amount of money (in the example $ 316.99) given a ten percent interest rate if it is used in the following way,

```
?- payment([A,A,A,A],316.99).

A = 100
```

It can also be used to compute the present value of a number of cash flows (in the example $ `100`, $ `110`, and $ `120`) given an interest rate of ten percent.

```
?- payment([100,110,120],PV).

PV = 271.98
```

This short and surprising program not only illustrates an important advantage (i.e., reversibility of arithmetic predicates), it also reveals two limitations if we write it in the following way:[3]

```
payment(List,Amount,Rate) :-
  List = [],          % = denotes normal unification
  Amount q= 0.        % q= denotes rational unification
payment(List,Amount,Rate) :-
  List = [Now|Then],
  Newamount q= Amount * (1 + Rate) - Now,
  payment(Then,Newamount,Rate).
```

The first limitation is rather obvious. `Rate` must be ground because otherwise the equation is not linear and as a consequence cannot be solved in Prolog III, CLP($\Re$), or CHIP. In CLP($\Re$)

[3]We write =, q=, and d= , to denote normal unification, rational unification and unification of finite domain restricted terms respectively.

non-linear equations are 'delayed' (cf. coroutining) automatically until new variable bindings make them linear. Both CHIP and Prolog III provide declarations similar to MU-Prolog's wait declarations that allow implementation of similar constructs.

The second limitation is less obvious. Apparently two types of unification are used: normal 'Robinson' unification, and unification of linear rational terms. In the first implementation the CLP system must decide which type of unification should be used. In other words, the CLP system must infer the types of the variables. In Prolog III and CLP($\Re$) constraints are detected automatically. In CHIP one must either use meta-declarations that state which type of unification is to be used or implement programs as in the second implementation of the payment program. The first approach seems to be more convenient than the CHIP approach. Unfortunately it is also unsound. Everything that looks like a constraint is also treated as a constraint. In some cases, however, one may want to use normal unification. This occurs for example in programs that symbolically manipulate arithmetic expressions.

The second example is taken from [21] and uses the CHIP language. It is the well-known SEND + MORE = MONEY puzzle which is part of the artificial intelligence folklore. The goal is to find an instantiation of the variables S,E,N,D,M,O,R, and Y using the digits 0...9 in such a way that the addition of SEND and MORE = MONEY. Each variable should have a different value. The problem is solved in CHIP (in approx. 17 ms.) using the following program,

```
sendmory([S,E,N,D,M,O,R,Y]) :-
  [S,E,N,D,M,O,R,Y] :: 0..9,
  alldifferent([S,E,N,D,M,O,R,Y]),
  S d!= 0,          % d!= denotes not equal
  M d!= 0,
  Send  = 1000 * S + 100 * E + 10 * N + D,
  More  = 1000 * M + 100 * O + 10 * R + E,
  Money =
  10000 * M + 1000 * O + 100 * N + 10 * E + Y,
  Send + More d= Money,
  labeling([S,E,N,D,M,O,R,Y]).
```

This example illustrates that programs in CLP languages can be short, readable and fast. 'Real life' problems are, of course, much more complicated. The *real* problem is often finding a suitable mathematical description of the problem. The advantage of the CLP approach is that it helps us in first finding a good model without having to worry about programming tricks and optimization early in the development process.

The example program is not fully declarative. Firstly, the domain declaration,

```
[S,E,N,D,M,O,R,Y] :: 0..9,
```

must be put first. This declaration is in fact a type declaration that states that the variables S,E,N,D,M,O,R and Y are all domain variables with domain 0...9. Secondly, the predicate `labeling/1` must be put after the constraints. The order of the constraints itself is not important. Swapping the constraints and `labeling/1` results in a pure *generate & test* program.

The constraints act as filters that remove values from the domains that cannot occur in a solution. The constraint solving procedures, forward checking and looking ahead, that are used cannot guarantee that all inconsistent values will be removed from the domains. In this sense the filtering process is incomplete. In other words, the constraint solver is not a decision procedure. It is for this reason that CHIP does not completely fit into the CLP scheme. To ensure correct results the labeling procedure is necessary. See [21] for more details.

4 Concluding remarks

Programming paradigms dictate styles and methods of programming and help to design and structure programs, resulting in shorter development times, lower development costs, and higher software integrity. Thinking in paradigms may also lead to inefficient use of resources and counter-intuitive or unproductive problem solutions. It often pays to be aware of the limitations of the paradigm that is used.

Several CHIP examples using the finite domains and Booleans have shown that an efficiency comparable to that of specialized constraint solvers (written in procedural languages) is possible [7, 20, 19]. In some cases CHIP even outperformed these specialized systems [18].

Efficient execution of linear rational term arithmetic can be attained. It is, however, unlikely that an efficiency comparable to that of specialized simplex packages will be reached. This is due to the fact that constraints are created dynamically. Moreover, the constraints are created in a non-deterministic environment.

Due to the declarative nature of CLP languages the development times and programs are short. However, present-day CLP language interpreters and compilers, are twice as large as their Prolog cousins, and are difficult to build and to extend. Moreover, the need for automatic storage reclamation is often hard felt. In CLP languages like Prolog III, and CHIP it is possible to express different types of constraints in one program. Unfortunately mixing them up is a bad idea because complete and sound type systems are missing.

We are confident that the advantages of the CLP approach outweigh the disadvantages. The exploitation of the CLP approach has just started. Undoubtedly numerous applications will be implemented in the near future in both industrial and academic settings.

Acknowledgement

This research was supported (in part) by the Netherlands Organisation for Scientific Research (NWO).

References

[1] R.J. Berndsen and F. Berthier. Goal seeking in qualitative reasoning: an implementation in Chip. In *IMACS Workshop, Qualitative reasoning and decision support systems*, Toulouse, 1991.

[2] J.M. Broek and H. Daniels. Application of constraint logic programming to asset and liability management in banks. *Computer Science in Economics and Management*, 4, 1991. (to appear).

[3] A. Colmerauer. Note sur Prolog III. In *Actes du seminaire 1986 - programmation en logique*, Tregastel, 1986.

[4] H. Daniels and A. Feelders. Model-based diagnosis of business performance: a constraint logic programming approach. In *Proceedings CSN*, Utrecht, 1990. (Published by Stichting Mathematisch Centrum, Amsterdam).

[5] Y. Deville. *A methodology for logic program construction.* Ph.D. thesis, University of Namur, 1987.

[6] M. Dincbas, P. van Hentenrijck, H. Simonis, A. Aggoun, T. Graf, and F. Berthier. The constraint logic programming language Chip. In *Proceedings of the international conference on fifth generation computer systems*, Tokyo, 1988.

[7] M. Dincbas, H. Simonis, and P. van Hentenryck. Solving the car sequencing problem in constraint logic programming. In *Proceedings European conference on artificial intelligence*, Munich, 1988.

[8] H. Gallaire. Boosting logic programming. In J-L. Lassez, editor, *Proceedings of the fourth international conference on logic programming*. The MIT Press, Cambridge, MA, 1987.

[9] T. Graf, P. van Hentenrijck, C. Pradelles, and L. Zimmer. Simulation of hybrid circuits in constraint logic programming. In *Proceedings IJCAI*, Detroit, 1989.

[10] J. Jaffar and J-L. Lassez. Constraint logic programming. In *Proceedings of the 14th ACM POPL Symposium*, Munich, 1987.

[11] J. Jaffar and S. Michaylov. Methodology and implementation of a CLP system. In *Proceedings of the 4th international conference on logic programming*, 1987. (The MIT Press).

[12] C. Lassez, K. McAloon, and R. Yap. Constraint logic programming and option trading. *IEEE Expert*, 2(3):42–50, 1987.

[13] J.W. Lloyd. *Foundations of logic programming*. Springer-Verlag, second edition, 1987.

[14] R.P. Minch. Logic programming as a paradigm for financial modeling. *MIS Quarterly*, 13(1), 1989.

[15] L. Naish. Automating control for logic programs. *Journal of Logic Programming*, 3:167–183, 1985.

[16] L. Naish. *Negation and control in Prolog*. Ph.D. thesis, University of Melbourne, Australia, 1985.

[17] E. Shapiro. Review of J. Lloyd's "Foundations of logic programming". *Computing Reviews*, 8608-0668, 1986.

[18] H. Simonis, N. Nguyen, and M. Dincbas. Verification of digital circuits using Chip. In *Proceedings IFIP*. Elseviers Science Publishers, 1988.

[19] P. van Hentenrijck and J-P. Carillion. Generality versus specifity: an experience with AI and OR techniques. In *Proceedings AAAI*, 1988.

[20] P. van Hentenrijck and M. Dincbas. Forward checking in logic programming. In J-L. Lassez, editor, *Proceedings of the fourth international conference on logic programming*. The MIT Press, Cambridge, MA, 1987.

[21] P. van Hentenrijck. *Constraint satisfaction in logic programming*. The MIT Press, Cambridge, MA, 1989.

A DECISION SUPPORT SYSTEM FOR PACKAGING LINES IN FOOD INDUSTRY

G.D.H. Claassen
Dept. of Mathematics (OR), Agricultural University Wageningen
Dreijenlaan 4, 6703 HA Wageningen, The Netherlands

1. Introduction

Scheduling and planning is a common activity in various environments. Due to the increasing complexity of industries and markets, this task becomes more and more important. The efficient generation of 'high quality' schedules, within a reasonable amount of time, can, especially in agri-business, be of crucial importance due to the stringent requirements with respect to freshness, extent of assortment and orders, decrease in quality, and other specific requirements of the market. Increasing flexibility of packaging lines should get a higher priority in the food industry in order to meet the due-dates, to gain shorter leadtimes, to maximize the utilisation of resources, to minimize the changeover costs etc.

The practice of scheduling packaging lines in food industry is rather simple and straightforward. In general it is a humen job in which just one solution is sought manually and the transfer and re-use of the acquired expertise to other (non)expert schedulers seldom takes place. Principles of developing a schedule are based on experience and are seldom analysed. Scheduling by hand follows an arbitrary backtracking process. At each step the violation of important constraints are checked before the process can proceed. To obtain a feasible schedule can be very time consuming and the procedure is mostly suboptimal. Once the schedule has been completed, it is extremely difficult to accomodate for rush orders within acceptable time.

The application of quantitative models in interactive planning-systems will only rarely take over the place from a planner. Nevertheless those systems could be very helpful in supporting the decision-maker. This paper describes an efficient approach to a scheduling and planning problem for the bottleneck packing facilities of a large dairy factory.

The problematic nature of the research could be formulated as to develop and evaluate a pilot **D**ecision **S**upport **S**ystem (DSS) in order to generate and present 'high quality' schedules within a reasonable amount of time. The pilot interactive planningsystem should combine the power of the human judgement and experience on the one hand with the accuracy and computing power of the computer on the other hand.

The cheese production division of the dairy company produces every week about 5 million pounds of cheese. After production and a maturation period between three weeks and two years in a large storage yard, the company offers about 400 hundred different kinds of varieties. On the packaging compartment the potential number of products increases expansively to 2500. In order to get through a throughput of five million pounds a week, the department under consideration has the disposal of ten packaging lines. The job arrival process can be classified as a deterministic dynamic shop. This means that the new jobs are periodically released to the shop floor and the processing times of the intermittently arriving jobs are known. In general the jobs can only be processed on one specific packaging line, however there are also jobs that can be processed on several, not identical, packaging lines with different capacities. According to Hax (1984) a flow shop consists of m-machines arranged in series and of n jobs that require m operations, each operation being performed on a different machine. In case a job has fewer (<m) operations, it may still be treated as an m operation job with zero processing times assigned correspondingly. However, the flow of work is unidirectional; each job must visit each machine in the prescribed order. It is not possible to interrupt a job's processing on a machine before completion. This is called non-preemptive. So the whole problem can be seen as a generalisation of an open, nonpreemptive, n-job m-machine flow shop problem.
Because all the machines of a packaging line are physically connected, the processing time of each job depends on the bottleneck operation to be performed.

Although the flow shop problem is the 'simplest' multistage scheduling problem, it turns out to be disappointingly difficult to solve (Hax, 1984). Garey (1976) proved that the nonpreemptive scheduling flow shop problem is NP-hard.

In order to break down the complexity of the stated problem, several researchers propose a decomposition of the problem into control levels. Hax (1984) describes the framework of Robert N. Anthony (1965). He classifies decisions into three categories: strategic planning, tactical planning and operational control. Strategic planning is mainly concerned with long-term decision making, related to investment decisions, product development etc. The emphasis of the tactical planning is an effective and efficient use of the resources. After making an aggregate allocation of the resources, it is necessary to deal with day to day operational decisions. This is called the operational control. Van Wassenhove (1983) also discusses a hierarchical framework for the development and implementation of a (similar) planning problem for a set of production facilities of a large chemical firm. Our research has only focussed on the management - (tactical) and operational control level.
This research showed that the developed pilot DSS supports the scheduler: he is able to generate 'high quality' schedules more effectively and efficiently.

2. Problem analysis

The ultimate goal of the management team was twofold. At first they want to support the decision-maker by setting up an effective and efficient working-schedule of the orderbook. Subsequently the system should also have a supporting task at the order entry level. If the sales manager has the disposal of a thorough overview of the orderbook or, even better, the working-schedule of the packaging department, the order-acceptance will be able to anticipate on the remaining capacity.

2.1. Starting points

In practice a scheduler has a restricted knowledge of the process of intermittently arriving jobs. In order to anticipate in an adequate way on the future demand, a packaging plan should not only be based on the jobs in the orderbook. If a reliable estimation of the future demand is taken into account, the system will be forced to level peak-production on the packaging department which is mostly related to some fixed days within the planning horizon. In this connection we presume that a rolling planning horizon of two weeks is long enough to anticipate on a short-term trend in orderbooking. An approximation of the future demand is based on the orderprocess of the last two weeks.

At the packaging department we define Standard Clusters (SC). Although the jobs within a SC consist of several unique operations, the outward appearance of the final product can be different. However, there are no changeover costs within each SC. Between the various SC's the jobs require different operations, each operation being performed on a different machine. So, when it comes to switching over from one SC to another, the changeover time on a packaging line will be substantially. For example. if the client wants the cheese to wraped up in paper the packaging line has to be enlarged by an automatic wrap-up-machine. Within this SC a switch over to an other kind of paper will force no intensive adjustment of the packaging line.
We distinguish about fifty different SC's; forty of them can be processed on only one packaging line. The other clusters can be worked up on several, not necessarily identical, lines working in parallel.

2.2. Tactical planning

On the tactical planning level a feasible (daily) 'master packaging schedule' of the orderbook is determined. The time horizon is subdivided into ten working days (two weeks). A Mixed Integer Linear Programming model (MILP) is the basis in this stage of the decision making process. In the objective function several, more or less conflicting, goals are considered.

The emphasis is to meet the duedates of the individual jobs (Just-In-Time). Early handling of orders is possible but, regarding the maturation period of the cheese (availability), restricted to a small extent. For this purpose the square of the deviation between the planned arrival time of each job on the shop floor and his duedate is minimized.

Furthermore it is desirable to minimize the changeover time on the packaging lines. Setup time reduction is achieved by scheduling the jobs daily to production lots of one or more standard clusters, within taking to account the availability and duedates of the individual jobs. Moreover, clustering the jobs to voluminous batches is conformable with the endeavour to minimize the remnants of the fixed lots in the storage yard.

As already stated, most of the jobs can only be processed on one packaging line. However, there are jobs that can be processed on alternative, not necessarily identical, packaging lines with different processing times. In order to optimize the capacity utilization, the elapsed time between the arrival and completion of a job on the shop floor (flow time) has to be minimized.

In general a crew of workers on the shop floor can operate only one specific packaging line, however the department under consideration has also the disposal of a special shift. This shift only works in the evening and is able to process all standard clusters on any packaging line. Strictly speaking the special shift is none overtime; the shift supply a shortage of capacity if necessary in a flexible manner. Moreover it is possible to extend the available capacity by overtime. An important goal is minimizing the hours of overtime and special shift. Hax (1984) describes an important shortcoming of the classical linear programming formulation: the relevant decision variables have to be converted to become measurable by a common unit (often money). In our case, the managerial decisons require the consideration of several goals, which are incommensurable with each other. For this purpose we approached the problem partly as a goal programming model. The hours of overtime as well as the special shift are modelled as deviational variables which are a part of the capacity constraints and the objective function. By weighing the variables in the objective function we are able to associate the goals with a priority.

2.3. Operational control

The tactical planning clusters the jobs into batches and allocate them to a particular packaging line within a feasible time-table. In this way the stated problem has been substantially reduced. Actually the remaining problem on the operational control level can be partitioned into two sub-problems. In both cases the problem is litterally the same as sequencing, however the measures of performance are fairly different. On the one hand the processing sequence of the clusters on each packaging line has to be determined. This problem, with sequence-dependent setup times, can be interpreted as the well-known 'asymmetric traveling salesman problem' for whose solution an heuristic approach has been chosen.

On the other hand a schedule of the sequence in which the individual jobs within a cluster are processed, has to be determined. The processing sequence depends on several (logical) rules. The enclosed planning criteria in descending order of importance are:

- In order to minimize the remaining lots in the storage yard, the quantity of the various cheese products ought to be in accordance with the fixed batches in the warehouse; at least as much as possible. For this purpose the orders within a batch are clustered to production code and article number. Together, these distinguishing marks make up an indication about the cheese product and packaging specification, ordered by the client.

- By clustering the jobs to customer-name, it is possible to preclude a large, intermediate inventory level on the expedition department.

- As the administrative realization of the orders (invoicing) can not start previous to the completion of the packaging process, the invoice clerks are served most by clustering the jobs to increasing extent. This working method precludes an excessive supply of orders on the invoice department at the end of the day.

3. Results

This section describes the judgement of the decision-makers after the pilot interactive planningsystem has been implemented and evaluated in a real world environment. For about two months the planning model has been run several times a day. Its major benefit is the generation of packaging line schedules in a more effective and efficient way. The quality of the final schedule turned out to be better than the solutions sought by hand. The efficiency enables the decision-maker to 'optimize' his own performance with respect to his mission.

Without the DSS the decision-maker can take just a few hours in order to finish the daily planning and scheduling problem at the agreed time. Occasionally he has to start the scheduling process even before all the jobs for the next day are booked. This working method implies that the remaining jobs, partly with a duedate of only one day ahead in the planning period, will never fit optimally into the completed schedule. Moreover to accomodate for rush orders is an extremely difficult job.

With the help of the interactive planningsystem a planner is able to generate schedules at any time and within a reasonable amount of time. So the decision-maker can delay the start of the scheduling process at least until all the orders with a duedate of the next day are booked. The system has also showed to be very useful in generating alternatives or revised plans when unforeseen disturbances occur; for example a breakdown of a packaging line or a sudden change in demand (rush-orders).

During the testphase the planners were delighted with the speed in which some time-consuming administrative actions and data processing were completed.

Because the planner always has the disposal of more information than the system, we have created the opportunity to review the generated schedule. In this connection the gain of time during the scheduling process is of great value. With the help of a menu-driven, User-Interface (UI) the planner is able to affect the, somewhat hidden, calculating modules in such a way that the solution will be tuned to the actual and future situation on the packaging department. In most cases the generated schedules have proven to be a good starting point and they are at least equal or even better than an average plan set up manually in the present situation. An additional advantage of the various utilities of the user friendly and fully interactive UI is the possibility to employ the human judgement and experience optimally, in order to improve the generated time-table.

The (daily) graphical presentation of the complete orderbook and the proposed final working-schedule to the salesmanager at the order entry level, has proven to be very valuable. It enables the orderacceptance to anticipate on the remaining capacity. As a result the interactive planningsystem has allowed for a better and smoother working-schedule for the packaging department.

4. References

Anthony, R.N., *Planning and control systems: a framework for analysis*, Graduate School of Business Administration, Harvard University, Boston, (1965).

Garey, M.R., Johnson, D.S. and R. Seth, Complexity of flow shop and job shop scheduling, *Mathematics of Operations Research*, Vol.1, No.2, (1976) pp. 117-129.

Hax, A.C. and Candea, D., *Production and inventory management*, Prentice-Hall Inc., (1984).

Wassenhove, L.N. van, Vanderhenst, P., Planning production in a bottleneck department, *European Journal of Operational Research*, Vol. 12, (1983) pp. 127-137.

Optimization-Based Decision Support System For Turbine Power Units Modelling and Design

J. DOLEŽAL, Z. SCHINDLER, J. FIDLER, O. MATOUŠEK[1]

Institute of Information Theory and Automation of the Czechoslovak Academy of Sciences, 182 08 Prague, Czechoslovakia

Introduction

Longer effort of the authors has resulted in a successful application of nonlinear mathematical programming methodology to turboprop power unit behaviour modelling and and design optimization. Highlights of the methodology and the gained experience were in the meantime published (DOLEŽAL et al. 1989, 1990a, 1990c). Based on the dynamic and thermodynamic equations and experimentally given characteristics of each component, the computer-aided system for modelling and analysis of the turbine power unit behaviour has been developed and implemented.

The steady-state, resp. the quasi-steady-state, regimes of the engine are described as a system of nonlinear algebraic equations and inequalities, which are treated as constraints in a certain nonlinear mathematical programming problem. In this way one can perform, if necessary, also optimal selection of design parameters and operating conditions, or to meet other existing physical or technological constraints. The transition regime simulation has been performed in analogical way by solving a system of nonlinear algebraic-differential equations.

Realization of the respective decision support system (DOLEŽAL et al. 1990b, SCHINDLER and DOLEŽAL 1990a, 1990b) is facilitated by the existence of the mentioned mathematical models. Their generality and efficiency is enhanced by the currently available user-friendly environment.

Solution Method

The suggested and practically tested approach to aircraft power units modelling exhibits many general aspects, which are common when dealing with other types of power units with gas turbine. It consists of the procedure of determination of a power unit behaviour using the known characteristics of each of its parts and the conditions how these parts interact.

The mathematical model of a considered power unit is based on the thermodynamic equations describing the fundamental cycle of working media, characteristics of all parts, mechanical arrangement of shafts, and conditions for steady-state and transition regimes. Characteristics of each parts used in calculations are assumed in the form given either by analytical functions or experimental data. This circumstance enables to solve the

[1] Aeronautical Research and Test Institute, Beranových 130, 199 05 Prague, Czechoslovakia.

mathematical model of the power unit using the real data of parts and to achieve more precise results. On the other hand, the needed approximations of experimental data can be source of additional difficulties during the solution process. e. g. increased amount of calculations, more probable numerical instabilities, etc.

The overall solution procedure can be summarized as follows:

1. Selection and definition of the fundamental isolated parts of the physical system.
2. Description of these parts by mathematical expressions obtained from experimental data.
3. Postulation of the principal relations to define mutual cooperation of the respective parts of the unit in steady-state and transition regimes.
4. Introduction of constraints to specify the allowed range of variables, validity of approximations, or additional specifications.
5. Solution of the obtained system of equations in the admissible region.
6. Analysis and evaluation of the obtained results.

For the steady-state regime of the engine, the following basic equilibrium conditions must be satisfied:

1) The mechanical arrangement of the engine, i. e. the mechanical link of the rotors of turbines and compressors, implies equalities of the respective shaft speeds.

2) Static pressures at the engine inlet and outlet are equal.

3) For the operating medium flow rates at the selected cross-sections mass conservation law holds.

4) For the compressor-turbine shaft systems in the steady-state energy conservation law holds.

During the transition regime, i. e. when the engine decelerates or accelerates, the requirements for engine instantaneous behaviour are determined again by conditions $1-3$. In addition, the change of speeds of the shaft systems in time, i. e. the dynamical behaviour of the unit, is determined by differential equations for shaft rotation caused by the available power overhead – see the references above.

Computation of steady-states or evaluation of right-hand sides of the respective differential equations is performed in iterative manner. Following strictly mathematical point of view it is necesssary to find a solution of the given system of nonlinear algebraic equations and inequalities either to determine the corresponding steady-state of the engine or to evaluate differential equations, i. e. the current quasi-steady-state.

Having in mind additional possibility of parameter setting with respect to certain optimality requirements, approach based on theory and algorithms of nonlinear mathematical programming (BARTHOLOMEW-BIGGS 1982, 1986, 1988) has been applied, i. e. the model is represented by a set of constraints in certain mathematical programming problem. Several tasks have been solved in this context (optimal compressor bleeding, maximal efficiency of propeller turbine, etc.).

It is not difficult to envisage that formal mathematical description and the subsequent simulation models of aircraft power unit behaviour cannot be principally too much different for conceptually and technologically similar power units. In the respective mathematical models such fact usually results in their partially similar inner structure and is reflected by an appropriate modularity of the implemented software. Then either for each power unit type it is possible to generate an adequate mathematical model or to implement a *generic* mathematical model for the possibly most technologically complicated case in the given class of power units. Many technologically simpler cases are then easily handled by the respective simplifying changes in the model input data.

For example, from the existing model of three-shaft turboprop power unit one can easily obtain two-shaft turboprop or two-shaft turbofan power unit models. Quite analogously it is possible to use a generic model of two-shaft bypass power unit to simulate its technologically simpler configurations.

Decision Support System **GoIPM**

Based on such fast and robust simulation models a problem-oriented user-friendly decision support system has been implemented featuring the extensive graphic environment to be run on personal computers. The system denoted as **GoIPM** (SCHINDLER and DOLEŽAL 1990a) exhibits a number of advanced options which are currently used by the designers in order to contribute to the efficiency of the design and test evaluation process. process.

These options include fast interactive evaluation or optimization of various design parameter influence on various operating conditions during steady-state and transition regimes, power unit reconfiguration, comparative analysis, etc. The mentioned modular structure of the implemented software system posesses enough generality and versatility to encompass related types of aircraft power units.

The existing computer system has been recently extended to support the fundamental design stages:

1. optimization of the aero-thermodynamic cycle;
2. determination of the overall engine behaviour using the approximated characteristics of each part;
3. adjustment of engine parameters to reach the satisfactory agreement with the realistic engine response;
4. analysis of the parameter changes during operation period of the engine.

Such closed system can be evidently exploited during the whole design process, from the introductory studies to the final follow-up of the produced power units. Especially in the connection with provided user-friendly graphic-supported interface such decision support system becomes an important design tool for turbine power units with positive impacts on each stage of their development.

The practical experimentation with the **GoIPM** system for various power unit configurations are quite promising and there exists an interest to further refine the mathematical models and to augment the user's support. As the result of such recent effort also the propeller characteristics have been implemented for steady-state regime silulation. Other requirements in this respect (inclusion of technological bounds on shaft speeds, temperature, fuel supply) will contribute to more realistic exploitation of the system, e. g. while developing a control unit.

Performed Implementations

The mathematical model has been originally applied to the turboprop power unit with twin-spool gas generator and free-turbine driven propeller shaft (Fig. 1). This structure has been considered for the following two reasons: (i) it represents one of the most complicated thermodynamic and mechanical arrangements, while the mathematical solution of less complicated types may be derived from it in a straightforward manner; (ii) for this turboprop unit, the corresponding technical and experimental data have been made available.

For the purpose of mathematical modelling, the power unit has been divided into the following basic parts (compartments) – see the functional scheme in Fig. 1: inlet diffuser

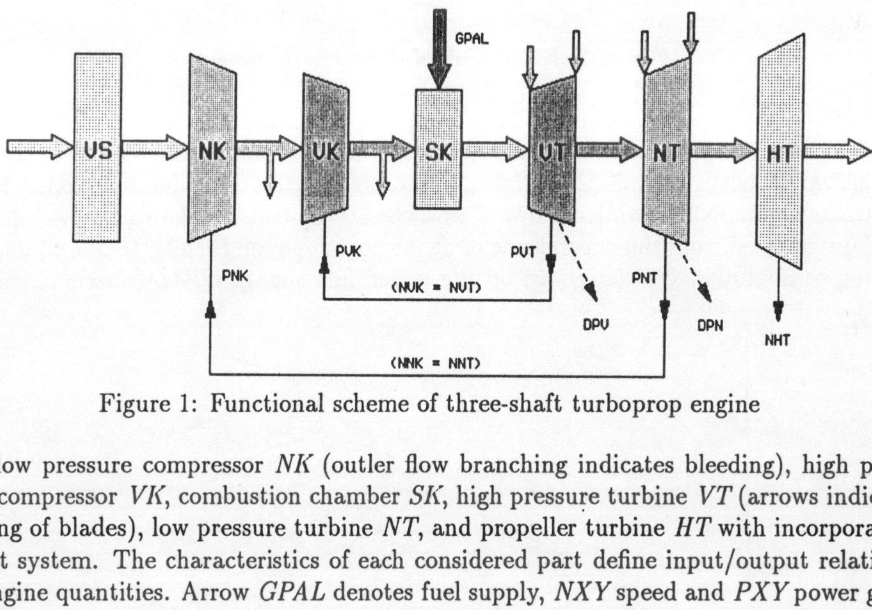

Figure 1: Functional scheme of three-shaft turboprop engine

VS, low pressure compressor *NK* (outler flow branching indicates bleeding), high pressure compressor *VK*, combustion chamber *SK*, high pressure turbine *VT* (arrows indicate cooling of blades), low pressure turbine *NT*, and propeller turbine *HT* with incorporated outlet system. The characteristics of each considered part define input/output relations on engine quantities. Arrow *GPAL* denotes fuel supply, *NXY* speed and *PXY* power generated or consumed on the part *XY*, and *DPN, DPV* are additional power consumptions on the shaft.

The initial data for calculations are ambient pressure and temperature and flight velocity. The fuel supply together with the propeller turbine speed determine the current operating conditions of the engine. The resulting data include all thermodynamic parameters at each of the chosen sections of the engine, low pressure and high pressure shaft speeds, the propeller shaft power, the additional reactive engine thrust, and the specific consumption. The details dealing with description of each considered part of the engine are collected elsewhere (DOLEŽAL et al. 1989, 1990a). Available experimental description of engine parts is converted to the appropriate analytical form using suitable data fitting algorithms.

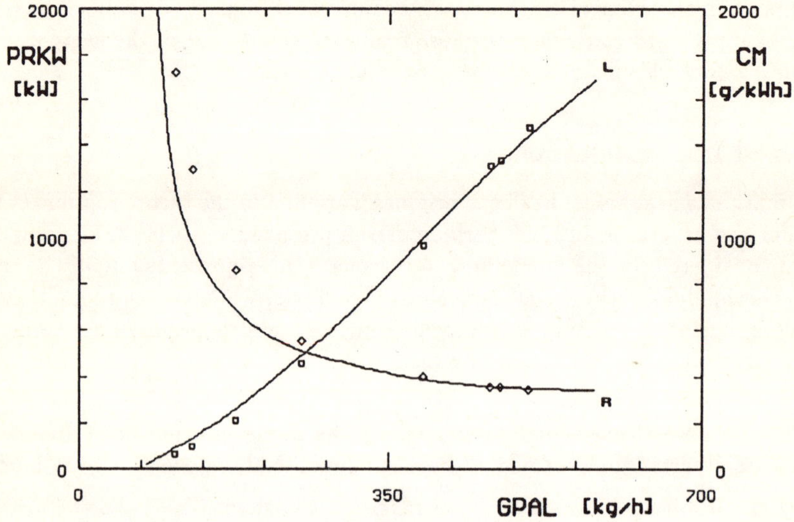

Figure 2: Evaluation of engine performance

Recently a propeller system has been adequately approximated and attached to provide the propeller quantities for steady-state regimes. (FIDLER et al. 1990). For the sake of illustration let us include the following two screen prints of simulation runs. Fig. 2 illustrates a good correspondence of the adjusted steady-state model to the real data as can be concluded from the dependence of of the engine power *PRKW* (curve L) and the specific consumption *CM* (curve R) on the varied fuel supply *GPAL* (nozzle character-

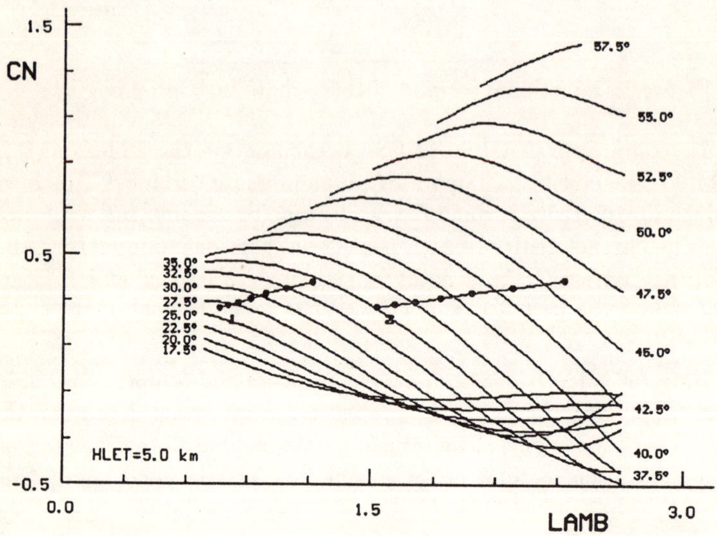

Figure 3: Operating lines in propeller characteristics

istics). By □, resp. ◇, are denoted experimental data collected on a special version of the power unit designed for the testing of mathematical models. Fig. 3 depicts analogical characteristics for the propeller power parameter *CN* in dependence on speed parameter *LAMB*. Optionally the respective propeller characteristics may be superposed. Assumed height of flight *HLET* = 5 km; curves 1 and 2 correspond to flying speed of 50 and 100 m/s, respectively.

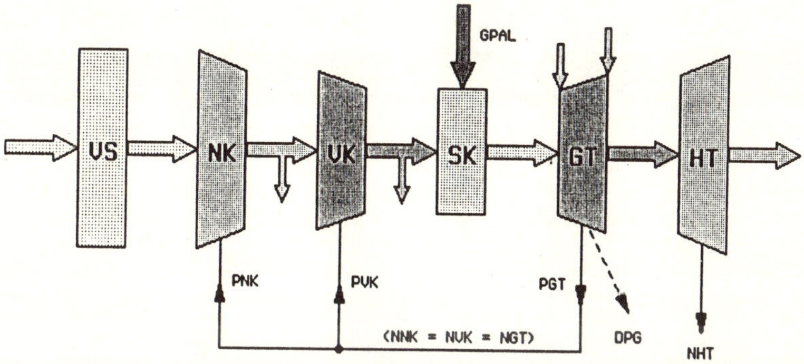

Figure 4: Functional scheme of two-shaft turboprop engine

Part of practical tests consists of using only a gas generator of the power unit, i. e. the propeller turbine is replaced by outlet nozzle only. Only simple change in input data makes it possible to obtain the model of such two-shaft jet power unit. Also other configurations can be easily derived (two-shaft turboprop, one-shaft jet). However, if the power unit has, e. g. two-stage compressor system on one shaft, one cannot immeaditely apply this approach as such coupling results in the change in steady-state conditions (equality of compressors speeds). Nevertheless, it is not difficult to implement the corresponding

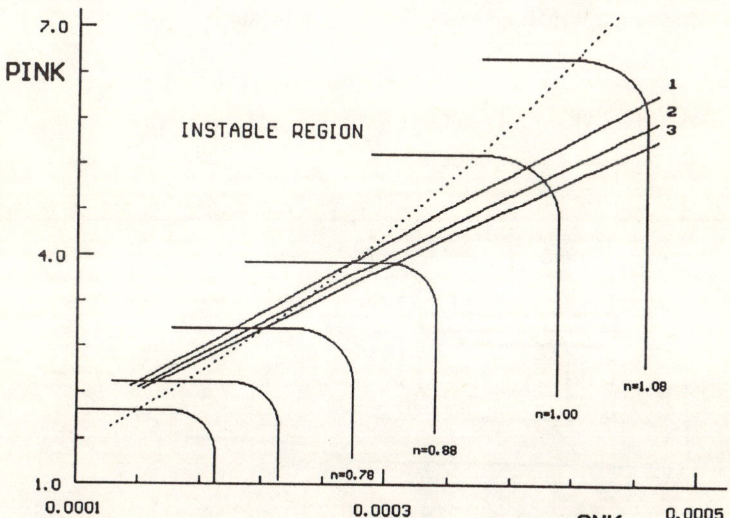

Figure 5: Operating lines in compressor characteristics

changes in the model to handle this case. The functional scheme of such power unit is given in Fig. 4. The meaning of all parts is analogical as in Fig. 1, only GT stands for single engine turbine.

In this way one can analyze power unit behaviour in early project stage based exclusively on the assumed characteristics of its parts. Operating lines in dependence on the varied fuel supply for three cases of high pressure compressor inlet area are in Fig. 5. They illustrate the influence of this parameter in the so-called pressure characteristics (dependence of pressure ratio $PINK$ on mass flow rate parameter QNK) of the low pressure compressor. Observe partial entry of the instable region (above the dotted curve representing the surge line) in the vicinity of idling regimes. Fig. 6 is full analogy of Fig. 2

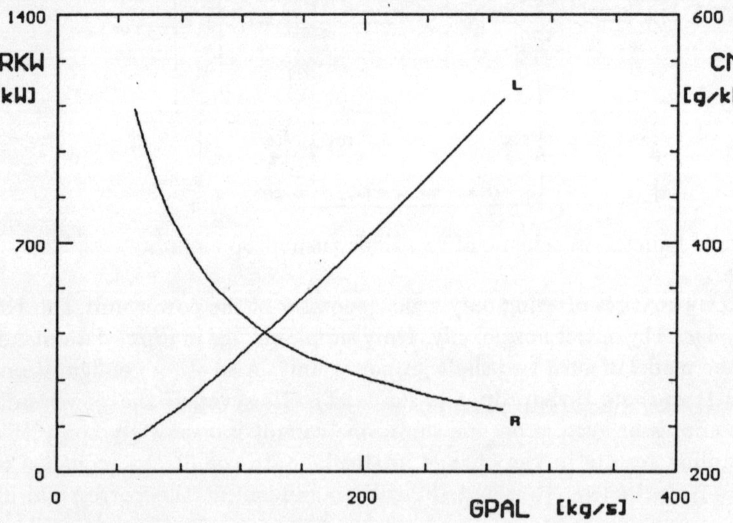

Figure 6: Engine performance dependence on fuel supply

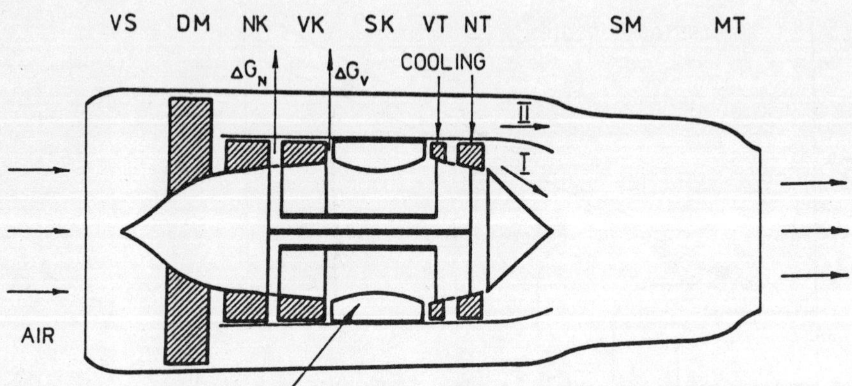

Figure 7: Technological structure of two-shaft bypass power unit

for this case. Fast generation of such lines is valuable for the designer and illustrates the evaluation and predictive power of the **GoIPM** system in this respect.

Above also the class of bypass power units has been mentioned. Let us briefly introduce this class. The mathematical model has been applied to the bypass power unit with twin-spool gas generator. The reason of considering this case were almost the same as in the turboprop case – advanced technological configuration and availability of experimental data. The fundamental technological scheme is depicted in Fig. 7 and the corresponding functional scheme in Fig. 8.

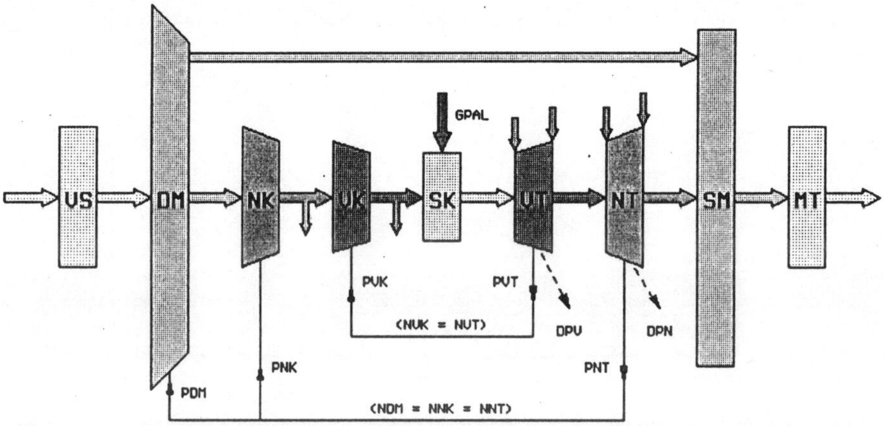

Figure 8: Functional scheme of two-shaft bypass power unit

From the point of view of mathematical modelling, the gas generator has similar structure as in Fig. 1 with the same meaning of basic parts denotation. In addition, there is a fan *DM*, which supports main engine flow *I* and bypass flow *II*. It has similar

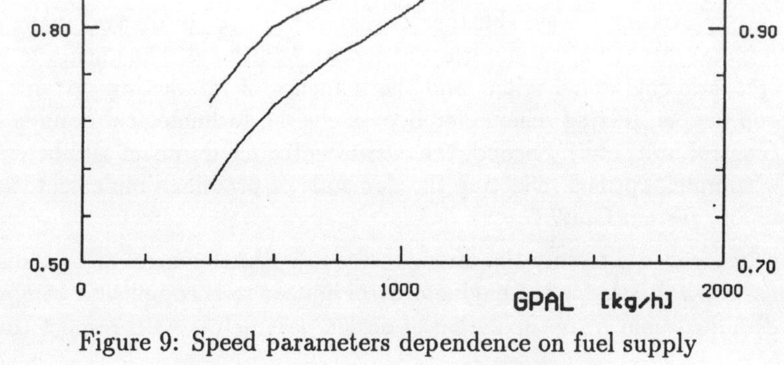

Figure 9: Speed parameters dependence on fuel supply

characteristics as compressors. Both flows enter mixing chamber *SM* and common flow leaves the engine via outlet *MT*. Other notation is fully analogical to the previously considered cases. For the mathematical model the crutial problem is an appropriate description of mixing processes. Details of this approach will be summarized and presented elsewhere (SCHINDLER et al. 1991).

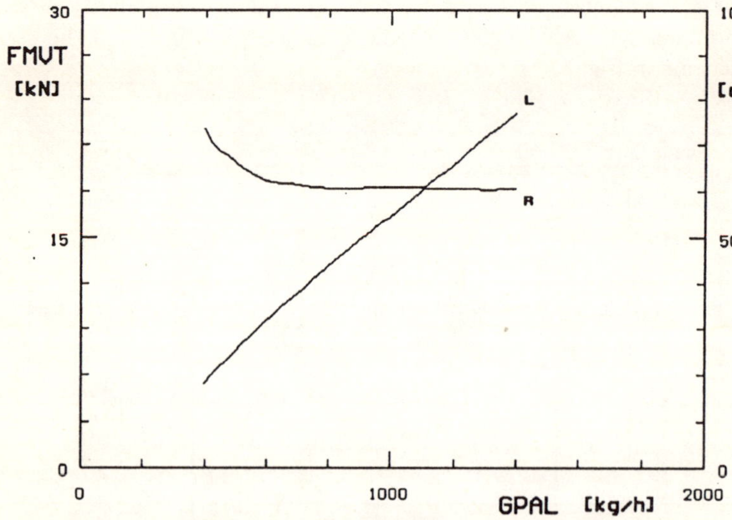

Figure 10: Engine performance dependence on fuel supply

Figs. 9 and 10 illustrate simulation runs for test input data. They depict the frequently considered dependence of shaft speed parameters *NPNK* (low pressure system – curve L) and *NPVK* (high pressure system – curve R) on the varied fuel supply *GPAL* as well as the dependence of engine thrust *FMVT* (curve L) and the specific consumption *CM* (curve R) on the same quantity.

Conclusions

From the presented results it may be concluded that the suggested aproach to power unit modelling offers a number of convenient features for its further development and subsequent implementation for real cases of power units. This methodology has shown fruitful especially for power units of smaller size, where the dimension aspects can be treated in an approximate way. Further developments will be in two main directions. First, the original mathematical models will receive additional refinements to reflect still better the realistic engine behaviour and the influence of interacting systems (propeller for turboprop engine, mixing scheme for bypass engine, technological bounds on certain quantities, control unit, etc.). Second, the user-oriented environment will be extended by adding new complex options reflecting the demands of practical implementations of the decision support system **GoPeM**.

Such options concern mainly the direct access to optimal control algorithms to determine optimal control laws for the engine control unit or to accomplish a computer-aided (automated) adjustment or optimization of design parameters with respect to the available experimental data. The gained experience with practical exploitation of such system in design and testing laboratories is promising and confrontation with real-world situations contributes to its further improvements. Moreover, such system is nowadays also used as an advanced and efficient education tool for students with mechanical engineering background.

References

BARTHOLOMEW-BIGGS M. C. (1982): *Recursive quadratic programming methods for nonlinear constraints.* In: *Nonlinear Optimization 1981*, M. J. D. Powell (Ed.), Academic Press, New York.

BARTHOLOMEW-BIGGS M. C. (1986): *Numerical examples of the behavior of REQP on nonlinear programming problems involving linear dependence among the constraint normals.* JOTA **48**, 215 - 227.

BARTHOLOMEW-BIGGS M. C. (1988): *A globally convergent version of REQP for constrained minimization.* IMA J. Numer. Anal. **8**, 253 - 271.

DOLEŽAL J., SCHINDLER Z., FIDLER J., MATOUŠEK O. (1989): *Mathematical model of turboprop engine behaviour.* ARTI Report Z-59, SNTL, Prague.

DOLEŽAL J., SCHINDLER Z., FIDLER J., MATOUŠEK O. (1990a): *Modelling and simulation of turboprop engine behaviour.* Acta technica ČSAV *35*, 1 - 27.

DOLEŽAL J., SCHINDLER Z., FIDLER J., MATOUŠEK O. (1990b): *Application of optimization methodology in technological system modelling: aircraft power unit design and evaluation.* In: *Modelling the Innovation: Communications, Automation and Information Systems*, M. Carnevale et al. (Eds.), North-Holland, Amsterdam, 549 - 555.

DOLEŽAL J., SCHINDLER Z., FIDLER J., MATOUŠEK O. (1990c): *Aircraft Turboprop Engine Simulation Based on a Mathematical Model.* In *14th IFIP Conference on System Modelling and Optimization*, H.-J. Sebastian, K. Tammer (Eds.), Springer-Verlag, Berlin, 919 - 928.

FIDLER J., DOLEŽAL J., SCHINDLER Z., MATOUŠEK O. (1990): *Interactive System* GoIPM *1.2 for Analysis of Power Units with Gas Turbine. Three-Shaft Turboprop Unit - Propeller Steady-States.* Institute of Information Theory and Automation, Prague. In Czech.

SCHINDLER Z., DOLEŽAL J. (1990a): *Interactive System* GoIPM *1.1 for Analysis of Power Units with Gas Turbine. Three-Shaft Turboprop Unit - User's Guide.* Institute of Information Theory and Automation, Prague. In Czech.

SCHINDLER Z., DOLEŽAL J. (1990b): *Interactive System* GoIPM *1.1 for Analysis of Power Units with Gas Turbine. Three-Shaft Bypass Unit - User's Guide.* Institute of Information Theory and Automation, Prague. In Czech.

SCHINDLER Z., DOLEŽAL J., MATOUŠEK O. (1991): *Optimization approach to the modelling of turbine aircraft engines.* 15the IFIP Conference on System Modelling and Optimization, Zurich, Sept. 2 - 6, 1991. To appear.

Search Based Planning for Decision Support

A.E. Eiben
Department of Mathematics and Computing Science
Eindhoven University of Technology
P.O.B. 513, 5600 MB Eindhoven
The Netherlands

Abstract

In this paper we discuss how search, and in particular optimization, can be used as a solution method in operational decision support systems. We first give a sketch of planning problems that can formally model operational decision problems. Thereafter we discuss how planning problems and search problems can be related and hereby the role of search is clarified. Optimization problems are identified as a special type of search problems having a special aim: finding the optimal value of a given object function. Search procedures to solve search problems are treated at last. We describe a General Search Procedure consisting of a constructive and an iterative part and enlighten how approximative optimization procedures are related to it.

Decision problems, also called planning problems, frequently occur in business environments. Computer systems providing support in decision or planning situations are called decision support systems (DSSs), cf. Bonczek, Holsappe and Whinston (1983), Sol (1985), Keen (1986), Anthonisse, Lenstra and Savelsbergh (1988). One mostly distinguishes strategical, tactical and operational decision problems although this classification is not strictly formal; whether or not a decision is considered to be strategic, tactic or operational is somewhat arbitrary. Nevertheless, in strategic and tactic decision situations there are so many factors to take into account and such an extent of uncertainty that attempts to model them formally have serious limitations. Therefore, we restrict ourselves to operational decision problems along this study, that is we consider problems where

- decisions have a short term impact (several hours to several days),
- a sound model of the decision situation can be given.

The role of a DSS can be described through its functions. We maintain the view presented in van Hee and Lapinski (1988), Eiben and van Hee (1990), and define a DSS as a system that can perform

- data management functions,
- evaluation of the effects of decisions proposed by the user,
- generation of decisions satisfying some user defined conditions.

The user defined conditions mentioned above can be *constraints* or *evaluation criteria.* A constraint is a qualitative condition, it is a property that might hold or not hold with respect to a decision. A decision that satisfies the given constraints is often labeled as *feasible*. An evaluation criterion is a quantitative measure on decisions. According to an evaluation criterion we can define a better–than relation between decisions and hence also *optimal* decisions can be defined.

Clusters of decisions are often called plans, therefore we shall use 'operational planning' and 'operational decision making' interchangeably. Accordingly, we shall talk in terms of plans instead of decisions in the sequel. Considering planning problems we distinguish three basic layers:

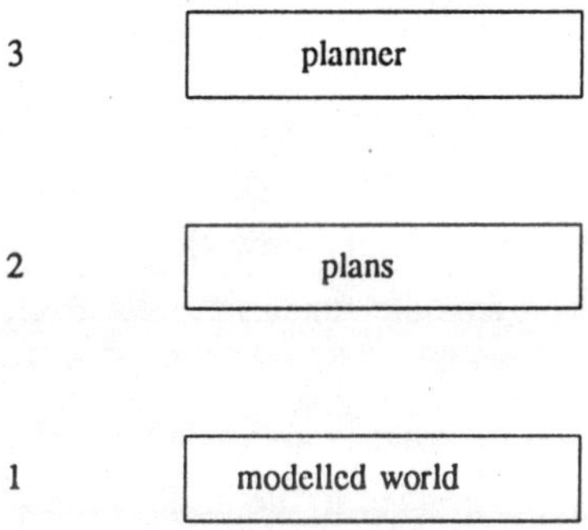

1) The lowest layer is formed by the world in consideration where a decision problem occurs. We assume that the world can be changing by itself and can also be changed by actions of actors, human or not.
2) The second layer is the level of plans constructed from elementary actions. Actions and plans are executable entities, their execution changes the world.
3) On the highest layer we find the planner or decision maker who wants to change the world in order to achieve some goals. Manipulating plans on the second layer he is working towards a desired plan to execute.

Notice that a planning problem (decision problem) can be defined in terms of layers (1) and (2), while it is handled on layers (2) and (3). It is important that manipulations acting on plans are strictly distinguished from actions that, when executed, modify the modelled world.

A crucial characteristics of planning problems is that time is involved. In Eiben (1989, 1991) there is a formal theory of planning problems, therefore we only give a simplified informal summary here. For the sake of simplicity let us restrict ourselves to such situations where the status of the world does not changes unless an action (or plan) is committed. Such a decision situation can be modeled by a formal *planning problem* that consists of the following:

1) a set of *world states*,
2) a set of *actions*,
3) a set of *time instances*,
4) a predicate *allowed* on actions with respect to states,
5) a function *effect* which assigns a state to the pair of a state and an action.
6) an *initial world state*,
7) a set of *goal states*,
8) a set of *evaluation criteria* with respect to plans.

Obviously, we also need certain general composition rules that specify how to construct plans from actions and how to extend the predicate *allowed* and the function *effect* from actions to plans.

A planning problem contains all the necessary information on what is given and what is wanted. A *solution of a planning problem* is a plan that – when applied to the initial state – leads to a goal state. An *optimal solution of a planning problem* is a plan that realizes an optimal value of the given criteria.

Search is a widely applied problem solving paradigm, see Simon (1983), Charniak and McDermott (1985). Our view about how to apply the space search concept for planning can be described stepwise.

i) We define a *search space* and the correspondence between the elements of the search space and plans. This latter is to guarantee that object in the search space mean something in the planning context. Notice that the search space can be identical to the set of all plans of a planning problem.

ii) We give *goal conditions* that specify a subspace of the whole search space. A solution of the search problem is meant as an element of this subspace; with other words it is an element that satisfies the goal conditions. Every element of the search space can be considered as a candidate for being a solution, therefore we call them *candidates* in the sequel. Obviously, the goal conditions must be given in such a way that solutions of the search problem correspond to solutions of the planning problem.

iii) There are *transition operators* or *manipulations* defined on the search space. Applying a transition operator (manipulation) to a candidate results in another candidate.

iv) A search problem is solved by traversing the search space by means of the transition operators (manipulations) defined in (iii), i.e. by stepping from candidate to candidate. A *search procedure* is a method that prescribes the way the consecutive steps are taken.

This view on planning by search brings a sophistication in the basic hierarchy described before. The modified taxonomy is depicted in the following figure:

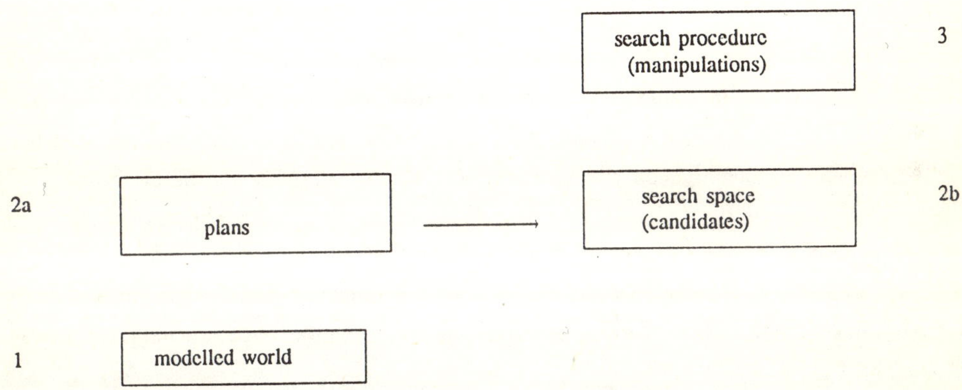

where (2a) and (2b) might coincide.

The arrow between (2a) and (2b) denotes that a mapping is fixed to define the correspondence between plans and candidates. Formally, if P is the set of all plans and the set C of candidates is the search space then we need a *representation function* $R : P \longrightarrow C$. Furthermore, we need to define a search problem in the context of C as a mirror image of the given planning problem such that solutions of the search problem deliver solutions for the planning problem through R. Notice that the actual search procedure belongs to the layers (2b) and (3); just like actions are the primitives of plans, manipulations stand for the elementary tools of the procedure.

By this approach we maintain a seemingly uncomplicated view about the activity of planning. At any point of the search space we have limited choices: we have to chose a possible manipulation at that point. The 'only' remaining difficulty is to decide which ones should be taken in order to reach a solution. It is typical for practical planning problems that the obtained search problem is mathematically intractable, cf. Garey and Johnson (1979), Papadimitriou and Steigliz (1982).

There is a natural division of these four points into two groups: (i) and (ii) contain **WHAT** is needed, while (iii) and (iv) specify **HOW** we are trying to obtain it. From the viewpoint of planning problems we can also justify this distinction of the two groups: (i) and (ii) embody a translation of the planning problem to the search context, (iii) and (iv) constitute a solution method to solve the resulted problem. This motivates our terminology: from now on we talk about a *search problem* referring to (i) and (ii), while a *search procedure* concerns (iii) and (iv).

The most natural choice for the search space is obviously the set of all plans. In practice, however, it can occur that one has a certain search procedure to be applied and this procedure can not directly handle plans. In this case we have to define the link between the planning problem and the algorithm by a search problem and a representation function.

In practical cases we have observed a resemblance in the way the candidates are defined. First, one defines elementary objects to construct the candidates from. Then one specifies a way of construction and defines candidates as complex objects correctly constructed from the elementary objects. The set of all correctly constructed objects called the *free search space*.

Example 1

Let us take a travelling salesman problem, cf. Garey and Johnson (1979), with n cities. In this case, any plan is a route description, that is a path trough k ($k \leq n$) cities. The elementary objects are thus edges (arcs) going between the given cities, the construction rule is 'concatenation of edges (arcs)'.

Observe that the free search space defined for a planning problem can be too wide, i.e. there can be candidates that we cannot interpret in the terms of the planning problem. A reason for this can be that the elementary objects and the construction rules to build the candidates are not defined sharp enough: there are meaningless or unwanted constructions that must be filtered out. In practice, such a restriction on the free search space is often expressed as a conjunction of more conditions that we shall call *constraints* in the sequel. Constraints to filter out impossible or meaningless candidates are considered as *hard constraints*, since they are rooted in the planning problem itself, they are not to express some subjective wishes. Nevertheless, there can be possible but unwanted candidates depending on the preferences of the planner. Constraints that are used to exclude such candidates are mostly called a *soft constraints*.

Example 2
Again for a travelling salesman problem, we can exclude incorrect routes by a hard constraint requiring that a plan does not contain cycli. A soft constraint can be for instance: 'the city nr. 5 is visited before the city nr. 2'.

A *feasibility condition* $\varphi_f : C \longrightarrow \{\text{true, false}\}$ over the free search space divides candidates into *feasible* and *infeasible candidates*. It is common for search methods that they restrict the search to the *feasible search space*

$$C_f = \{ c \in C \mid \varphi_f(c) = \text{true} \}.$$

Let us remark that within a search problem there is no difference between the soft and the hard constraints that specify φ_f. Practically, however, they play a different role: the hard constraint must be satisfied by the planner, while he has the freedom to modify (add or delete) soft constraints.

To define the goal of the search we have to specify which candidates are satisfactory to terminate with, that is the solutions of the search problem need to be defined. Therefore we also use a *goal condition* $\varphi_g : C \longrightarrow \{\text{true, false}\}$ over the free search space.
A *search problem* is a 3–tuple $(C, \varphi_f, \varphi_g)$, where C is a set of candidates, the free search space, φ_f and φ_g are the feasibility condition and the goal condition, respectively. A *solution of a search problem* is a candidate $c \in C$ for which

$$\varphi_f(c) = \text{true} \quad \text{and} \quad \varphi_g(c) = \text{true}$$

holds. Notice that modifying the soft constraints we change the search problem, since according to these modifications the feasibility condition changes.

Now we can articulate the formal basis of applying search for planning. If for a given planning problem we can define a search problem and a representation function R such that

- feasible candidates yield allowed plans through R^{-1} and
- solutions of the search problem yield solutions of the planning problem through R^{-1}

then we can look for a search procedure that finds a solution of the search problem.

By an *optimization problem* we mean a minimization problem. A *minimization problem* is a pair (C, f), where C is an arbitrary set, $f : C \longrightarrow \mathbb{R}$ is the so called *object function.* The aim in a minimization problem is to find a minimum of f over C, that is a $c \in C$ such that

$$\forall d \in C : f(c) \leq f(d).$$

It is clear that optimization problems can be seen as search problems: an optimization problem (C, f) can be expressed as a search problem $(C, \varphi_f, \varphi_g)$, where

$$\varphi_f(c) \equiv \text{true},$$

$$\varphi_g(c) = \text{true} \Leftrightarrow \forall d \in C : f(c) \leq f(d).$$

Observe that in the definition of a minimum there is a universal quantifier that ranges over the whole C. This means that verifying that a certain $c \in C$ is a minimum can be very difficult even if C is finite. Furthermore, in practice it is not always needed to find an absolute minimum of f. Therefore one often considers a *simplified optimization problem,* where only

$$f(c) \leq D$$

is required for a boundary D given in advance. Let us remark that such a simplified optimization problem is not necessarily easy to solve. A great deal of the NP–complete problems listed in Garey and Johnson (1979) is a simplified optimization problem in the above sense.

When can we apply optimization for solving decision problems ? The answer is straightforward:

- either if there are evaluation criteria given in the problem (eg. for travelling salesman problems a feasible plan is needed with a minimal route length);
- or if we can define an object function in a natural way, such that optimizing this function coincides with satisfying the original goal conditions (eg. for time table problems a plan is a solution if each lecture is scheduled, i.e. if the number of unscheduled lectures is 0).

In any of these two cases we can couple an evaluation criterion as an object function f to the set of all plans P, hence we obtain an optimization problem (P, f) that transforms to $(C, R \circ f)$.

Next we study search and optimization methods by one model. To solve search problems we consider (stochastic) iterative generate–and–test search procedures. Distinguishing their most crucial components we make up a General Search Procedure (GSP) maintaining a list of candidates in each iteration cycle. This list is called a *population.* The rough outlines of the GSP are:

```
Construct initial population
WHILE NOT stop DO
  BEGIN
      Choose elements of the population
      Produce new elements from the selected ones
      Extend the population by adding the new elements to it
      Select elements of the extended population to survive for the next cycle
  END
```

Without going into details we remark that by setting the components ***construct, stop, choose, produce*** and ***select*** appropriately, we can obtain different well–known methods as instances of the GSP. The formal definitions of the components and the instantiations leading to Genetic Algorithms and Simulated Annealing are described in detail in Aarts, Eiben and van Hee (1991). In Eiben (1991) Depth–first Search, Breadth–first Search, Best–first Search and Threshold Accepting are also discussed; in van Hee and Nuijten (1991) a Prolog implementation of GSP is given.

The advantage of using the GSP as a framework to specify search procedures is that of generality. First, the above mentioned methods can be defined and used problem independently to a big extent, which allows the re–use of a previously defined procedure. Notice that this does not forbid one to incorporate problem dependent knowledge into the solution method, but it leaves one free to do or not to do it. Secondly, the generality of the scheme of GSP permits (re)defining the search components within the same framework, thus it supports using different solution methods within the same DSS. These latter features make the GSP not only theoretically, but also practically applicable for being used in automated decision support.

As a matter of fact a search procedure (an instance of GSP) consists of two important components: a *constructive part* and an *iterative part*. The constructive part is to create an initial population, containing one or more candidates. This construction part is likely to be highly problem dependent, relying on the special structure of the given problem. After having at least one (feasible) candidate the iteration part can begin. The iteration steps posses a problem independent inner structure as the above WHILE loop exhibits it: in our vision every iteration procedure contains a choice, a production and a selection step.

Just as optimization problems are seen as special search problems we can consider optimization procedures as special search procedures. If the given search problem is an optimization problem then the iteration should yield still better candidates and approximate the optimum. Therefore, in such a case the name *improvement* for the iterative part of a search procedure is appropriate. When emphasizing the feature that iteration methods are approaching an optimum the name *approximation* is often used.

Obviously, it is a crucial question about improvement procedures whether they actually find an optimum of the given object function. For stochastic procedures this question should be understood as asking about probabilistic convergence properties of a procedure. In Eiben (1991) we present a couple of convergence results stating that under several general conditions any instance of the GSP finds an optimum with probability 1. In Aarts, Eiben and van Hee (1991) these results are interpreted for genetic algorithms, cf. Goldberg (1989), and simulated annealing, see Aarts and Korst (1989).

Literature

Aarts, E.H.L., Eiben, A.E. and van Hee, K.M., Global Convergence of Genetic Algorithms: A Markov Chain Analysis, Proceedings of the International Workshop Parallel Problem Solving from Nature, Springer–Verlag, 1991. (in press)

Aarts, E.H.L. and Korst, J., Simulated Annealing and Boltzmann Machines, J. Wiley and Sons, 1989.

Anthonisse, J.M., Lenstra, J.K. and Savelsbergh, M.W.P., Behind the screen: DSS from an OR point of view, Thechnical report 11.88/02, NFI, 1988.

Bonczek, R.H., Holsappe, C.W. and Whinston, A.B., Specification of modelling and knowledge in decision support systems, in Sol, H.G. (ed.), Processes and Tools for Decision Support, North–Holland, 1983.

Charniak, E. and McDermott, D., Introduction to Artificial Intelligence, Addison–Wesley, 1985.

Eiben, A.E., Modeling Planning Problems, in: Lecture Notes in Computer Science, Vol. 364: Proceedings of MFDBS 89, Springer–Verlag, 1989.

Eiben, A.E. and van Hee, K.M., Knowledge Representation and Search Methods for Decision Support Systems, in: Gaul, W. and Schader, M. (eds.), Data, Expert Knowledge and Decisions, NATO ASI Series, Vol. F 61, Springer Verlag, 1990.

Garey, R.M. and Johnson, D.S., Computers and Intractability: A Guide to the Theory of NP–Completeness, Freeman and Co., 1979.

van Hee, K.M. and Lapinski, A., OR and AI Approaches to Decision Support Systems, Decision Support Systems 4 (1988), pp. 447–459.

van Hee, K.M. and Nuijten, W.P.M., A Decision Generator Shell in Prolog, Proceedings of CISM–IIASA Summer School on Methodology, Implementation and Applications of DSS, Udine, 1990, in press.

Goldberg, D.E., Genetic Algorithms in Search, Optimization and Machine Learning, Addison–Wesley, Reading MA, 1989.

Keen, P.G.W., Decision Support Systems: The Next Decade, in McLean, E.R. and Sol, H.G., Decision Support Systems: A Decade in Perspective, North–Holland, 1986.

Papadimitriou, C.H. and Steiglitz, K., Combinatorial Optimization: Algorithms and Complexity, Prentice –Hall, Englewood Cliffs, N.J., 1982.

Simon, H.A., Search and Reasoning in Problem Solving, Artificial Intelligence 21 (1983), pp. 7–29.

Sol, H.G., DSS: Buzzword or OR challenge?, European Journal of Operational Research 22 (1985), pp. 1–8.

User-Oriented Optimization System OptiA for the Solution of Mathematical Programming Problems

J. FIDLER, J. DOLEŽAL, J. PACOVSKÝ

Institute of Information Theory and Automation of the
Czechoslovak Academy of Sciences, 182 08 Prague, Czechoslovakia

Introduction

The presented version of the OptiA system represents a user-friendly interactive *environment* for the definition, solution and analysis of mathematical programming problems. This menu-driven system is implemented on PCs and supports all stages necessary for the fast and efficient treatment of various classes of such problems: unconstrained, constrained, quadratic, global, and nonsmooth. Support includes the source code edition, its compilation (Fortran, Pascal, C) and linking with the selected numerical method and other modules, and finally execution and analysis of results.

The system is equipped by a number of efficient algorithms illustrating the power of mathematical programming techniques. User can easily incorporate his favourite algoritms to be supported by this environment, which is *open* with respect to both, the number of the methods in the given class and the number of the supported classes of mathematical programming problems. Many existing numerical methods are thus made accessible also to non-expert users in other areas of education, science and technology. The system can be alternatively considered as a support tool for efficient solution of decision-making and design problems involving parameter optimization subproblems.

Basic Problem Formulation

Theoretical and numerical developments in the field of nonlinear mathematical programming in the last two decades contributed to a large extent to the availability of powerful methods and numerical algorithms for the solution of various classes of mathematical programming problems. The most frequent form of such problems assumes

$$\min \; f(x_1, \ldots, x_n),$$

subject to the equality and inequality type constraints

$$\begin{aligned} g_i(x_1, \ldots, x_n) &= 0, \quad i = 1, \ldots, m_e, \\ g_i(x_1, \ldots, x_n) &\leq 0, \quad i = m_e + 1, \ldots, m. \end{aligned}$$

Needless to say that many practical problems can be brought to such form and treated in a unified way.

However, it must be realized that many of the available methods still require fairly deep mathematical programming and related numerical analysis background for their successful implementation. This cicrumstance prevents large-scale exploitation of many methods by an avarage user. Therefore many optimization packages and libraries came to their existence in the past, being mostly limited for the use on mainframes. Recent achievements in PC technology made it possible to run most of the existing optimization codes on such hardware, and to take full advantage of their interactive and graphical capabilities. Then various kinds of the supporting user-friendly systems can be developed and the available power of optimization methods may be nowadays brought to the disposal of non-expert users. Menu-driven facilities with extensive explanatory help system to a considerable extent substitute the earlier necessity of sufficient theoretical knowledge. In this way the applicability areas of mathematical programming methodology are considerably promoted and increased.

OptiA System Description

The current version of the **OptiA** software system (DOLEŽAL et al., 1990a) is based on the recently distributed prototype (FIDLER et al., 1988) and the previous effort of the authors to unify and implement a number of available methods for numerical solution of nonlinear mathematical programming problems (FIDLER et al., 1987a, 1987b). The system enables the user to perform fast and efficient solution of the following fundamental classes of problems:

1. Unconstrained (local) minimization of a function of several variables.
2. Minimization of a function of several variables under the equality and inequality type constraints.
3. Quadratic programming.
4. Global minimization of a function of several variables on an interval in R^n.
5. Minimization of a nonsmooth (locally Lipschitz) function.

For each such class of mathematical programming problems usually several methods are available to provide straightforward performance comparison and experimentation when solving a particular problem. Moreover, the algorithm base (source codes in Microsoft[1] Fortran, Pascal or C programming language, resp. their compiled object modules) is constructed as an *open* library, so that the existing user's own methods can be easily added satisfying only the simple compatibility requirements. Alternatively, it is not difficult to augment the system capabilities to handle other classes of optimization problems, e.g. data fitting problems, multicriteria optimization, min-max problems, etc., with full support of the **OptiA** system.

The implemented environment prepared in C programming language is basically dedicated to support all routine solution steps. Namely, the menu-driven system navigates the user when setting up and then solving the given problem. The so-called

[1]registered trademark

prototypes of possible problem description (*definition*) and control codes (*main, monitor*) decrease the extent of editing. In this context any favourite editor (Edlin[2], Norton Editor[2], Kedit[2]) can be used. The prepared problem description and the control program are compiled by the user-licenced Fortran, Pascal or C compilers, which are also used to generate supplied *object modules* of all included minimization codes.

The user need not to bother with the details of compiling the problem description and the respective control programs by anyone of the mentioned compilers (not necessarily by the same one), of linking with the selected method object module, and of executing the resulting module. Input/output information is provided in an interactive mode and its extent is determined by the user, who can invoke any time the context sensitive help to obtain the respective option description and explanation.

The course of calculations is monitored on the display and there is always an opportunity to interupt the program execution, to analyse the intermediate results, to change the control parameters or to switch to any other method. Simultaneously, also a solution *protocol* is prepared according to the user's specifications. The existing disadvantage of the compulsory compilation of any problem description (suitable and efficient interpreter not yet available) offers, on the other hand, the user considerable amount of flexibility when optimization results are only the intermediate stage of calculations and further manipulation with the current data cannot be avoided.

OptiA System Implementation

Because of the memory limitation for some methods, the number of variables (n) and of constraints (m) is generally limited to 20. Such limit is fully acceptable in academic and many practical applications. For a mathematical programming problem from any of the above mentioned classes a computer code is generated according to the user's instructions. This code consists of the four specific files:

1. *Main program.* It provides the input of initial and control parameters and calling of the selected solution method available in the subroutine form. Alternatively, user's optional calculations may be inserted here.
2. *Problem definition.* It contains several subroutines necessary for the support of the selected solution method. It includes the evaluation subroutine for the function to be minimized and according to the type of the solution method also the evaluation subroutines for constraints, gradients of all functions (analytical or adaptive difference formula), Hessian matrix, etc.
3. *Minimization method.* It contains a minimization algorithm selected by the user.
4. *Monitoring subroutine.* It provides the current information of calculation status on the display, or the communication with solved problem during its solution by a minimization method. Either standard system version or user supplied alternative can be used.

[2]registered trademark

The current version enables the user mixing of these source files written in the above mentioned programming languages except of the selected minimization method available, as a rule, only in the object form. User's own methods can be written again in any supported language. For the OptiA system internal communication the subsequent notation is introduced. Each filename begins with four characters, i. e. ABnn*.xxx. However, this usage is not obligatory, and it is mostly dictated by mnemonic aspects. The user can run the system providing his substitutes of these filenames in the system configuration file. The character combination AB determines the class of the solved problem. For the considered five classes it means:

1. UC — Unconstrained Optimization
2. CO — Constrained Optimization
3. QP — Quadratic Programming
4. GO — Global Optimization
5. NO — Nonsmooth Optimization

The next two figures nn specify a particular method in the given class. In the context with xxx = FOR, resp. PAS, resp. C, or xxx == OBJ there is a unique denotation of a file containing the respective method. Such notation then appears in the menu-lists. To each method the corresponding prototype files for supported compilers are supplied. Denotation *prototype* stands for the prefabricated fundamental structure of the Fortran, Pascal or C source module for the respective main program, monitoring program and problem definition. These modules contain all necessary statements for the initialization of the selected minimization method and optional calculations. Only those statements specific for the given problem are to be inserted into the offered prototypes.

Definition of a particular problem and setup of calculation course in the system is provided by the appropriate selection of four problem specific files from the following set:

MYPROBL.MAF	MAin program source Fortran file
MYPROBL.MAP	MAin program source Pascal file
MYPROBL.MAC	MAin program source C file
MYPROBL.MAO	MAin program Object file
MYPROBL.DEF	problem DEfinition source Fortran file
MYPROBL.DEP	problem DEfinition source Pascal file
MYPROBL.DEC	problem DEfinition source C file
MYPROBL.DEO	problem DEfinition Object file
MYPROBL.MOF	MOnitoring subroutine source Fortran file
MYPROBL.MOP	MOnitoring subroutine source Pascal file
MYPROBL.MOC	MOnitoring subroutine source C file
MYPROBL.MOO	MOnitoring subroutine Object file
MYPROBL.EXE	EXEcutable problem file

As a result of compilation-linging cycle the executable module MYPROBL.EXE is created. Information concerning the available solution methods and the available files for the solution definition is provided via the system control file MYPROBL.EXM. This file can be any time modified by the user to register new items or to delete unnecessary ones.

As pointed out earlier, during the problem setup, i. e. preparation of the main, monitor and definition files, the user can, in principle, select various supported compilers without any restriction. The same is true if an alternative solution method, provided by the user, is being developed and tested on the existing examples.

Optimization Methods

For the sake of the reader's better orientation in the possibilities of the **OptiA** system let us include the list of available methods in current version of the system. First item in the row is the *filename*, second the *solution method*, and third the **OptiA**-*menu* name.

1. Unconstrained local minimization of a function of several variables

   (a) Derivative-free methods

UC01	Powell	`Powell`
UC02	Nelder-Mead	`Nelder-Mead`

   (b) Methods using a derivative

UC11	Davidon-Fletcher-Powell	`Dav.Fletch.Pow.`
UC12	Broyden	`Broyden`
UC13	Pearson 2	`Pearson_2`
UC14	Pearson 3	`Pearson_3`
UC15	Newton with gradient proj.	`Newton_proj.`
UC16	Fletcher-Reeves	`Fletch.Reeves`
UC17	Goldstein-Price	`Goldst.Price`
UC18	Newton	`Newton`

2. Local minimization of a function of several variables with constraints

C001	Davidon-Fletcher-Powell	`Dav.Fletch.Pow.`
C002	Biggs	`Biggs_I`
C003	Biggs (modification)	`Biggs_II`
C004	Powell with variable metric	`Powell_var.met.`
C005	Powell – watch dog	`Powell_WD`
C006	augmented Lagrangian	`Aug.Lag.Proj.`
C007	Nelder-Mead	`Nelder-Mead`
C008	Schittkowski	`Schittkowski`

3. Quadratic programming

QP01	Powell	`Powell_quad.`
QP02	Schittkowski	`Schitt_quad.`

4. Global minimization of a function of several variables on an interval in R^n

G001	based on cluster analysis	`Glob.opt.`
G002	Monte Carlo	`Mt.Carlo_glob.`
G003	Bayes	`Bayes_glob.`
G004	LP-search method	`LP-Search_glob.`
G005	Zilinskas' method	`Zilinskas_glob.`

5. Minimization of a nonsmooth (locally lipschitzian) function of several variables

N001	bundle without constraints	Lemarechal_unc.
N002	bundle with constraints	Lemarechal_cons.

Because of the limited extent of this contribution let us include at least the description of the fundamental stage as seen on the screen (Fig. 1), where the selected class of constrained minimization methods is depicted together with the specified method (variable metric method of Powell – C004). Upmost line informs about the existing basic options further specified in the subordinated menu windows.

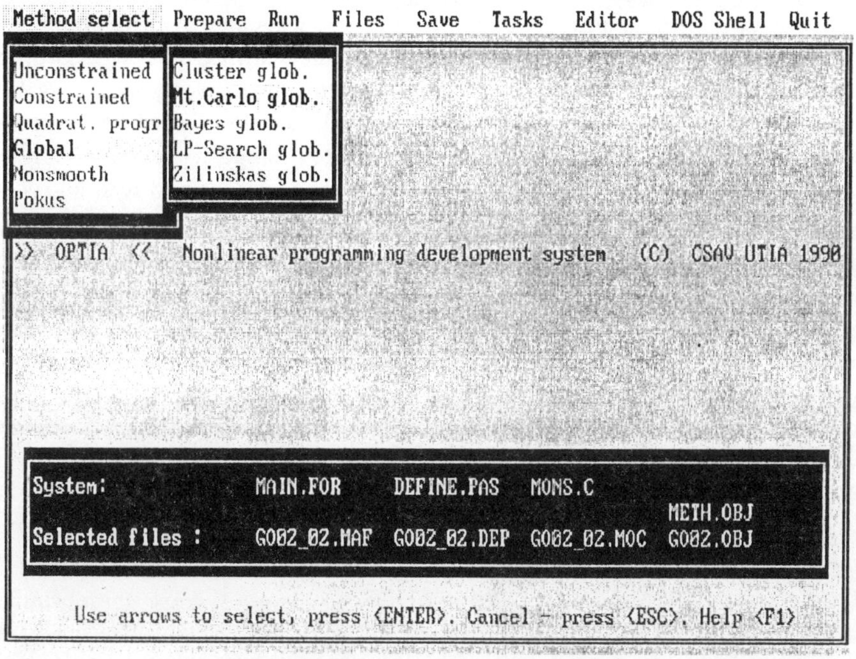

Fig. 1. **OptiA** system fundamental screen

Dark window in the lower part of the screen provides the information concerning the currently selected files for a particular problem formally denoted C004_03 (third line) and the solution stage status, e. i. if the respective file is available in the source (extension FOR, PAS, C) or object form (extension OBJ) – first and second line, respectively. The performed selection shows that combination of all possible source files is feasible, maybe this not being the most frequent case. All necessary details can be found in the updated *User's Guide* (DOLEŽAL et al., 1990a).

Using the **OptiA** system is fairly simple and straightforward. Due to the authors' experience it can be managed in a very short time using the step-by-step solved explanatory *Examples* (DOLEŽAL et al., 1990b). This fact predetermines the existing interest to use the **OptiA** system as an advanced educational tool by a number of universities. Also the choice of a suitable method for special applications can be easily performed by the system on a typical case prepared according to the **OptiA** conventions. In fact, the system can handle practically any program appropriately included in the *main* file. Then the selected method can be used with the user's original program independently.

Conclusions

The **OptiA** system can be implemented on any IBM compatible PC (XT and higher) equipped with a hard disk. For this application area also arithmetic coprocessor is highly recommended. The system is under current development, the prepared version will provide additional efficient algorithms for user's experimentation. New classes of methods will deal with min-max and multicriterial mathematical programming problems. In this context is it necessary to point out the fact that **OptiA** system is primarily *user-oriented integrated environment* equipped by an illustrative collection of the appropriate numerical algorithms, which were developed and distributed by many people. Their inclusion into the system should facilitate further promotion and wider application of optimization techniques in various areas of education, science and technology.

Similar optimization systems are nowadays developed on several places. Let us mention at least the EMP (Expert for Mathematical Programming) system (SCHITTKOWSKI, 1987) featuring certain *expert-like* support for the user and nowadays implemented also on mainframe computers, general DISO (DIalogue System for Optimization) system (EVTUSHENKO et al., 1988) exhibiting built-in interpreter and automatic differentiator, or user-friendly PADMOS (PAscal Automatic Differentiation München Optimization System) system (KREDLER et al., 1990) available also in a commertial version. Let us note that PADMOS implements automatic differentiation analogous to FISCHER (1987), however the distributed collection of minimization methods is still limited and TurboPascal implementation allows linking with Turbo C routines only.

It is worth to observe longer effort, e.g. see DIXON and PRICE (1986), EVTUSHENKO et al. (1988) or SCHITTKOWSKI (1990), to equip the existing optimization techniques and systems with automatic differentiation option, which is by far superior to somewhat clumsy symbolic differentiation (GRIEWANK, 1989). Seemingly such approach was first appropriately described by RALL (1981). Together with parallel development of problem-oriented interpreter module (precompiler) such effort results in implementation of optimization systems not necessarily bound to any specific compiler.

Such options, on the one hand, can enable more comfortable solution for a given class of problems with no compilation or linking. On the other hand, it has to be realized that not negligible part of system generality and flexibility will be lost. Also less convenient solution time can be expected. It seems therefore practical to implement such options only alternatively for the sake of comparison or illustration and to preserve the existing freedom in running practically any program involving parameter optimization under the existing user-friendly optimization environment. Analogous options including also graphic-like module for visualization of various computational stages are planned for future versions of the **OptiA** system aiming to support also the solution of optimal control problems.

References

DIXON L. C. W., PRICE R. C. (1986): *The truncated Newton method for sparse unconstrained optimisation using automatic differentiation.* Technical Report No. 170, The Hatfield Polytechnic, Hatfield.

DOLEŽAL J., FIDLER J. , PACOVSKÝ J. (1990a): *Dialogue-Oriented System* OptiA *for Minimization of Functions of Several Variables. Version 2.8 - User's Guide.* DFG Report No. 243, Universität Bayreuth, Bayreuth 1990.

DOLEŽAL J., FIDLER J. , PACOVSKÝ J. (1990b): *Dialogue-Oriented System* OptiA *for Minimization of Functions of Several Variables. Version 2.8 - Examples.* DFG Report No. 244, Universität Bayreuth, Bayreuth 1990.

EVTUSHENKO Y., MAZOURIK V., RATKIN V. (1988): *Multicriteria optimization in DISO system.* In: *System Modelling and Optimization,* M. Iri, K. Yajima (Eds.), Springer-Verlag, Berlin-Heidelberg-New York, pp. 231–240.

FIDLER J., DOLEŽAL J., SCHINDLER Z. (1987a): *User-Oriented Package for Constrained Minimization of Functions of Several Variables.* Research Report No. 1429, Institute of Information Theory and Automation, Prague. In Czech.

FIDLER J., DOLEŽAL J., SCHINDLER Z. (1987b): *PC Implementation of User-Oriented Package for Constrained Minimization.* Research Report No. 1480, Institute of Information Theory and Automation, Prague. In Czech.

FIDLER J., PACOVSKÝ J., DOLEŽAL J., SCHINDLER Z., OUTRATA J. (1988): *Dialogue-Oriented System* OptiA *for Minimization of Functions of Several Variables. Version 2.0. User's Guide.* Institute of Information Theory and Automation, Prague.

FISCHER H. (1987): *Some Aspects of Automatic Differentiation.* Technical Report No. 107 Institut für Angewandte Mathematik und Statistik, Technische Universität München, München.

GRIEWANK A. (1989): *On Automatic Differentiation.* In: *Mathamatical Programming: Recent Developments and Applications,* M. Iri, K. Tanabe (Eds.), Kluwer Academic Publishers, Dordrecht-Boston-London, pp. 83–108.

KREDLER CH., GREINER M., KÖLBL A., PURSCHE T. (1990): *User's Guide for PADMOS.* Institut für Angwandte Mathematik und Statistik, Technische Universität München, München.

RALL L. B. (1981): *Automatic Differentiation: Techniques and Applications.* Springer-Verlag, Berlin-Heidelberg-New York.

SCHITTKOWSKI K. (1987): *EMP: An Expert System for Mathematical Programming.* Mathematisches Institut, Universität Bayreuth, Bayreuth.

SCHITTKOWSKI K. (1990): Private communication.

Probabilistic Analysis of Algorithms for Stuck-at Test Generation in PLAs

John Franco
Department of Computer Science
University of Cincinnati
Cincinnati, OH 45221-0008

June 20, 1991

Abstract

A collection of fast algorithms for generating test vectors for PLAs is presented and analyzed. It is shown that, in some sense, complete sets of test vectors for almost all such circuits which are irredundant, primal, and non-tautological can be generated quickly.

1 Introduction

It has been known for some time that logic optimization can produce circuits that are completely testable for all stuck-at faults. The relationship between testability and Boolean minimization for two-level combinational circuits dates back to the Quine-McCluskey algorithm [8]. The notions of primality and irredundancy were generalized for multi-level circuits in [1]. Recent work in synthesis for testability has been able to ensure complete multiple-fault testability for multi-level combinational logic circuits [5]. All of these results only show in varying ways that with unlimited computational resources test vectors could be generated for all stuck-at faults in a circuit; however, in practice the testability of a circuit is that which can be found with relatively modest computational resources.

Because the testability problem is NP-complete [6], there probably are no algorithms for testability which are sufficiently fast for every input. However, in practice it is often noticed that that test vector design is actually "easy." This paper presents formal evidence that full testability is extremely easy for nearly all randomly generated two-level circuits. Two-level circuits are of interest because they are naturally implemented in programmable-logic arrays (PLA's).

The AND/OR structure of a two-level circuit corresponds naturally to sum-of-products structure of disjunctive-normal-form (DNF). In such circuits all single and multiple stuck-at faults are testable if all single stuck-at-faults on the inputs and outputs of the AND gates are testable [7]. Finding a test vector for the output of AND gate is equivalent to finding a truth assignment that falsifies all clauses in the corresponding DNF expression, except for the clause that corresponds to the node under test, and sets that clause to *false* if a stuck-at-1 test is being generated or *true* if a stuck-at-0 test is being generated.

What we intend to show is that, in some sense, a large class of prime and irredundant circuit instances are provably testable in polynomial time. Thus, for a class of circuit instances complete testability is strongly associated with easy testability. We do this by showing that test vectors can be obtained in polynomial time for almost all prime and irredundant instances generated by a standard probabilistic model.

It should be noted that there are some remaining problems in the direct application of this work to testing PLA's. The first is that the testing of PLA's in current technologies typically requires testing for shorts and cross-point faults, as well as stuck-at faults; furthermore, to address these additional faults specialized design for testability methods such as those described in [4] may be used. Secondly, the optimization approach used in some of the current heuristic two-level logic optimizers, such as [2], could theoretically generate stuck-at fault test vectors as a side effect, although in current practice test vectors are generated by auxillary tools. Despite these practical limitations we feel that this work is well motivated by the need to improve our understanding of the relationship between complete testability and ease of testability, and that it is natural to begin a study of this problem in the better understood domain of two-level circuits.

2 Preliminaries

A Boolean variable can take two values, *true* and *false*. A literal is either a negated or unnegated Boolean variable. If the literal is negated its value is opposite the value of the corresponding variable. Otherwise the literal has the same value as the corresponding variable. If v is a Boolean variable its negated literal is $\bar{v}$. The literals v and $\bar{v}$ are said to be complementary.

A DNF Boolean expression is a disjunction of conjunctions of literals. We represent DNF expressions as a collection of sets of literals. Each set of literals is called a clause. A clause is satisfied and has value *true* if one of its literals has value *true*. A clause is falsified and has value *false* if all its literals have value *false*.

Definition:

The *functionality* of an expression I containing r Boolean variables is a mapping $F_I : B_1 \times B_2 ... B_r \rightarrow \{true, false\}$ where B_i, $1 \leq i \leq r$, is the Boolean value of variable v_i such that $F_I(t) = true$ if and only if at least one clause in I is satisfied by truth assignment t.

Definition:

A clause c in expression I is *irredundant* if removal of C from I changes the functionality of I.

Definition:

A literal l in clause c of expression I is *primal* if removal of l from c changes the functionality of I.

It is not the case that primality implies irredundancy. For example, each literal of each clause of $(a, \bar{b}), (\bar{b}, c), (\bar{a}, c)$ is primal but functionality is not changed if the clause $(\bar{b}, c)$ is dropped. It is also not the case that irredundancy implies primality. For example, each of the clauses of $(a, \bar{b}), (a, b)$ is irredundant but removal of neither literal b or $\bar{b}$ changes functionality.

We talk about testability of a DNF expression with the understanding that there is a direct mapping to the testability of the PLA based on that expression.

Definition:

> A DNF expression is ***completely testable*** if, a) for every clause there exist two truth assignments which satisfy and falsify the clause and falsify all other clauses; b) for every literal l in a clause c there exist two assignments which cause all other literals in c to have value *true*, cause l to have value *true* and *false*, and falsify all other clauses.

A clause for which both truth assignments do not exist is said to be not testable. A literal for which both truth assignments do not exist is said to be not testable.

DNF expressions that are irredundant and primal are completely testable. For suppose there is a clause e that is not testable. Then either there is one value that e may take such that all assignments inducing this value satisfy at least one other clause or there is a value that e may never take. In the second case e is redundant so we only consider the first case. Setting e to the opposite value does not change functionality hence e is redundant. A similar argument holds for testing literals.

3 The Probabilistic Model

The probabilistic model we use generates DNF Boolean expressions consisting of n independent clauses, each of which is constructed as follows. Let $V = v_1, v_2, ..., v_r$ be a set of r Boolean variables. For all $1 \leq i \leq r$, with probability p the clause contains v_i, with probability p the clause contains $\bar{v}_i$, and with probability $1 - 2p$ the clause contains neither. We call this model $M(n, r, p)$. An expression generated by the model will be called a random expression.

In a random expression it is possible for a clause to contain no literals. Such a clause will have no effect on the functionality of the expression. If p is set too low then all clauses contain no literals with probability tending to 1.

Lemma 1 *If* $\lim_{n,r\to\infty} pnr = 0$ *then a random expression contains only empty clauses with probability tending to 1.*

Proof:

The probability that a clause is empty is $(1-2p)^r$. The probability that all clauses are empty is $(1-2p)^{rn} = 1 - 2prn + O((prn)^2)$. The lemma follows. □

For a certain range of p there is at least one unit clause in a random expression.

Lemma 2 *If* $\lim_{n,r\to\infty} prn = \infty$ *and* $p < (1-\epsilon)\ln(n)/(2r)$ *for any* $\epsilon > 0$ *then the probability that there is a unit clause in a random expression tends to 1.*

Proof:

The probability that a particular clause is a unit clause is $\binom{r}{1}(2p)(1-2p)^{r-1}$. Hence the probability that a random expression contains no unit clauses is $f(p,r,n) = (1-2pr(1-2p)^{r-1})^n$. The expression $2pr(1-2p)^{r-1}$ has a maximum at $pr = 1$. We consider the endpoints $prn = k$ where k is large and $p = (1-\epsilon)\ln(n)/(2r)$ of the range specified by the hypothesis. If $prn = k$ then the probability that the expression contains no unit clauses is less than $e^{-2prn(1-2p)^r} < e^{-2k(1-k/n+O(1/n^2))}$. This tends to 0 as k increases. If $p = (1-\epsilon)\ln(n)/(2r)$ then the probability is less than $e^{-2prn(1-2p)^r} = e^{-(1-\epsilon)n\ln(n)(1-2p)^r} < n^{-(1-\epsilon)n^{1-(1-\epsilon)}} = n^{-(1-\epsilon)n^\epsilon}$. This tends to 0 as $n \to \infty$. Since $f(p,r,n) \to 0$ at the interval endpoints and $2pr(1-2p)^{r-1}$ increases from the low endoint to a maximum at $pr = 1$ and then decreases until the upper endpoint the lemma is proved. □

Over this range of p there are redundant clauses with high probability.

Lemma 3 *The probability that the literal of a unit clause is contained in another clause of a random expression tends to 1 if* $\lim_{n,r\to\infty} pn = \infty$ *and* $p < (1-\epsilon)\ln(n)/(2r)$ *for any* $\epsilon > 0$.

Proof:

From Lemma 2 the probability that there is a unit clause tends to 1. The probability that a literal which is the unit clause is not in any other clause is $(1-p)^{n-1}$. In the limit this is e^{-pn}. The lemma follows. □

From Lemmas 2 and 3, if $pn \to \infty$, and $p < (1-\epsilon)\ln(n)/(2r)$ then almost all random expressions have redundant clauses.

A tautology is not a reasonable PLA function. We restrict our attention to the range of p for which almost all random expressions are not tautologies.

Lemma 4 *The probability that a random truth assignment falsifies all clauses of an expression generated by $M(n,r,p)$ is greater than $(1-(1-p)^r)^n$.*

Proof:

The probability that a random truth assignment does not satisfy a clause is the probability that at least one of the literals in the clause is falsified or the clause contains no literals. This is greater than the probability that at least one of the literals in the clause is falsified which is one minus the probability that each of the r variables in V is either not in the clause or is in the clause but only as the literal that is made *true* by the truth assignment. This probability is $(1-(1-p)^r)$. The probability that all clauses are falsified is therefore greater than $(1-(1-p)^r)^n$. □

Lemma 5 *If $p > (1+\epsilon)\ln(n)/r$ for any $\epsilon > 0$ then a random expression is not tautological with probability tending to 1.*

Proof:

From Lemma 4 the probability that all clauses are falsified by a random input vector is greater than $(1-(1-p)^r)^n$. By comparing the Talyor series expansion of e^{-p} with $1-p$ we have $(1-(1-p)^r)^n \geq (1-e^{-pr})^n$. By hypothesis we have $(1-e^{-pr})^n \geq (1-e^{-(1+\epsilon)\ln(n)})^n = (1-n^{-(1+\epsilon)})^n$. But $\lim_{n,r\to\infty}(1-n^{-(1+\epsilon)})^n = e^{-n^{-\epsilon}} = 1$. Thus, the probability that a random truth assignment is a falsifying truth assignment, if $p > (1+\epsilon)\ln(n)/r$, is 1 in the limit. Hence, a random expression is not tautological with probability tending to 1 if $p > (1+\epsilon)\ln(n)/r$ for any $\epsilon > 0$. □

On the other hand,

Lemma 6 *If* $p = c\ln(n)/r$ *for any* $c < 1$ *and* $\lim_{n,r\to\infty} n^{1-c}/r = \infty$ *then a random instance is tautological with probability tending to 1. If* $p = \alpha(n)\ln(n)/r$ *where* $\alpha(n) = o(1)$ *and* $\lim_{n,r\to\infty} n/r = \infty$ *then a random instance is tautological with probability tending to 1.*

Proof:

The probability that a random truth assignment satisfies a clause is the probability that the clause has at least one literal and each variable in V is either not in the clause or is in the clause but only as the literal that is made *true* by the truth assignment. The probability that a clause contains at least one literal is $(1-(1-2p)^r)$. The probability that a clause is satisfied given it contains at least one literal is no less than $(1-p)^r$. Hence the probability that a random truth assignment satisfies a clause is no less than $(1-p)^r(1-(1-2p)^r)$ and the probability that a random truth assignment does not satisfy a clause is no greater than $(1-(1-p)^r(1-(1-2p)^r))$. The probability that a random truth assignment does not satisfy every clause is no greater than $(1-(1-p)^r(1-(1-2p)^r))^n$. The average number of truth assignments that do not satisfy every clause is no greater than $2^r(1-(1-p)^r(1-(1-2p)^r))^n$. Finally, the average number of truth assignments that do not satisfy every clause is an upper bound on the probability that there exists such a truth assignment. If $p = c\ln(n)/r$, where $c < 1$, then the average number of truth assignments that do not satisfy every clause is no greater than $e^{r\ln(2)-n^{1-c}}$. But $\lim_{n,r\to\infty} e^{r\ln(2)-n^{1-c}} = 0$ if $\lim_{n,r\to\infty} n^{1-c}/r = \infty$. If $p = \alpha(n)\ln(n)/r$ then the average number of non-satisfying truth assignments tends to 0 if $\lim_{n,r\to\infty} n/r = \infty$. □

In this section we have found conditions under which random expressions are redundant or tautological with probability tending to 1. To summarize, if $p < (1-\epsilon)\ln(n)/(2r)$, $\epsilon > 0$, and $pnr \to 0$ then almost all random expressions only have empty clauses. If $p < (1-\epsilon)\ln(n)/(2r)$, $\epsilon > 0$, and $pn \to \infty$ then almost all random expressions have redundant clauses. If $p = \alpha(n)\ln(n)/(2r)$, $\alpha(n) = o(1)$, and $n/r \to \infty$, then almost all random expressions are tautologies. If $p = c\ln(n)/r$ for any $c < 1$ and $n^{1-c}/r \to \infty$ then almost all random expressions are tautologies.

In the next section we consider testability in the remaining parameter space.

4 Algorithms For Testability and Analysis

In this section we consider the performance of algorithms for the testability of random DNF expressions.

If $p > c\ln(n)/r$ for every fixed c then testability is very easy. All we need to do for each clause is set its literals to *true* to test for stuck-at-0 (separately, set one literal to *false* to test for stuck-at-1) and then randomly select the remaining truth assignments. We call this the *random-method*.

Lemma 7 *If $p = \alpha(n)\ln(n)/r$ where $\alpha(n)$ is any growing function of n then the random-method finds a complete set of test vectors for a DNF expression generated according to $M(n,r,p)$ with probability $n^{-O(\alpha(n))}$.*

Proof:

> Since clauses are independent, the assignment is random with respect to all clauses but the one under test. Hence the probability that all clauses but the tested one are falsified by the assignment is greater than $(1-(1-p)^r)^n$. The average number of times such assignments fail to generate a valid test vector is less than $2n(1-(1-(1-p)^r)^n)$ since the total number of tests is $2n$ (stuck-at-0 and stuck-at-1 for each clause). This is an upper bound on the probability that at least one truth assignment fails to generate a valid test vector. Let $\alpha(r)$ be any function that increases with r. Let $p = \alpha(r)\ln(n)/r$. Then the probability that at least one truth assignment fails to generate a valid test vector is bounded from above by $2n(1-e^{-e^{-\alpha(r)\ln(n)}n}) = 2n(1-e^{-n^{1-\alpha(r)}}) = n^{-O(\alpha(r))}$. □

Since the random-method needs to be used $2rn + 2n$ times to generate all tests, the average number of times the method fails to produce a test is less than $rn^{-O(\alpha(r))}$. This is an upper bound on the probability of failure and tends to 0 as $n, r \to \infty$ if $n > r^\epsilon$ for any $\epsilon > 0$.

In the previous section we showed that random expressions are redundant if $pn \to \infty$ and $c < 1/2$. If $\lim_{n,r\to\infty} pn \neq \infty$, $c < 1/2$, and $\lim_{n,r\to\infty} n^{2-4c}/r = \infty$ then with probability tending to 1 the number of unit clauses in an expression is greater than $\sqrt{r^{1+\epsilon}}$ for any $\epsilon > 0$. If the number of unit clauses is greater than $\sqrt{r^{1+\epsilon}}$ then with probability tending to 1 there is at least one pair of unit clauses that is identical or one pair that is complementary. Then the expression is redundant or tautological.

Lemma 8 *If the number of unit clauses in a random expression e is greater than $\sqrt{r^{1+\epsilon}}$ for any $\epsilon > 0$ then with probability tending to 1 either there is an identical pair of unit clauses in e or else there is a complementary pair in e.*

Let m be the number of unit clauses The probability that there are no two clauses that are identical or complementary is $r!r^{-m}/(r-m)!$. By applying Stirling's approximation for factorials this is less than $(1-m/r)^{m-r}e^{m}$. In the limit this is $e^{-m^2/r}$. The lemma follows. □

Lemma 9 *If $p = \alpha(n)\ln(n)/r$ where $\alpha(n) < 1/2$, and $\lim_{n,r\to\infty} n^{2-4\alpha(n)}/r^{1+2\delta} = \infty$ for any $\delta > 0$ then with probability tending to 1 the number of unit clauses in a random expression is at least equal to $\sqrt{r^{1+2\delta}}$.*

The number of unit clauses is binomially distributed with mean $2pr(1-2p)^{r-1}n$. By the Chernoff bound for the binomial distribution the probability that the number of unit clauses is less than $1 - r^{-\delta/2}$ times the mean is less than $e^{-r^{-\delta}2pr(1-2p)^{r-1}n}/3 = \delta'(n,r)$. Let the mean be greater than $\sqrt{r^{1+2\delta}}$. Then the probability that the number of unit clauses is less than $\sqrt{r^{1+\delta}}$ is bounded from above by $\delta'(n,r) \to 0$. The mean is greater than $\sqrt{r^{1+2\delta}}$ if $\lim_{n,r\to\infty} n^{1-2\alpha(n)} > \sqrt{r^{1+2\delta}}$. The lemma follows. □

On the other hand, if $\lim_{n,r\to\infty} pn \neq \infty$, $c < 1/2$, and $\lim_{n,r\to\infty} n^{2-2c}/r = 0$ then variables are in so few clauses that with probability tending to 1 every clause contains either a literal that is not present in any other clause or contains a literal l such that every other clause that contains l or its complement also contains a literal that is not present in any other clause. We call this property of instances property P. A literal that appears in only one clause is said to be solitary.

An instance with property P, is either redundant or testable in polynomial time. To generate a stuck-at-1 test for a particular clause h in an irredundant expression, set all solitary literals to *false* and their complements to *true* then set all unset literals satisfying property P in clauses not yet falsified to *false* and their complements to *true*. As a result, all clauses will have value *false*. To generate a stuck-at-0 test for h, set all literals in h to *true* and their complements to *false*. Then set all solitary literals, excluding those of h, to *false* and their complements to *true*. Next, set all unset literals satisfying property P in clauses not yet falsified to *false* and their complements to *true*. All the clauses that have not yet been falsified contain literals that satisfy property P and have value *true* (from h); and/or do not satisfy property P. For such clauses, if there are no literals of the latter kind then the instance is redundant; if there are such literals, pick one that is unset and set it to *false* and its complement to *true*. If some clause other than h is still not falsified then h is redundant. Otherwise a test has been generated.

We now show that almost all random instances have property P under the conditions stated.

Lemma 10 *If* $p = \alpha(n)\ln(n)/r$ *where* $\alpha(n) < 1/2$, *and for any* $\epsilon > 0$, $\lim_{n,r\to\infty} n^{2-2\alpha(n)}/r^{1+\epsilon} = 0$ *then a random expression has property* P *with probability tending to 1.*

Consider any clause a and suppose it has x literals. We shall say that a is semi-valid if a contains no literals or or there is another literal in a which does not appear in any other clause. We find the result only for semi-valid clauses; this will bound the result stated in the hypothesis. The probability that a has x literals is $\binom{r}{x}(2p)^x(1-2p)^{r-x}$. The probability that a variable does not exist in a clause other than a is $(1-2p)^{n-1}$. Hence, the probability that at least one literal of a is not in any other clause given a has x literals is $1-(1-(1-2p)^n)^x$. The probability that a is semi-valid

$$\sum_{x=1}^{r}\binom{r}{x}(2p)^x(1-2p)^{r-x}(1-(1-(1-2p)^n)^x)+(1-2p)^r$$
$$= 1-\sum_{x=1}^{r}\binom{r}{x}(2p)^x(1-2p)^{r-x}(1-(1-2p)^n)^x$$
$$= 1-(1-2p+2p(1-(1-2p)^n))^r+(1-2p)^r$$
$$= 1-(1-2p(1-2p)^n)^r+(1-2p)^r.$$

Applying the binomial theorem and summing gives

$$1-(1-2p(1-2p)^n)^r+(1-2p)^r = 1-pn(1+O(pn))\sum_{i=1}^{r}\binom{r}{i}2i(-2p)^i$$
$$= 1-4p^2nr(1-2p)^r(1+O(pn)).$$

Thus, the probability that a is not semi-valid is $4p^2nr(1-2p)^r(1+O(pn))$. The average number of such clauses is $4p^2n^2r(1-2p)^r$. This is an upper bound on the probability that some clause in a random expression is not semi-valid. By the conditions of the hypothesis this is less than $4c^2(\ln(n))^2n^{2-2\alpha(n)}/r$. The lemma follows. □

From Lemmas 8,9,10 and the results of Section 2 we conclude that either there exist algorithms which find complete test sets for random expressions with probability tending to 1 or such expressions are redundant or tautological with probability tending to 1 if $p < \ln(n)/(2r)$. We now concentrate on the last remaining range of p.

If $p = c\ln(n)/r$, $c > 1/2$, and $\lim_{n,r\to\infty} n^{1-c}/r = 0$ then random instances are not tautological and do not possess property P with probability tending to 1. In this case we can use a variant of an algorithm called *UNSAT-FINDER* to generate complete tests with probability tending to 1. *UNSAT-FINDER*, takes a DNF Boolean expression I as input and either finds a truth assignment which does not satisfy I or gives up. Let V be the set of Boolean variables from which a random expressione I is constructed. Let L denote the set of literals associated with V. Let $var : L \to V$ be a mapping from literals to their associated variables. Let $T : V \to \{true, false, unset\}$ be a mapping from variables to Boolean values. T specifies a truth assignment to the variables in I; the value *unset* is treated as a *don't care*. It is constructed and returned by *UNSAT-FINDER* if the algorithm does not give up.

UNSAT-FINDER(I):
For all $v \in V$, set $T(v) = unset$
Repeat
Let C_{min} denote the collection of clauses in I with the least number of literals
Randomly select literal l from C_{min}
If l is positive set $T(var(l)) = false$, Otherwise set $T(var(l)) = true$
set $I = \{c - comp(l) | c \in I, l \notin c\}$
Until there exists a null clause or $I = \Phi$
If $I = \Phi$ then return T, Otherwise give up

It should be clear that if *UNSAT-FINDER* returns a truth assignment, that truth assignment falsifies the original expression I. It should also be clear that *UNSAT-FINDER* runs in time bounded by a polynomial in the length of I. The conditions for which the probability that *UNSAT-FINDER* gives up tends to 0 are also the conditions for which random instances are not tautological. We wish to find those conditions when $p < \ln(n)/r$ (since we already know that instances are not tautological in probability when $p > \ln(n)/r$). The result is similar to a dual result on CNF Boolean instances and a "unit-clause" algorithm that was presented in [3]. However, that result is not strong enough to be applied here. Therefore, in what follows we strengthen the result of [3] and adapt it to *UNSAT-FINDER* while lifting some lemmas directly from that paper.

For the sake of simplifying the analysis we suppose that *UNSAT-FINDER* selects a literal from a smallest clause only if there exist clauses of size less than $\ln(2pr)$ (recall that $2pr$ is the average size of clauses). Otherwise, *UNSAT-FINDER* selects a literal randomly from the set of unset literals. In the analysis below references to *UNSAT-FINDER* are to this modified version.

We need to find the probability that no null clauses are generated by *UNSAT-FINDER*. We do so by modeling the flow of clauses through various states during execution of the algorithm. During each iteration of *UNSAT-FINDER* clauses containing the chosen literal are removed from I (because they are clauses that become falsified by the assignment $T(var(l))$) and occurrences in I of the complement of the chosen literal are removed (because they represent literals that have value *true* as a result of the assignment $T(var(l))$). Let $C_i(j)$ denote the collection of clauses in I containing exactly i literals at the start of the $j+1^{st}$ iteration. Let $J(x,y,z)$ denote the probability distribution over DNF Boolean expressions where x clauses are chosen uniformly and independently from the set of all possible z-literal clauses that can be constructed from y Boolean variables.

Theorem 1 *Given* $|C_i(j)| = n_i(j)$, *for all* $1 \leq i \leq r-j$, *the clauses in* $C_i(j)$ *are distributed according to* $J(n_i(j), r-j, i)$ *independently of the clauses in* $C_l(j)$, $l \neq i$.

Proof:

This is certainly true for the case $j = 0$. Suppose it is true for all $0 \geq j \geq m$. There are two ways the $m+1^{st}$ selected literal is chosen: from the set of smallest clauses $C_k(m)$ if there exists a $k < \ln(2pr)$

such that $C_k(m) \neq \Phi$, and randomly from the set of unassigned literals otherwise. Consider the second case. By hypothesis, if h_i clauses of $C_i(m)$ contain the selected literal or its complement, the remaining $n_i(m) - h_i$ clauses of $C_i(m)$ are distributed according to $J(n_i(m) - h_i, r - m - 1, i)$. If g_{i+1} clauses of $C_{i+1}(m)$ contain the complement of the selected literal, stripping occurrences of that literal from those clauses results in a collection of g_{i+1} clauses distributed according to $J(g_{i+1}, r - m - 1, i)$. Combining the two collections results in $n_i(m) - h_i + g_{i+1}$ clauses distributed according to $J(n_i(m) - h_i + g_{i+1}, r - m - 1, i) = J(n_i(m + 1), r - (m + 1), i)$. Now consider the case that a literal is selected from $C_k(m)$, $k < \ln(2pr)$. Except for the clause from which this literal was selected, the clauses of I are independent of the selected literal. Hence the previous argument applies. □

Let X be a random variable and let $E\{X\}$ denote the expectation of X. Let $w_i(j)$ denote the number of clauses entering $C_i(j + 1)$ as a result of selecting the $j + 1^{st}$ literal (there is no dependence on instance given here since we will soon take expectations). Let $z_i(j)$ denote the number of clauses leaving $C_i(j)$ as a result of selecting the $j + 1^{st}$ literal. Let $n_i(j) = |C_i(j)|$. A set of recurrence relations for $E\{r_i(j)\}$, $1 \leq i, j \leq r$, in terms of $E\{w_i(j)\}$ and $E\{z_i(j)\}$ can be developed as follows:

$$E\{n_i(j + 1)\} = E\{n_i(j)\} + E\{w_i(j)\} - E\{z_i(j)\}. \tag{1}$$

Because of Theorem 1, for all $\ln(2pr) \leq i \leq r$

$$E\{z_i(j)\} = E\{E\{z_i(j)|n_i(j)\}\} = \sum_{l=0}^{\infty} \frac{i \cdot l}{r - j} Pr(n_i(j) = l) = \frac{i \cdot E\{n_i(j)\}}{r - j}.$$

Also, $E\{w_r(j)\} = 0$ and for all $\ln(2pr) \leq i < r$

$$E\{w_i(j)\} = E\{E\{w_i(j)|n_{i+1}(j)\}\} = \sum_{l=0}^{\infty} \frac{(i + 1)l}{2(r - j)} Pr(n_{i+1}(j) = l) = \frac{(i + 1)E\{n_i(j)\}}{2(r - j)}.$$

The recurrence relations for $1 \leq i < \ln(2pr)$ depend on $p_i(j)$, the probability that the selected literal l is chosen from $C_i(j)$. In this case we have

$$\begin{aligned} E\{z_i(j)\} &= E\{z_i(j) | l \notin C_i(j)\}(1 - p_i(j)) + E\{z_i(j) | l \in C_i(j)\} p_i(j) \\ &= \frac{iE\{n_i(j)\}}{r-j} + p_i(j)\left(1 - \frac{i}{r-j}\right) \end{aligned}$$

and

$$\begin{aligned} E\{w_i(j)\} &= E\{w_i(j) | l \notin C_{i+1}(j)\}(1 - p_{i+1}(j)) + E\{w_i(j) | l \in C_{i+1}(j)\} p_{i+1}(j) \\ &= \frac{(i+1)E\{n_{i+1}(j)\}}{2(r-j)} - p_{i+1}(j)\frac{i+1}{2(r-j)}. \end{aligned}$$

From Theorem 3.3 of [3] we have

Lemma 11 *For all* $\ln(2pr) \le i \le r$ *and* $1 \le j \le r$,

$$E\{n_i(j)\} = \binom{r-j}{i}(2p)^i(1-p)^j(1-2p)^{r-i-j}n. \tag{2}$$

Since the number of literals in a clause of a random expression is binomially distributed,

Lemma 12 *For all* $1 \le i \le r$

$$E\{n_i(0)\} = \binom{r}{i}(2p)^i(1-2p)^{r-i}n$$

From Lemma 10 the conditions which insure $E\{w_{\ln(2pr)-1}(j)\} < r^{-\epsilon}$ for any $\epsilon > 0$ can be obtained.

Lemma 13 *For any* $\epsilon > 0$, *if* $e^{\ln(2)+2+(p\ln(2)+\ln(pr))/(1-p)-pr}n/r < r^{-\epsilon}$ *then for all* $1 \le j \le r$, $E\{w_{\ln(2pr)-1}(j)\} < r^{-\epsilon}$.

Proof:

$$E\{w_{\ln(2pr)-1}(j)\} \leq \frac{\ln(2pr)E\{n_{\ln(2pr)}(j)\}}{2(r-j)}.$$

The maximum of $E\{n_{\ln(2pr)}(j)\}/(r-j)$ can be found by determining the value of j which makes

$$\frac{(r-j)E\{n_{\ln(2pr)}(j+1)\}}{(r-j-1)E\{n_{\ln(2pr)}(j)\}} = 1$$

and substituting that value in (2). Thus, we want j such that

$$\frac{(r-j)E\{n_{\ln(2pr)}(j+1)\}}{(r-j-1)E\{n_{\ln(2pr)}(j)\}} = \frac{(r-j)\binom{r-j-1}{\ln(2pr)}(2p)^{\ln(2pr)}(1-p)^{j+1}(1-2p)^{r-\ln(2pr)-j-1}n}{(r-j-1)\binom{r-j}{\ln(2pr)}(2p)^{\ln(2pr)}(1-p)^{j}(1-2p)^{r-\ln(2pr)-j}n}$$

This is satisfied by $j = j_{max} = r - (1-p)(\ln(2pr)-1)/p$. Making use of Stirling's approximation in the third step below we have,

$$\begin{aligned}
&\frac{E\{n_{\ln(2pr)}(j_{max})\}}{(r-j_{max})} \\
= \; & \frac{p}{(1-p)(\ln(2pr)-1)}\binom{(1-p)(\ln(2pr)-1)/p}{\ln(2pr)}(2p)^{\ln(2pr)}(1-p)^{r-(1-p)(\ln(2pr)-1)/p} \\
& \times(1-2p)^{(1-p)(\ln(2pr)-1)/p-\ln(2pr)}n \\
\leq \; & \frac{p}{(1-p)\ln(2pr)}\frac{(2\ln(2pr))^{\ln(2pr)}}{\ln(2pr)!}(1-p)^{r-(1-2p)\ln(2pr)/p}(1-2p)^{(1-2p)\ln(2pr)/p}\left(\frac{1-p}{1-2p}\right) \\
< \; & \frac{p}{(1-p)\ln(2pr)}(2e)^{\ln(2pr)}(1-p)^{r}\left(\frac{1-2p}{1-p}\right)^{(1-2p)\ln(2pr)/p}e^{2}n \\
< \; & \frac{p}{(1-p)\ln(2pr)}(2e)^{\ln(2pr)}e^{-pr}e^{-(1-2p)\ln(2pr)/(1-p)}e^{2}n \\
< \; & \frac{p}{\ln(2pr)}e^{\ln(2)-pr+p\ln(2pr)/(1-p)+2}n.
\end{aligned}$$

Thus, for all $1 \leq j \leq r$

$$E\{w_{\ln(2pr)-1}(j)\} \; < \; pne^{\ln(2)+2+p\ln(2pr)/(1-p)-pr} < e^{\ln(2)+2+(p\ln(2)+\ln(pr))/(1-p)-pr}n/r.$$

The lemma follows. □

Lemma 5 says that non-tautological instances are produced with probability tending to 1 only if $\lim_{n,r\to\infty} e^{-pr}n/r = 0$. Lemma 12 says that $E\{w_{\ln(2pr)-1}(j)\} < r^{-\epsilon}$ for all $1 \le j \le r$ if $\lim_{n,r\to\infty} e^{-pr}n/r^{1+\epsilon} = 0$ for any $\epsilon > 0$. Thus, in some sense for almost all non-tautological instances, $E\{w_{\ln(2pr)-1}(j)\} < r^{-\epsilon}$ for $1 \le j \le r$. It will be shown that if $E\{w_{\ln(2pr)-1}(j)\} < r^{-\epsilon}$ for $1 \le j \le r$ and any $\epsilon > 0$ then with probability tending to 1 *UNSAT-FINDER* will find a truth assignment for each clause such that the clause has value *true (false)* and all other clauses have value false. Thus, with *UNSAT-FINDER* it is possible to generate a complete set of test vectors for a PLA with probability tending to 1.

The following theorem will make our work much easier.

Theorem 2 *The probability there exists a clause of size less than* $\ln(2pr)$ *in a random instance tends to 0 if* $p = c\ln(n)/r$ *where* $c > 1/2$.

Proof:

The probability that a clause has size no greater than $\ln(2pr)$ is

$$\sum_{l=0}^{\ln(2pr)} \binom{r}{l} (2p)^l (1-2p)^{r-\ln(2pr)}.$$

Since $\ln(2pr)$ is much less than the mean pr, this sum is less than $(2pre)^{\ln(2pr)}e^{-2pr}$. Thus, the probability that all clauses have size greater than $\ln(2pr)$ is at least

$$\left(1-(2pre)^{\ln(2pr)}e^{-2pr}\right)^n.$$

If $p = c\ln(n)/r$ this is

$$\left(1-(2pre)^{\ln(2pr)}n^{-2c}\right)^n > e^{-(4pre)^{\ln(2pr)}n^{1-2c}}.$$

But $(2pre)^{\ln(2pr)} = (2ec\ln(n))^{\ln(2c\ln(n))}$ cannot grow as fast as n^ϵ for any $\epsilon > 0$. Hence the exponential tends to 1 if $c > 1/2$ and the lemma is proved. □

Suppose after creating a random instance we set $n_i(j) = 0$ for all $1 \le i \le \ln(2pr) - 1$ (that is, we eliminate all clauses of length less than $\ln(2pr)$). With probability tending to 1 we do not have to do so. Hence the result will apply to almost all random expressions.

Lemma 14 *For all* $1 \leq i \leq \ln(2pr) - 1$, $\lim_{n\to\infty} p_i(j) \to E\{w_i(j)\} - E\{w_{i-1}(j)\}$

Proof:

$$p_i(j) = pr(C_l(j) = \phi, l = 1,2,...,i-1) - pr(C_l(j) = \phi, l = 1,2,...,i).$$

Since $Ew_{\ln(2pr)-1}(j) < r^{-\epsilon}$ the average number of iterations between successive occurrences of the event that a clause moves from C_i to C_{i-1} increases with increasing n and r. Hence, asymptotically, the probability that there is at least one clause in $C_l(j)$, $l = 1,2,...,i-1$, is the flow of clauses into $C_{i-1}(j)$. This is $E\{w_{i-1}(j)\}$. Similarly, the probability that there is at least one clause in $C_l(j)$, $l = 1,2,...,i$, is $E\{w_i(j)\}$. Hence, $p_i(j)$ tends to $(1 - E\{w_{i-1}(j)\}) - (1 - E\{w_i(j)\}) = E\{w_i(j)\} - E\{w_{i-1}(j)\}$. □

Then we can write for $1 \leq i \leq \ln(2pr) - 1$, $1 \leq j \leq r$

$$\begin{aligned} E\{n_i(j+1)\} &= \left(1 - \frac{i}{r-j}\right) E\{n_i(j)\} + \left(1 - \frac{i}{r-j}\right) E\{w_{i-1}(j)\} + \frac{i}{r-j} E\{w_i(j)\} \\ &= \left(1 - \frac{i}{r-j}\right)\left(1 + \frac{i}{2(r-j)}\right) E\{n_i(j)\} + \frac{i}{r-j} E\{w_i(j)\} \\ &\leq \left(1 - \frac{i}{2(r-j)}\right) E\{n_i(j)\} + \frac{i(i+1)}{2(r-j)^2} E\{n_{i+1}(j)\}. \end{aligned}$$

Theorem 3 *Let* $E\{n_i(0)\} = 0$ *for all* $1 \leq i < \ln(2pr)$. *For all* $1 \leq i < \ln(2pr)$, $1 \leq j \leq r$, $\epsilon > 0$

$$E\{n_i(j)\} < \frac{(\ln(2pr))^{\ln(2pr)}}{i^i (r-j)^{(k-i)}} \binom{r-j}{\ln(2pr)} (2p)^{\ln(2pr)} (1-2p)^{r-\ln(2pr)-j} n$$

if $\lim_{n,r\to\infty} e^{-pr} n / r^{1+\epsilon} = 0$.

Proof:

By double induction. The basis step at each i holds since $E\{n_i(0)\} = 0$. The induction step proceeds as follows:

$$\begin{aligned}
E\{n_i(j+1)\} &= \left(1 - \frac{i}{2(r-j)}\right) E\{n_i(j)\} + \frac{i(i+1)}{2(r-j)^2} E\{n_{i+1}(j)\} \\
&< \frac{(2(r-j)-i)(\ln(2pr))^{\ln(2pr)}\binom{r-j}{\ln(2pr)}(2p)^{\ln(2pr)}(1-2p)^{(r-\ln(2pr)-j)}n}{2(r-j)i^i(r-j)^{(\ln(2pr)-i)}} \\
&\quad + \frac{i(i+1)(\ln(2pr))^{\ln(2pr)}\binom{r-j}{\ln(2pr)}(2p)^{\ln(2pr)}(1-2p)^{r-\ln(2pr)-j}n}{(i+1)^{(i+1)}(r-j)^{(\ln(2pr)-i-1)}2(r-j)^2} \\
&= \frac{(\ln(2pr))^{\ln(2pr)}\binom{r-j}{\ln(2pr)}(2p)^{\ln(2pr)}(1-2p)^{r-\ln(2pr)-j}n}{2(r-j)^{(\ln(2pr)-i+1)}}\left(\frac{i}{(i+1)^i} + \frac{2(r-j)\cdot}{i^i}\right. \\
&= \frac{(\ln(2pr))^{\ln(2pr)}\binom{r-j}{\ln(2pr)}(2p)^{\ln(2pr)}(1-2p)^{(r-\ln(2pr)-j)}n}{i^i 2(r-j)^{(\ln(2pr)-i)}}\left(1 - \frac{i(1-e^{-1})}{2(r-j)}\right) \\
&\leq \frac{(\ln(2pr))^{\ln(2pr)}\binom{r-j}{\ln(2pr)}(2p)^{\ln(2pr)}(1-2p)^{(r-\ln(2pr)-j-1)}n}{i^i 2(r-j)^{(\ln(2pr)-i)}} \cdot \frac{(r-j)^{\ln(2pr)-i}}{(r-j-1)^{\ln(2pr)}}
\end{aligned}$$

This proves the theorem. □

Theorem 4 *Let $E\{n_i(0)\} = 0$ for all $1 \leq i < \ln(2pr)$. For any $\epsilon > 0$, all $p < c\ln(n)/r$, and $1 \leq j \leq r$,*

$$E\{w_1(j)\} \leq \frac{(\ln(2pr))^{\ln(2pr)}n}{r^{\ln(2pr)}}$$

if $\lim_{n,r\to\infty} e^{-pr}n/r^{1+\epsilon} = 0$.

Proof:

From the previous theorem

$$E\{w_1(j)\} \leq (\ln(2pr))^{\ln(2pr)}\binom{r-j}{\ln(2pr)}(2p)^{\ln(2pr)}(1-2p)^{(r-\ln(2pr)-j)}n.$$

Using the technique of Lemma 13 we find that this expression has a maximum at $j = r - 1/2p$. Substituting back into the expression gives the result. □

Theorem 5 *The probability that UNSAT-FINDER does not find a falsifying truth assignment is bounded from above by* $\ln(n)\ln(r)E^*\{w_1\}$ *where* $E^*\{w_1\}$ *is the maximum flow of clauses into* C_1.

Proof:

Similar to the proof of Theorem 3.4 in [?]. □

From Theorems 4 and 5 we have the probability that *UNSAT-FINDER* does not find a falsifying truth assignment is bounded from above by

$$\frac{\ln(n)\ln(r)(\ln(2pr))^{\ln(2pr)}n}{r^{\ln(2pr)}} \qquad (3)$$

if $p = c\ln(n)/r$, $c > 1/2$, and $\lim_{n,r\to\infty} n^{1-c}/r = 0$. This is less than $1/(r^{1+\epsilon}n)$ if $n < 2^r$. If $n > 2^r$ falsifiability may be found in polynomial time by exhaustive search.

We make use of *UNSAT-FINDER* to generate tests in the same way that we made use of the random-method except that we use *UNSAT-FINDER* for generating the truth assignments. Since we have to make $2rn + n$ tests the average number of failed tests is less than $O(\ln(n)n^2/r^{\ln\ln(n)})$ from (3). This is an upper bound on the probability that a test fails and tends to 0 as $n, r \to \infty$ under the conditions stated.

5 Conclusions

In this paper we have examined the impact of primality and irredundancy on the ease of testability of two-level circuits. We have shown that for a large class of prime and irredundant circuits that with probability tending toward 1, the circuit may be fully tested in polynomial time. Thus for this restricted class of circuits we have shown that full testability does indeed imply easy testability with high probability .

References

[1] K. Bartlett *et al.*, Multilevel logic minimisation using implicit don't cares, ***IEEE Transactions on Computer-Aided Design of Integrate Circuits and Systems*****, 17**, 6 , pp. 723-740, June , 1988 .

[2] R. K. Brayton and C. McMullen and G. D. Hachtel and A. Sangiovanni-Vincentelli, ***Logic Minimization Algorithms for VLSI Synthesis***, Kluwer Academic Publishers, 1984 .

[3] J. Franco, and Y. C. Ho, Probabilistic performance of a heuristic for the Satisfiability problem, ***Discrete Applied Mathematics*****, 22**, pp. 35-51, 1988/89 .

[4] H. Fujiwara, ***Logic Testing and Design for Testability***, MIT Press, Cambridge MA 1985 .

[5] G. D. Hachtel and R. M. Jacoby and K. Keutzer and C. R. Morrison, On the relationship between area optimisation and multifault testabilty of multilevel logic, ***Proceedings of the International Workshop on Logic Synthesis***, June, 1989.

[6] D. S. Johnson, The NP-Completeness column: an ongoing guide, ***Journal of Algorithms*****, 6**, pp. 291-305, 1985 .

[7] I. Kohavi and Z. Kohavi, Detection of multiple faults in combinational logic networks, ***IEEE Transactions on Computers*****, C21** , 6 , pp. 556-568, June , 1972.

[8] E. J. McCluskey, Minimisation of Boolean functions, ***Bell Lab. Technical Journal***, Bell Lab., **35**, pp. 1417-1444, November, 1956.

"Decision Support on Logistic Networks"

- needs and developments -

Lorike Hagdorn - van der Meijden

Department of Business Administration
Erasmus University Rotterdam
P.O. Box 1738
3000 DR Rotterdam, The Netherlands
Tel : 31 - (0)10 - 4082025
Fax : 31 - (0)10 - 4523595

Abstract

Since the last decade, both Logistics and Decision Support Systems are main points of interest in business environment. A Decision Support System is developed for strategic planning on logistic networks. In this paper, this Decision Support System is applied on the design of a logistic network for a manufacturer of copiers and faxes. From this case-description, suggestions are made for advanced functionalities of Decision Support Systems. From the point of view of logistics, connections between Decision Support Systems on strategic, tactical and operational levels are needed. Moreover the assistance of a Decision Support System in splitting complex decision problems in manageable subproblems is very useful. There is also a heavy need for support in developing, administrating and comparing the results of scenario's.

Keywords

logistics, distribution, networks, planning, decision support system

1. Introduction

During the last decade, logistics has become a main point of interest in business. Especially an integral view on logistics is gaining ground because of its impact on improvement of customer service and reduction of logistic costs (production-costs, handling-costs, inventory-costs and transportation-costs). This paper gives an overview of some needs for and developments of Decision Support Systems in the field of integral logistic networks (see figure 1).

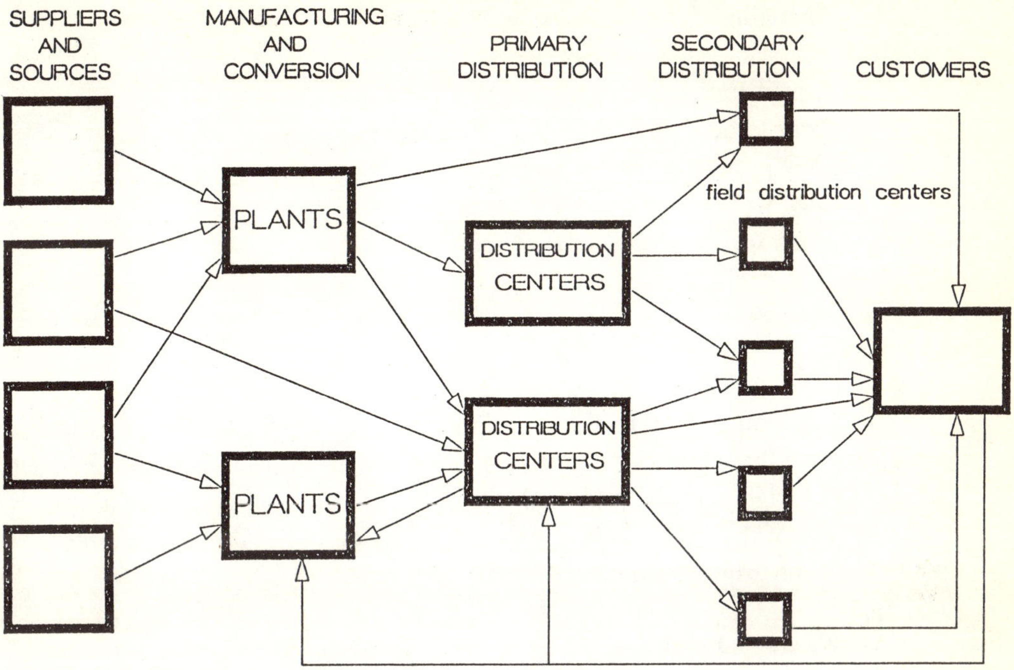

figure 1. *Example of a logistic network*

Not only designing these networks, but also improving the effectiveness and the efficiency of these networks with assistance of Decision Support Systems are subjects in this paper. First, some important trends in logistics and the needs for Decision Support from the point of view of logistic managers are described. Based on these needs, some essential functionalities of Decision Support Systems are dealt with.
A case - situation of structuring a logistic network for a manufacturer of copiers and faxes is described globally.

2. Needs for Decision Support on Logistic Networks

Logistic Management is paying large attention to logistic costs on one hand and on customer service on the other hand. To find a balance between the highest customer service and the lowest logistic costs is one of their main points of interest. In relation to this subject, they are dealing with questions like :

How can we prepare for and get the benefit of :

Globalisation of markets

Changing demands
Increasing customer service
United Europe
Door to door concepts
New production technologies
EDI
Make or buy - decisions
etc.

2.1 Strategic Planning

Insight in the structure of the total logistic process from supplier to customer is a first step in answering these questions. Decision Support Systems can assist management in improving this insight and can give them tools to evaluate consequences of alternatives for the structure of their total logistic process. In the design of the logistic process the following question are of main interest :

- Supply
  - Where and how ?
    - number and location of suppliers
    - delivery times
    - reliability of deliveries
    - flexibility
    - buy or make ?
- Production
  - Where and how ?
    - number and location of plants
    - allocation of production
    - technical concept (flexibility)
    - buy or make ?
- Distribution
  - Where and how ?
    - number and location of logistic centres
    - tasks of logistic centres
    - buy or do ?
- Integration
  - Where and how ?
    - decentralized / centralized organization
    - information management

Example of strategic planning in logistic networks
A international operating company, producing copiers and faxes, has three plants in Europe (located near London, Lille and Venray). All three plants are producing different types of copiers and faxes and all three plants are distributing all products to all European countries. In every country a so-called 'National Warehouse' is functioning as national distribution centre. The national warehouses are responsible for distributing the products to the regional centres and to final customers. (see figure 2a and 2b)

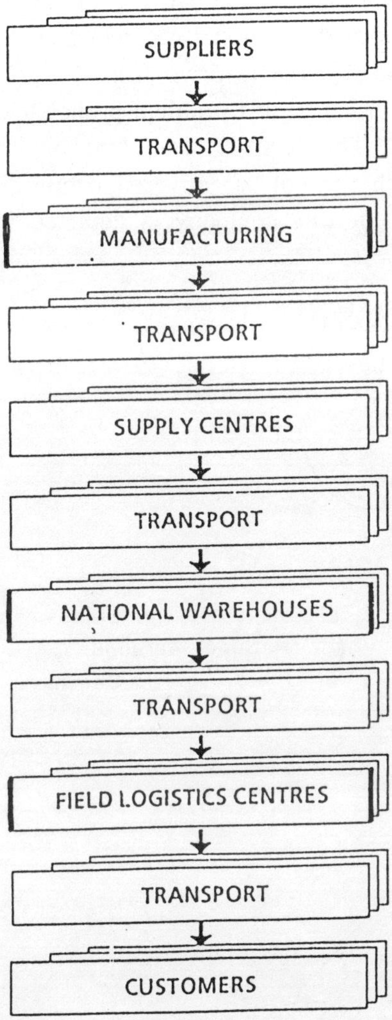

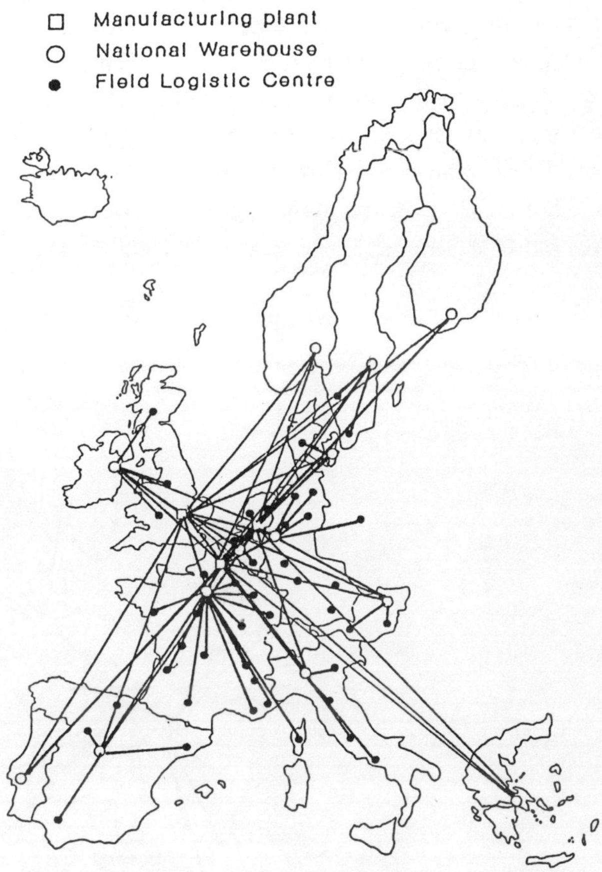

figure 2a *Present distribution network, schematic view*
figure 2b *Present distribution network, realistic view*

The logistic management is wondering about the way they distribute their products to their customers. It seems, their present distribution structure is very expensive from the point of view of transportation, handling and inventory costs. Moreover they are investigating in decreasing their leadtimes from 3 - 5 days deliveries to '24 hours delivery'.

Based on their experience, the logistic management suggests to introduce the concept of direct delivery from plants to regional centres instead of distribution via national warehouses and to introduce the concept of 'cross-docking' (transportation of products between plants and then coordinated distribution from one plant to a dedicated region in Europe). The logistic management is aware of the contradiction between the direct delivery concept (direct delivery from the factories to the regional centres) and the introduction of 24-hour service in Europe : it is impossible to drive from Lille or Venray to the south of Italy within 24 hours! A solution to this problem probably is the introduction of European Logistic Centres. This centres can function as distribution centres for the regions in Europe which can not be delivered within 24 hours. A possible new logistic network-structure for this company is depicted in figure 3.

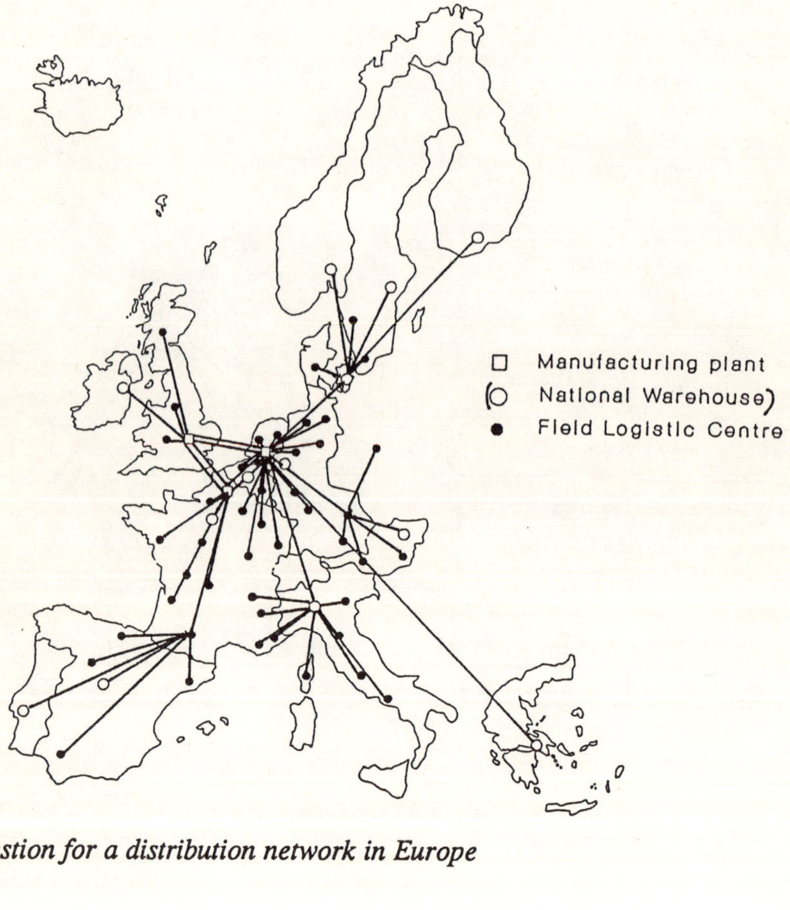

figure 3 *Suggestion for a distribution network in Europe*

This type of decisions can be supported by a Decision Support System very effectively. The use of a Decision Support System in this example stimulated creative thinking and generated and evaluated new concepts in logistic networks for this company. Moreover, a Decision Support System is used to support the discussion with the regional centres and the national warehouses on the introduction of the new structure of the distribution network.

2.2 Tactical and Operational Planning

Not only strategic questions about the structure of the logistic network which fits closely to the trends in markets and challenges of the company are of great importance.

Also an effective and efficient organization and control of the logistic process from suppliers to customers contributes largely to the productivity of a company and gives opportunities for the improvement of the cost-level and the quality-level of the products and services.

At this level, management can be assisted by Decision Support Systems which deal with :

delivery frequencies of suppliers in relation to MRP systems
transportroutes from suppliers to plants
plant lay-outs
performance measurement and interpretation at plants
production planning
stock policies
delivery frequencies at logistic centres
lay-out of logistic centres
performance measurement and interpretation at logistic centres
delivery frequencies at customers
transport routing
co-loading in transport
return flows
etc.

3. Functionalities of Decision Support Systems in logistics

Based on the management needs for Decision Support Systems in logistics, some elements of the functionality of DSS are discussed.

3.1 *Relation between different DSS's on different planning levels and different problems?*

Based on the different type of questions in logistics, which are described above, we can distinguish the need for DSS at operational level, tactical level and strategic level. The decisions in relation to these three planning levels are often considered at several departments and by several people, although all these questions are closely related to each other !
So, in an ideal situation there has to be relations between the different DSS's on logistics which are used in an organization. In this relations one can distinguish two components : data interchange and decision interchange.
These relations are only useful if they are closely related to the plannings cycles for strategic, tactical and operational within the company. (figure 4)

figure 4 *Relation between Decision Support Systems and planning cycles*

3.2 *Decomposition of problems ?*

When a subdivision into strategic, tactical and operational problems is made, then still the problems can be too complex to analyze at once. So, some support is needed for the way you can make a decomposition of problems in smaller parts, without loosing the integral aspects of logistics. For instance, for the strategic problem of structuring the logistic network from supplier to customer, a subdivision can be made into the different levels of the logistic chain e.g. :

step 1. structuring at the level of plants
step 2. structuring at the level of suppliers
step 3. structuring at the level of logistic centres

When working on the improvement of the structure one level, e.g. of the plants, it is important to evaluate the effects of the decisions on this level, on the quality of the structure of the chain on the other two levels (logistic centres and suppliers).

3.3 *Scenario-support (development and comparison)*

An other very important functionality of DSS's in general is the way they support developing and comparing scenario's and alternatives. There is a strong need , also for DSS in logistics, for a clear support on developing scenario's and report facilities to compare the results of different scenario's. In logistics, costs, service and flexibility are three important key-elements for comparing alternatives.

References

Hagdorn, E., Nunen. J. van (1989) Nieuwe distributiestructuren in Europa na 1992 : een analysemethodiek, in : Hamerslag, R., Weenink, A.J.H. (eds), *Bundel Verlvoerslogistike werkdagen 1989*, EVO Zoetermeer, pp. 359 - 372. (in Dutch)

Keen, P.G.W., Scott-Morton, S. (1978) *Decision Support Systems, an organizational perspective*, Addison Wesley Publ. Comp., London.

Magee, J.F., Copacino, W.C., Rosenfield, D.B. (1985) *Modern Logistics Management*, John Wiley & Sons.

Nunen, J. van, Benders, J. (1980) A decision Support System for location and allocation problems within a brewery, *Operations Research Proceedings*, Springer Verlag Berlin Heidelberg, pp. 96 - 105.

Turban, E. (1990) *Decision Support and Expert Systems, Management Support Systems*, Macmillan Publ. Comp., New York

Towards better understanding of the model concept in the context of information systems development.

R.J.M. Hartog and C.A.J. Meijs
Wageningen Agricultural University
Computer Science Department
Dreijenplein 2 6703 HB Wageningen

April 1991

Abstract

This paper draws attention to the fact that the meaning of the term 'model' and the meaning of many related terms such as 'representation', 'object system' is not satisfactorily defined in the context of information systems development. We argue that the importance of key concepts like the model concept justifies repeated attempts to clarify its meaning. Firstly a better understanding of the term 'model' is important for effective communication with managers and users during the development of information systems and secondly research areas like model management and metamodelling will benefit from an investigation into the essential aspects of the modelconcept. Understanding what a model *is* will at least be very difficult if one does not know what one can do with a model. We will argue that the difference between 'a model' and 'a body of information' is based primarily on meta-information which can be used by a user, or an automated modelmanager.

1 Introduction

In every information systems development methodology (ISD Methodology) models play a crucial role. Firstly information systems themselves are often considered to be models of reality. Secondly the core of most intermediate documents which are delivered by the end of each phase during information system development is formed by models of different types. And finally information systems developers become more and more aware of the role which mental models play in the communication between those who are participating in information systems development. Thus it is not surprising that the terms 'model' and 'modelling' are being used abundantly in ISDM literature.

All taken together one would wish that both the *use* as well as the *development* of ISD Methodologies is based on a common understanding of the model concept. However in most descriptions of ISDM's an explicit definition of the term 'model' or a pointer to a handbook definition of the term 'model' is lacking.

It has often been pointed out that not all concepts or terms can be defined. In fact it is amazing how much science has advanced in areas where key concepts were not very well defined. ([Simon] pp 20). On the other hand the search for sharp, preferably operational, definitions of key concepts has always been an essential scientific activity and the general acceptance of a definition of a key concept is usually regarded as a landmark in scientific history.

Clearly 'model' is such an undefined key concept in the context of information systems development. Since the creation and maintenance of most models in an ISD context is nowadays computer-aided, a shared definition of what a model actually *is* becomes more relevant.

Furthermore not only the term 'model' asks for clarification but also terms such as 'representation','system','universe of discourse', 'object system','level of abstraction'; this becomes apparent when we try to make connections between these concepts. We believe that the ISD research community should invest more effort in clarifying the meaning of those terms for several reasons. The first reason is that so many participants in ISD have different backgrounds: one only has to think of the background differences of managers, end-users and programmers, but in the case of development of 'less traditional' information systems such as expert systems and decision support systems the model concepts of physicists, mathematicians and operational researchers often play an important role. A second reason for reattempting to clarify the meaning of the term 'model' is the fact that our ideas about 'thinking' 'communication' and 'complexity' and many related concepts have been changing considerably over the last decades. A third reason for stimulating this discussion about the model concept is the importance it bears for automatic modelmanagement: modelmanagement becomes more and more an important issue in the world of decision support and computer simulation. It seems likely that modelmanagement will benefit from a better articulation of *what* has to be managed. Finally the increasing attention for metamodelling calls for a more consequent use of the term 'model'

In this paper we do not claim to be able to present adequate definitions for terms like 'model', 'system' etc. Our main purpose is to draw attention to the fact that it is apparently difficult to define the term 'model' while at the same time the ISD research community uses this term so often very lightly as if everybodies' concept of a model is the same. In our view an important aspect of a model which discriminates a model from 'a body of information' is the fact that a model contains meta-information, i.e. information which conveys the structure and the boundaries of the actual body of information. This meta-information enables the model to function as a model i.e. to avoid bandwidth problems. This meta- information also plays a crucial role in automated modelmanagement. Finally this view on meta-information leads in a natural way to a view on meta-models.

2 Some definitions of the modelconcept

In the introduction we mentioned that it is surprisingly difficult to find a definition of the term 'model' which is referred to by many researchers in the discipline of ISD. This section offers a small selection of definitions and 'almost-definitions' which can be regarded as fairly typical.

2.1 Definitions outside ISD context

Because the term model as it is used in the context of information systems development is apparently adopted from older disciplines let us start with a few definitions from these 'older' sources. [Bertels 69] offers a compilation of definitions of the term model. We have selected from this list the following definitions:
'A material model is the representation of a complex system by a system which is assumed simpler and which is also assumed to have properties similar to those selected for study in the original complex system.' [Wiener]
and:
'A formal model is a symbolic assertion in logical terms of an idealized relatively simple situation showing the structural properties of the original factual system' [Wiener]
'The word *model* is used as a noun, adjective and verb, and in each instance it has a slightly different connotation. As a noun 'model' is a *representation* in a sense in which an architect constructs a small-scale model of a building or a physicist a large-scale model of an atom. ...' [Ackoff 62]
Bertels and Nauta themselves present in [Bertels 69] the following definition of (logic *and* non-logic models :
'when one uses a known system K, which is independent of a system O, to obtain information about O, then K is a model of O.'
(However it must be noted that [Bertels 69] concludes with the statement that THE modelconcept does not exist.)
In [Stafford Beer] a chapter is dedicated to the model concept containing the following (somewhat implicit) definition on page 100 :
'Let us call this mental representation that is not direct perception of the world a *model* of the world.'
And about this representation Beer says: 'This representation is not an account of what *is* the case but a continuous prognosis of what is about to be reported to us as being the case.'

2.2 Definitions in ISD context

It is remarkable that we have not been able to find a definition of the term 'model' *as such* in the information systems development literature. While this does not

imply that such definitions can not be found at all, it certainly suggests that explicit definitions of the concept *model* sec are uncommon in ISD literature.
[Wieringa] provides us with the following definitions:
A *conceptual model* of a Universe of Discourse is an abstract entity which embodies a common understanding among the relevant people of the Universe of Discourse.
A *descriptive model* of a Universe of Discourse is an abstract system which represents the entities in the Universe of Discourse at a certain level of approximation.

2.3 Discussion

As we said before definitions of the model concept are rather sparse, in particular in the context of information systems development. On the one hand it is apparently not easy to find definitions of the term model while on the other hand it is uncommon to refer to one standard definition.

It is clear that the definitions quoted in section 2 do not give satisfactory answers to these questions. This is partly due to the fact that these definitions rely mostly on concepts which have themselves no generally accepted meaning or are themselves not operationally defined. In relation to a satisfactory understanding of what a model *is* we are interested in answers to questions like: What functions can a model perform? What can be done with a model during any of the ISD phases? How should a model be used?

If we interpret the definition of Bertels and Nauta themselves also as an implicit definition of what 'representation' means (i.e. a system is a representation of another system when it is used to obtain information about this other system) we may conclude that most authors regard a model as a representation of a system. Note that [Wieringa] regards a model as an *abstact* system.

But systems exist in a variety of concrete or abstract forms. We have been inspired by *the meaning triangle* of Ogden and Richards [Ogden]. In the low left corner of the triangle is the *symbol*, which stands for the *referent* (i.e., the thing one wants to describe). The referent is placed in the low right corner of the triangle. The relation between the symbol and the referent is coupled through a *reference* (i.e., a concept or a thought). The symbol symbolizes the reference, and the reference refers to the referent.
This triangle implies three types of systems (for the moment we assume for simplicity that a system is a collection of interrelated entities):

- empirical sytems: systems in which entities are objects from a concrete or abstract system.

- conceptual systems: the entities of these systems are thoughts or things in the minds of people

- representations or symbolic systems: representations symbolizes the entities of the conceptual system.

It is important to be aware that representations are not directly related to the objects of the empirical system, because the used symbols may have several *meanings* which lead to different objects. For the information system to be a good representation of the emperical system, it must contain a representation of the *meaning* of reality. In other words, some characteristics of reality are invariants of the information system developments transformations.

In the following section we will use the definition of Bertels and Nauta and *the meaning triangle* as a basis for further clarification.

3 Towards a better understanding of the term 'model'

3.1 The boundaries of a body of information

This subsection discusses first some relevant aspects of information systems themselves. An information system can provide us with information, usually on request. In order to be able to use this information effectively and efficiëntly the members of the user organisation must be aware which questions one can reasonably pose to the information system and which not. In other words the problem is : how to convey to the members of the user organisation what information can be found in the information system and what not? This problem is closely related to the following problem:
given some arrangement of information systems organized in an information architecture, what information can be found in which system?
And finally this problem is strongly related to the problem of model management i.e. : how to store models in a modelbase in such a manner that easy retrieval of the right model at the right moment is possible. In fact any automated model manager will have to contain built-in knowledge about what information is contained in which model in order to be able to answer any questions posed by the user.
Presenting a print out of all information which is represented in the information system to the user is only seldom a feasible solution. It must be clear that we have to present to the user some form of meta-information which is much easier to communicate to the user than the whole body of information contained in the system. Furthermore it must also be clear that we cannot give any meta-information if there *is* no meta-information about the contents of the information system.

3.2 Discrimination between 'model' and 'non-model' information

In our view it is precisely this meta-information which discriminates between what can be called 'a model' and what should not be called 'a model'. In other words:

if a body of information can be described by means of such meta-information the user is sufficiënty supported in discriminating which information is contained in the information system and which is not, *then* the information in the information system is in the form of a model.
A definition of the modelconcept which is based on this aspect of bodies of information would highlight the fact that models play an important role in *communication.*

3.3 About models and communication

In our view the main factor limiting the usability of information systems in the next decades will be the narrow bandwidth of communication channels. In the context of this article the relevant communication channels are: firstly the communication channels between people, secondly the communication channels between external memories and processors (such as the communication channel between a person and some form of external memory like a scratchpad or a screen).
The wordrate of human speech as well as the wordrate of human reading is very limited just as the bitrate of the usual communication channels at the technical level. (For instance we easily forget that, although storage costs drop rapidly it still takes more than 46 days to read all the data of a cd-rom given a bitrate of 9600). While we may expect that the bandwidth of communication channels at the technical level will be considerably enlarged by technological advances the corresponding limitations in human communication will probably remain.
These bandwidth limitations are apparent in all stages of the information systems life cycle: in the first stages we find that it always takes much time to communicate company specific information from managers and end-users to analysts, and in later stages we find that it always takes (too) much time to read the documentation of the system.
Modelling plays an important role in solving or avoiding the bandwidth problem. Modelling implies that bodies of information are structured in such a way that meta-information can be communicated to indicate the structure and the boundaries of the body of information to the user respectively to the modelbase manager. Of course this implies that the user respectively the modelmanager must interpret this meta-information correctly. At the same time this implies that discrimination between models and non-models depends on the relevant persons or processors: if the relevant persons do not have the knowledge to interpret the meta-information then the actual body of information does not constitute a model for *these* persons.
A model offers the user (or an automated model manager) several ways to reduce the load of the communication channel: firstly the meta-information can be used to convey which information can be obtained from the model and which not; secondly it helps the user (or automated model manager) to obtain precisely that information which is needed instead of all the information available; thirdly the meta-information is often a basis for compression and decompression: in particu-

lar a mathematical model can be very easily communicated while anyone who has learned to interpret such a mathematical model can obtain a wealth of information from it.

4 Essential elements of models in ISDM's

4.1 Elements for representing ontological constructs

In order to make the concept of meta-information which discriminates between 'model' and 'non-model' information more tangible we performed a investigation into those bodies of information which are usually called 'models' by researchers in the disciplines of information systems development, (including development of decision support systems and expert systems). This has shown that these 'models' can be constructed with the following elements:

- a set of variables
- a set of domains corresponding to these variables
- a set of relationships usually expressible as constraints
- a set of rules for transforming relationships
- a set of operational definitions
- a set of rules of correspondence
- an indication of the relevant object system

The conceptualization of a empirical system, should result in a definition of the problem and the intended range of application of the system. Identification of the information requirements delivers sets of variables and domains. These variables are *user* variables;they are related to the situation in which the user finds himself. According the systems approach, we make a distinction in environmental, decision and output variables. Decision variables are those factors within the system, which the user can alter to exercise control. Operational definitions should precisely state the relations between environment, decision and output variables.

In view of the going discussion of the function of models in solving the bandwidth problem we conclude that the meta-information must explicitly contain (or at least enable the receiver to infer) how the first 5 sets in the list are to be instantiated for a particular model.

While the list of elementary constructs for 'models' is mainly a result of investigating what sort of bodies of information are called 'models' in the discipline of information systems developers the choice of elements is heavily biased by experiences with modelling in science. In order to compensate for this bias we want to make a quick comparision of our ideas on the essential elements of a model with the list of ontological constructs presented in [Wand]. In our essential elements list the variables, domains, relationships (constraints) and transforming rules are the only elements for representing ontological constructs. At first sight it may seem surprising that we are so easily satisfied with only four elements for representation of ontological constructs while the representational model in [Wand] contains 25 ontological constructs. However when one takes into account those representational elements which are usually not provided for (cf the corresponding evaluation of the Entity-Relationship Model for Ontological Completenes in [Wand] this difference is explained to the extent that we can at least skip 15 ontological constructs from Wand and Webers' representational model. Note that these differences are largely due to the different representation of time. The same can be said of the remaining difference because the remaining difference can be traced back primarily to the ontological construct 'state' which is supposed to be explicitly represented in the representational model in [Wand] and only more implicitly with the elements in the list we presented.

4.2 Meta-models and model management

In the foregoing subsections we argued that models contain meta-information which reveals the boundaries and structure of a body of information.

In the database world it is common practice to re-use parts of datamodels, which are stored in the datadictonary of a database managementsystem. A datadictionary contains actually meta-information, concerning the corporate data. Sometimes slightly modifications to the definitions of entity types, attributes or constraints, as defined in the data-dictionary, are necessary. For this coördination and maintenance of corporate data a new function has been introduced in organisations: the data-administrator.

On the contrary the re-use of decision-models in a DSS context is not so widely supported by model managementsystems. There are only some prototypes which can support modelmanagement,see for example [Liu]. The availability of model managementsystems may be stimulated by using meta-models.
Starting-point for the meta-models could be *the meaning triangle*, with three kind of systems. The entities of the empirical system correspond in this context with the concepts of a certain decision model. Conceptualisation of these concepts delivers a meta-datamodel. With regard to modelling and decision support the representation takes the form of relations, see [Blanning]. Other possible schemes are represented by symbols of logic, semantic nets or frames.

The understanding of the concept *meta* is fundamental. According the meaning defined in Webster dictionary, the greek prefix *meta* is usually meaning: after, beyond or higher. A meta-concept describes a class of concepts at a higher level. In other words a concept is an instance of the meta-concept.
An example of combining this interpretation of meta-concepts with the classification of systems in three types, will be shown in the next section.

5 A discussion of some examples

5.1 Maps

Maps or charts are usually called models and indeed it is possible to communicate with a minimum amount of meta-information which information one can retrieve directly from a certain map and which not, provided that the receiver of this meta-information is able to interpret this meta-information correctly. The basis of correct interpretation of meta-information about maps is mainly the analogy between certain types of maps and the fact that the receiver of meta-information is supposed to have learned what information a certain type of map contains. Furthermore, while the legend is primarily meant to show how to read the map it generally gives also some clues as to what can be read from the map.
Typical aspects for maps and charts are:

1. few timepoints are represented
2. most domains are unordered sets
3. almost no rules for transforming relationships
4. relatively many operational definitions
5. relatively few rules of correspondence

If the meta-information associated with a map would be enhanced with meta-meta-information revealing the boundaries and structure of the meta-information we could recognise a meta-model. For instance if the index and the legend would constitute all the meta-information and if there was additional information on the structure an de the boundaries of the index and legend these latter two could be regarded as a metamodel.

5.2 Critical path analysis

Considering the modelling of a familiar problem of a critical path analysis, a well known representation model of this problem is the PERT/CPM network diagram. The directed lines in this diagram indicates the activities which have to be performed, the nodes are the points in time reached when all activities leading into them have been completed, and the stucture of the network shows which activities have to be completed before others can start.
Some important variables are: tasks (activities that make up the project), immediate predecessors, time estimates for completing the task and budgeted cost. An operational definition of the *Time Expected* is :

$$TE = (a + 4m + b) / 6$$

where a = optimistic time estimate, b = pessimistic time estimate, and m = most likely time estimate.

For the construction of a meta-datamodel in this field of operational research we use the techniques of Entity Relationship Modelling [Chen].

The empirical system contains the concepts *node* and *arrow*, which are modelled as entity types in our meta-datamodel:

We consider the empirical system at the low right corner of *the meaning triangle*, containing the concepts of the node-arrow diagram. The meta-datamodel has the entity-types *node* and *activity*, referring to these concepts. Two relationships R1 and R2 can be distinguished. Where R1 has the properties:

- A *node* may be the start of many *activities*
  An *activity* has one and only one start *node*

and R2 has the properties:

- A *node* may be the end of many *activities*
  An *activity* has only one end *node*

Transforming this ER-Model to well-normalized tables, conform the relational principles, results in two tables (identifying attributes are respectively: activity letter and node number):

ACTIVITY TABLE (*activity letter*, START NODE NUMBER, END NODE NUMBER, OTHER ATTIBUTES)

NODE TABLE (*node number*, OTHER ATTIBUTES)

At this point it is interesting to compare the results of the meta-modelling practice (the data structure) with those commonly used. An important difference of this approach is that it will lead to two ways of identifying activities. Our meta-model has the possibility of having more than one activity with the same start and finish nodes. This situation causes problems for computer programs developed with the traditional appoach. The analysis at the meta-level allows us to make an judgement if this is an important and desirable facility.

5.3 Informationplanning

Most matrices which are made during information planning are often regarded as map-like. Their likeliness with maps is based on the fact that time is not represented, most domains are unordered sets, they contain no rules for transforming relationships. Unfortunately there is much difference with maps because these matrices contain almost no operational definitions and rules of correspondence are overwhelmingly important. They are only a model of the enterprise insofar the participants in information planning have learned to read such a matrix and are able to recognise the analogy between the matrices: the meta-information information about a matrix relating dataclasses and functional areas can only be understood by those who have learned the rules of correspondence in a process of creating these matrices.

6 Conclusion

In this paper we have drawn attention to the fact that the modelconcept does play an important role in research on ISD. We argued that a better understanding of the modelconcept will be benificiary in research areas of ISD and in particular in modelmanagement and metamodelling. We have reviewed a few typical definitions of the term 'model' and elaborated one of these by highlighting the role which models play in communication. This brought the meta-information which reveals the structure and boundaries of a body of information into focus. Also it provided us with a new definition of the meta-model concept.

In this paper we did not address the problems of compaction and computational complexity. While in more traditional information systems computational complexity and the degree of compactness of models is not very important, these aspect are much more important in decision support systems with features based on the discipline of operational research . It will be clear that compact models themselves do not require a substantial bandwidth in order to be communicated. This would seem to imply that for compact models communication of meta-information is less relevant because the bandwidth problem does not occur, i.e. we can easily 'send' the model itself to the receiver. Research in the field of artificial intelligence however seems to indicate that compact models sec are pretty useless and that compact models must be accompanied by very much procedural information. Also history of science research suggests that - precisely for compact models - the rules of correspondence cannot be formulated compactly. This is in keeping with statements in [Blanning] or [Finlay] which imply that mathematical models without a corresponding datamodel are meaningless.

The going suggests that it could be usefull to define some sort of *degree of compactness* and to relate this to different forms of meta-information necessary to communicate to the user respectively the modelbase manager what information a model contains. Such a definition would be primarily related to different types of constraints and the types of domains.

Another important aspect which is suggested by our view of the model concept is the role which education in our society will play or will have to play: because models are only models insofar the relevant people can understand the corresponding meta-information the value of models depends to a large extent on the result of society's educational activities. An important question is thus: which models should everyone learn to interpret?

References

[Ackoff 62] Ackoff R.L.
Scientific Method London 1962

[Ackoff 78] Ackoff R.L.
The Art of problem Solving Wiley and Sons 1978

[Bertels 69] Bertels K., Nauta D.
Inleiding tot het model begrip. Bussum 1969.

[Blanning] Blanning R.W.
A relational framework for information management.
in: "Decision support systems: a decade in perspective" Mclean E.R., Sol H.G. (eds.). Elseviers Science Publishers; IFIP 1986.

[Chen] Chen, P.P., The Entity Relationship model - Toward a unified view of data. ACM Transactions on Database Systems, vol. 1, nr. 1, pp 9-36, 1976.

[Finlay] Paul N. Finlay
Decision Support Systems and expert systems: a comparison of their components and design methodologies. Computers Opns Res Vol 17 No 6 pp 535-543, 1990.

[Liu] Liu J, Yun D., and G.Klein
An Agent for Intelligent Model Management
in: Journal of Management Information Systems, Vol.7 No.1 1990.

[Ogden] Ogden C. , Richards I.
The meaning of meaning, Routledge and Kegan Paul LTD, London 1923.

[Simon] Simon H. A. The Sciences of the Artificial M.I.T. Mass 1981 second edition

[Stafford Beer] Stafford Beer
Decision and Control Chichester Wiley and Sons 1966

[Wand] Wand Y. Weber R.
Toward a theory of the deep structure of information systems.
DeGross J., Alavi M., Opelland H. eds Procs 11th ICIS Copenhagen 1990

[Wiener] Rosenblueth A., Wiener N.
The Role of models in Science in: Phil of Science, 12 (1945): 316-321

[Wieringa] Wieringa R.
Three roles of conceptual models in information systems design and use.
in: "Information Systems Concepts: An in-depth Analysis" Falkenberg E.D. and Lindgreen P. (eds.) Elseviers Science Publishers; IFIP 1989.

GLOBAL-DETECTOR: KNOWLEDGE-BASED ANALYSIS AND DIAGNOSIS OF ECONOMICAL PERFORMANCE ON DAIRY FARMS

Wil H.G.J. Hennen & D.W. de Hoop
Agricultural Economics Research Institute
Section of Animal Husbandry
P.O.B. 29703, 2502 LS Den Haag, Holland

ABSTRACT

The financial performance of a farm is nowadays more dependent on the farmer's technical knowledge and management skills. To support management, microcumputer programs can be used.
The Agricultural Economics Research Institute (LEI) developed the knowledge-based computer system GLOBAL-DETECTOR for globally analysing economical and technical bookkeeping-data and to give advice for improvement. This system, which software is programmed in the language muLISP, covers all returns and variable costs. For analysing the data, farm-adjusted standards are used. The acquisition and presentation of knowledge for the diagnosis of performance is done by a method (IMAGINE) which is developed especially for this research.
GLOBAL-DETECTOR supports decision-making. In this perspective, the extensive explanation-facilities possessed by the system are crucial. First experiences with the system seem positive. Although farmer's individual whishes and demands cannot be fulfilled easily with computer systems, GLOBAL-DETECTOR may be used on a large scale on account of the flexibility and user-friendliness.

INTRODUCTION

Due to the milk quota system which is currently applied in the EC, the farmer's point of view has changed from increasing the scale of the farm (by strategic decisions), to more attention of lowering production costs (Poppe, 1986). Tactical decisions gain growing interest in this new situation. The financial performance of a farm is nowadays more dependent on the farmer's technical knowledge and management skills (Brand et al., 1986). In this perspective, it can be noticed that farmers aim at milking their full quota at the lowest possible cost by keeping an eye upon the total return- and cost-image (De Hoop et al., 1988).

De Haan (1991) compared two groups of dairy farms with the same area of land (about 37 hectare), number of cows (about 100) and milk production (about 6800 kg per cow). The first group of 40 farms (out of 283 random selected Dutch farms) had the highest gross-margin (total returns minus total variable costs) of about 340,000 Dutch guilders per farm. This group can be considered as the "best" fifteen percent of farms. The average gross-margin of the second group which consisted of 43 farms with a low gross-margin, was about 25% lower than the first. This difference of more than 100,000 Dutch guilders indicates for a great part distinct levels of management. According to King and Sonka (1988), farm management is the process by which decisions about allocating a farm's resources to meet desired ends are analyzed, made and implemented. Thorough studies on Dutch arable farms done by Zachariasse (1974) and on Dutch horticulture farms done by Alleblas (1988), showed that farm-results depend on management. Differences in management on dairy farms were also found in literature (e.g. Roep et al., 1991; De Hoop et al., 1988).

The main activity of a manager is decision making (Zachariasse, 1990b). Prerequisites for good decisions are not only information, but also creativity and decision power. However, information is the key element in the decision making process (Zachariasse, 1990b; Batte et al., 1990; Morahan et al., 1989).
Good managerial decisions need professional analysis of the available data (e.g. farm-data from bookkeeping) to yield the necessary information. But it mostly lacks good performance figures and good farm comparison (De Hoop et al., 1988). Party therefore, the use of accounting-data has not been very popular among farmers, although the need and demand for information will grow (Poppe, 1991a). This increase is due to changes in the farm's environment (e.g. King and Sonka, 1988), which makes the decision making process increasingly complex, resulting in a farmer's necessity for good information systems (Harsh et al., 1990).
The reports from external organisations display numerous data, but there is mostly a lacking of a thorough analysis from all these data (De Hoop et al., 1988). From this it is obvious that the farmer all by himself[1] has difficulties in analysing and drawing conclusions from the report. McGrann et al. (1989) note therefore: "Economics and finance are areas where expertise is often limited, leading to inadequate use of data and analysis tools by producers, lenders and educators. Expert systems offer a significant delivery technology.".
Since advances in computer hardware and software have increased the potential for effective computer-based support of farm management decisions (King et al., 1990), there are opportunities to bring data analysis and interpretation to microcomputer programs (McGrann et al., 1989). A number of these programs concern the financial structure of the farm. McGrann et al. give a description of the Agricultural Financial Analysis Expert System (AFAES), which includes software to make analysis summaries, graphic presentations of the analysis and a diagnostic analysis of the financial statement data. Dobbins and King (1988) show how the

[1]Only for the authors' convenience, the farmer, expert, user, etc. will be assumed to be male.

reports from the FINANX program (developed at the University of Minnesota) were interpreted by experts whose protocols provided the structure of an expert systems' knowledge-base. Longchamp et al. (1990) give a description of ANFI: an expert system for financial analysis. This system may give the farmer a good idea about the way the farm is managed. The expert system FinARS, as is described by Boggess et al. (1989), supplies from a minimum dataset a "quick and easy" evaluation of the financial health of a farm business and "... it can be used as a diagnostic tool for farmers (...) to provide an initial interpretation of their firm's financial situation, diagnose its potential problems, and furnish suggested alternatives for improving the firm's financial situation". Philips and Harsh (1987) have developed an expert system similar to FinARS for analysing and interpreting the financial condition of a dairy farm. According to Dobbins (1988), diagnostic analysis provides the managers the information that will allow them to improve the performance.

A preliminary investigation of the Agricultural Economics Research Institute (LEI) proved to have a beneficial impact of knowledge-based computer systems on management support for one detailed economic function (Hennen, 1989 and Breé and Hennen, 1989). However, "For a good analysis of the whole farm, data from many functions have to be used together." (Breé and Hennen, 1989). In order to support the dairy management covering all returns and variable costs and thereby improving the economic performance, an expert system (GLOBAL-DETECTOR) has been developed for globally analysing economical and technical bookkeeping-data. The analysis may be followed by a great number of graphical presentations, a "quick and easy" diagnosis of the strong and weak aspects of the management, and a presentation of possible ways for improving the economical performance. The goal of this paper is to describe and discuss GLOBAL-DETECTOR. A new method for knowledge acquisition will be of special interest. The scope of GLOBAL-DETECTOR will cover all aspects of gross-margin; fixed costs will be included later. The farmer's concern is the returns and variable costs, whereas the long-term decisions will only occur incidentally (De Hoop et al., 1988). The internal management of dairy farms is primarily focussed on efficient production, expressed in the gross-margin (Zachariasse, 1990a). Zachariasse observes that decisions concerning production are not only numerous, but they are also difficult to transfer to others. This is due to the complex circumstances in which these decisions take place. Because production is closer to the daily interest of the farmer and has an important impact on the financial results, the analysis and diagnosis of the financial structure of the farm (likewise above mentioned expert systems ASEAS and FinARS) has provisionally been left out of GLOBAL-DETECTOR.

GENERAL DESCRIPTION OF GLOBAL-DETECTOR

The analysis and diagnosis of the economical performance on a dairy farm can be carried out by the knowledge-based computer system GLOBAL-DETECTOR (GLOBAL Discursive Expert for the Technical and Economical Control, Testing and Opinion-formation of Results), developed at the LEI in 1990. This system, which must be consulted with a microcomputer (PC), is intentionally meant as a tool for supporting farm management. However, it may also possess an educational value for farmers, advisors and students.

GLOBAL-DETECTOR consists of two parts: analysis and diagnosis[2]. The system analyses the accounting-data from bookkeeping reports, taking in it's scope all aspects of the gross-margin. The results from the analysis are presented in graphs, tables, overviews, texts and lists and are joined up with the relevant explanation. Analysis may be followed by knowledge-based diagnosis. Expertise in this part is necessary, since it requires integral judgement.

The analysis and diagnosis is globally executed; only the most important data are used. Detailed analysis and diagnosis certainly produces better results, but by doing so the system would grow to an unmanageable magnitude caused by combinatorial explosion. The objective of GLOBAL-DETECTOR is to present the dairy farmer the strong and weak aspects of the farm management in a "quick and easy" manner and to give advice for improvement of the tactical decisions of the farm management.

A prerequisite for a proper use of such system is that the farmer must have a good idea of the way how the system operates and comes to its conclusions. This is important in order to increase the farmer's insight in his farm, to improve his knowledge and management capabilities, and to increase acceptance of the system. The explanatory facilities of GLOBAL-DETECTOR are therefore crucial.

It should also be evident that the system is made as user-friendly as possible, since computer-novices must be able to work with the system without any troubles.

---

[2]In the Netherlands the method "Information Engineering" is used in all branches of agriculture to describe relationships between decision processes and information requirements (Zachariasse, 1990b; De Hoop, 1988; Poppe, 1991b). The LEI has taken part in the identification of common data requirements and decision processes across firms. Among other things, this led the detailed Information Model of the cluster "Analysis and Diagnosis": a detailed description of how financial farm data can be analysed to gain an impression of strong and weak aspects of the management (LEI/VLB, 1989).

TECHNICAL SPECIFICATION

In nearly all cases special computer programs called "shells" or "tools" can be used for building up expert systems as well as the exploitation of knowledge. There are numerous commercially available software packages, which can speed up the development of expert systems. However, the analysis part of GLOBAL-DETECTOR is the major part and this part does not need software suitable for expert systems. The use of a "shell" in combination with this software, will undoubtedly be a heavy burden on the memory capacity of the microcomputer. On the other hand, the diagnosis part needs expert system's software. But a "shell" for the diagnosis part is not used for some reasons:

1. A "shell" in combination with the more conventional software for the analysis part gives problems with the internal memory of the computer. This disadvantage became visible during the development of an earlier expert system at the LEI (Hennen, 1989).
2. Most "shells" lack the flexibility necessary for such a hybrid system as GLOBAL-DETECTOR. The many functions this system possesses and bearing in mind some future developments, a flexibel programming environment is inevitable.
3. Software or a "shell" capable of implementing and using knowledge acquired by the method IMAGINE[3], is not existing.
4. Users may have to pay a large amount of money for the royalties of the "shell", or must even purchase an expensive "shell" to consult the expert system.

Like the expert system decribed by Evans et al. (1989), GLOBAL-DETECTOR is also developed "from scratch", which makes use of an Artificial Intelligence's language. This language, muLISP (Soft Warehouse), is a dialect of the standard language Common LISP (Steele, 1984). muLISP consumes only a small amount of memory and is relatively fast. For all functions of GLOBAL-DETECTOR, software is developed in muLISP, i.e. software for user-interface; for calculation of standards; for making tables, graphs and bar-diagrams; as well as explanation-facilities; for the application of IMAGINE and the inferring of advices. No additional software packages are used. In anticipation of future developments, an inference engine[4] for backward- and forward chaining[5] is also programmed and may be added to GLOBAL-DETECTOR in due course.

---

[3]IMAGINE will be described later on in this paper.

[4]An inference engine is part of a knowledge-based system or expert system that contains the general problem-solving knowledge. This inference engine processes the domain knowledge (located in the knowledge base) to attain new conclusions (Waterman, 1985).

[5]Backward chaining is an inference method where the system starts with what it wants to prove and tries to establish the facts which are needed to prove the conjecture. Forward chaining is an inference method where the premisses of the "IF...THEN" rules are matched against facts to establish new facts (Waterman, 1985).

All software for control, inferences, graphical output etc. have been programmed domain-independent, which means that the system can be used as a "tool" or "shell" for developing similar systems in other domains, even outside agriculture.

GLOBAL-DETECTOR can be consulted on a IBM PC or compatible computer. A hard-disk is recommendable. About 400 kByte of internal- and about 350 kByte of external memory will be sufficient. These modest requirements make it possible to use this system on a large scale.

THE ANALYSIS PART

Different methods for analysis

Analysis is necessary for providing insight into the strong - and weak parts of the farm (Dobbins, 1988) and is therefore the focal point of any record-keeping activity (James and Stoneberg, 1986). Generally, analysing management practices can be done by using:

- averages of a group of comparable farms (external comparison);
- farm-inherent standards (internal comparison);
- historical farm-data (internal comparison).

External comparison is a method which, although easy to apply, has the difficulty of defining the comparable groups and the diversity within a group, since farms differ in many aspects. Farm-inherent standards are used for internal comparison and can be the result of planning or normative calculations. They are often used in management-information systems. Historical farm-data are useful for detecting trends, but they fail to show the relative position of a particular farm with respect to other farms.

In GLOBAL-DETECTOR, farm-adjusted standards have been used. These "hybrid" standards are in fact combinations of external and internal standards. Farm-adjusted standards have been developed and described by De Haan (1991). Data from more than 300 specialized Dutch dairy farms (random selected) were used to calculate algorithms by means of regression analysis. This resulted in separate algorithms for nearly all returns and variable costs. Each algorithm has an inherent set of independent variables and can be used to calculate a farm-adjusted standard for that particular aspect. The farm's actual values of the independent variables may be placed in that algorithm, followed by the calculation of the farm-adjusted standard value. This value may

be considered as the value of an average Dutch farm for that particular aspect, while this average farm has the same values of independent variables as the farm under consideration. Farm-adjusted values can be compared with the actual values. Deviations might be an indication of bad performance.
Algorithms for the calculation of farm-adjusted standards are developed for each distinct year. These algorithms are therefore year-dependent. For a particular aspect, farm-adjusted standard values can be calculated in a couple of years. Comparing these values for that aspect in those years with the comparable actual values may result in different deviations in the distinct years. Detection of trends - based on these historical farm-data - can be carried out by GLOBAL-DETECTOR.

Farm-adjusted standards derived from empirical material are not meant as a goal or target. They are merely corrected averages. For example, according to the Dutch extension service the amount of concentrates fed are too high on most farms, mostly resulting in high costs. The cost on an average Dutch farm will therefore also be too high, which means that the farm-adjusted standard may not be used as a target value. However, with this standard value for the cost of concentrates, the farmer knows his position in relation to other farms.
The standards can indirectly be used as a goal in two ways. For some aspects, algorithms were also developed for the 25% highest and the 25% lowest performing farms with relation to that particular aspect. For a certain farm, the 25% highest standard for a return-aspect or the 25% lowest standard for a cost-aspect can be the goal to achieve. The second way is to let an expert make use of the deviation and other relevent data to elicit advices as to what actions the farmer can take to procure a certain goal. This is the advice-part of GLOBAL-DETECTOR, which will be explained later on.

Results from the analysis part

The farmer or advisor may use GLOBAL-DETECTOR to carry out the analysis. After having started the system, the bookkeeping-data from a chosen year are read in from a disk, which is followed up by the calculation of farm-adjusted standard values and other relevant variables. Then series of possibilities appear on the display which can be used to select the specific information the user wishes to go into. The menu-structure appears to be user-friendly.
An overview of the realised and farm-adjusted standard values of all returns and variable costs, which are part of the gross-margin, is displayed in Fig. 1. Deviations are also given; favourable ones are indicated by , whereas unfavourable ones are indicated by !. All aspects are expressed

in the same reference: guilders per hectare. This is a justifiable point of view, since it might be expected that the milk quota per hectare will not change in the short term on one particular farm and farmers aim at milking their full quota at the lowest costs as possible (De Hoop et al., 1988). The milk quota per hectare is thus one of the most important facts on a Dutch dairy farm.

The user might also be interested how an aspect is affected by an independent variable. A few dozens of graphs are at his disposal. One example is the influence of the milk production per cow (corrected for the percentage of fat and protein) on the gross-margin per hectare (Fig. 2). All other independent variables are kept constant. In the traject from 5000 to 10000 kg milk, the milk quota per hectare is also kept constant. This means that the number of cows per ha has to decrease when the milk yield per cow increases. It is obvious from the graph that for this particular farm the farm-adjusted standard for gross-margin will not always increase when the milk production per cow increases. Very high milk productions, e.g. more than 9,000 kg, seem to be unfavourable for this farm, mainly due to low cattle-credits, the high costs for purchasing concentrates at such a high level and the rather low milk quota per ha. At that high milk yield per cow, the stocking rate is low and there will be a surplus of own roughage. Daatselaar (1988) came to comparable conclusions in his research.

DETECTOR (L.E.I.)

RESULTS IN DUTCH GUILDERS PER HA	RESULT	STANDARD	DEV.	● !
Gross margin	9059	8772	287	●
Y I E L D S				
Milk reciepts	10740	10802	-62	!
Cattle credits	1843	1605	238	●
Remaining	279	323	-43	!
D I R E C T C O S T S				
Add. Feeding c.	2233	2339	-106	●
Veterinary	311	225	86	!
Insemination	177	130	47	!
Milkrec.+Herdbook	106	78	28	!
Interest	353	368	-15	●
Milk products	105	157	-52	●
Contract rearing	0	0	0	
Other cattle c.	28	113	-85	●
Seeds+Chemicals	130	144	-14	●
N-fertiliser	288	288	0	
Other fertilisers	61	74	-13	●
Other. c. crops	14	15	-1	
Minerals,etc.	0	27	-27	●

Press a button, please.....

Fig. 1. Realised values, standard values and deviations for gross-margin, returns and variable costs. Output from GLOBAL-DETECTOR.

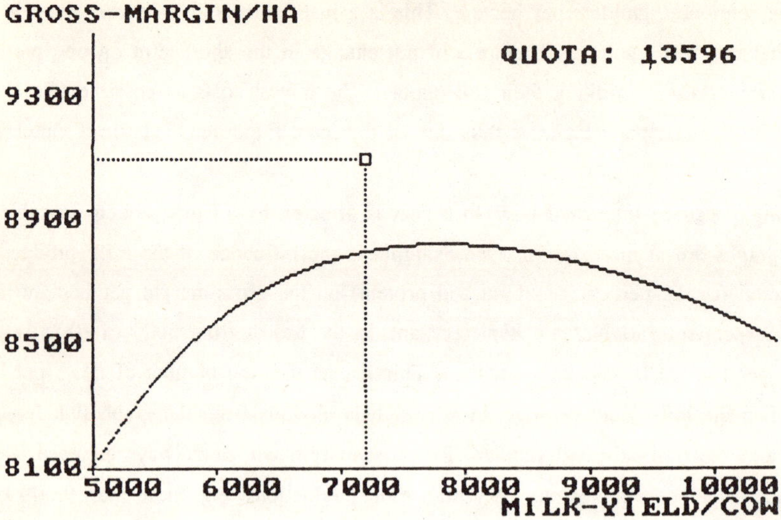

Fig. 2. Relation between the milk production per cow (X-axis) and the gross-margin per hectare (Y-axis); and the position of farm x having a milk qouta of 13596 kg per ha. Output from GLOBAL-DETECTOR.

The farm under consideration, displayed by a small block in Fig. 2, has not only realized a favourable gross-margin, but the milk production nearly reached an "optimal" level. Although not shown, each graph is accompanied by the necessary information.

As indicated before, some graphs do not only display average lines, but also lines for the highest and the lowest performing 25% percent of the farms for that aspect. Fig. 3 displays the influence of the corrected milk production per cow on the cattle-credits per cow. The upper line shows the farm-adjusted standard for the highest (or best) 25% of the farms corrected for the same independent variables. This farm is better than a comparable average farm, but has a worse performance than the average of the best quarter of farms. Reaching the highest standard may be a goal.

Although very informative for analysing, the dozen bar-diagrams and tables which can be displayed, will not be described in detail in this paper. The bar-diagrams are useful for a quick glance at a couple of related aspects to discover easily the favourable and unfavourable ones, e.g. components of feeding costs. Tables are useful to display quantitive information and results which cannot be displayed graphically.

The user has the possibility to skip easily to another year for analysis. Data from that year are read in from the database. The calculations that follow are done by means of farm-adjusted standard and standard prices for that particular year. As far as a very recent year is concerned, and having no algorithms for farm-adjusted standards available at the moment, the most recent algorithms are used in combination with price-indices. Deriving algorithms by regression-analysis can only be done if the data from a great number of farms are available at that moment.
It is also possible to ask GLOBAL-DETECTOR for an overview of three years in succession. Fig. 4 shows such an overview. Realised values as well as deviations from farm-adjusted standard values from all aspects are displayed over three years. Some simple heuristics are implemented to make a trend analysis of the data in this table. Results are displayed to the user.
Finally, the user can ask for a display of the most striking features of the farm, combined with the way GLOBAL-DETECTOR has inferred these. The function of this overview is to give the farmer or an advisor a quick idea of some outranging data in order to pin-point them in the report at hand. This may be important for the identification of problems.
Algorithms for inferring the most striking features are derived from both descriptive statistics and plain heuristics from an expert. The displayed features are no strong or weak aspects, they are merely characteristics worth mentioning when an expert takes a quick glance at the report. Strong and weak aspects of the farm management are the result of the expert system in the diagnosis part of GLOBAL-DETECTOR.

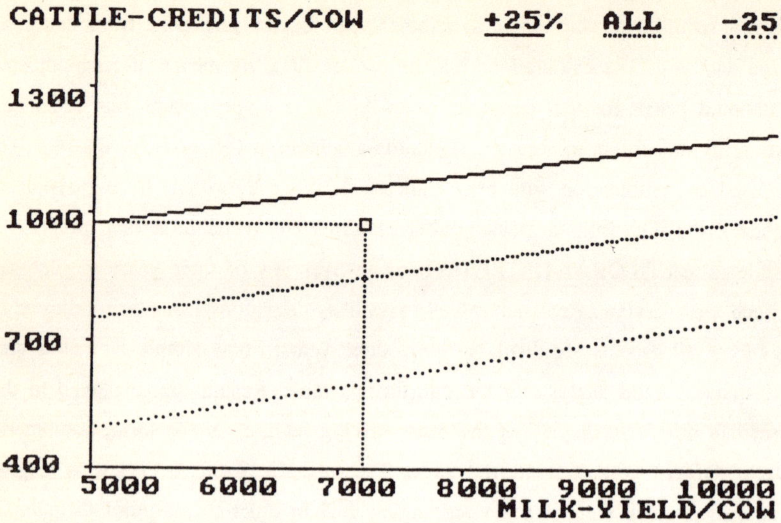

Fig. 3. Relation between the milk production per hectare (X-axis) and the cattle-credits per cow (Y-axis); and the position of farm x. Output from GLOBAL-DETECTOR.

DETECTOR (L.E.I.)

RESULTS FROM 3 YR (FL./HA)	RES *86*	DEV.		RES *87*	DEV.		RES *88*	DEV.	
Gross margin	7456	-838	!	7831	-560	!	9059	287	●
Y I E L D S									
Milk reciepts	12080	-183	!	10926	-23	!	10740	-62	!
Cattle credits	1067	-415	!	1194	-175	!	1843	238	●
Remaining	0	-81	!	158	-49	!	279	-43	!
D I R E C T C O S T S									
Add. Feeding c.	3771	121	!	2741	326	!	2233	-106	●
Veterinary	335	104	!	275	64	!	311	86	!
Insemination	165	31	!	183	67	!	177	47	!
Milkrec.+Herdbook	113	35	!	98	26	!	106	28	!
Interest	387	-31	●	373	-23	●	353	-15	●
Milk products	80	-17	●	110	-9		105	-52	●
Contract rearing	0	0		0	0		0	0	
Other cattle c.	19	-111	●	31	-91	●	28	-85	●
Seeds+Chemicals	90	-31	●	125	-34	●	130	-14	●
N-fertiliser	556	0		401	0		288	0	
Other fertilisers	163	75	!	63	-12	●	61	-13	●
Other. c. crops	10	1		14	-1		14	-1	
Minerals,etc.	0	-19	●	29	-4.		0	-27	●

Press a button, please.....

Fig. 4. Realised values and deviations from standards for gross-margin, returns and variable costs in three successive years. Output from GLOBAL-DETECTOR.

THE DIAGNOSIS PART (EXPERT SYSTEM)

Negative deviations don't necessarily imply weak aspects. For example, a high cost factor may result in a high return factor. Knowledge or expertise is indispensable for evaluating deviations in combination with other factors to make a sound diagnosis of the performance. Dobbins (1988) emphasizes the role of an "expert" for this task.

The objective of diagnosis is to find out what is wrong in the economical and/or technical situation of the farm (Longchamp et al., 1990) in order to provide the manager with information that will allow performance to be improved (Dobbins, 1988). The diagnosis part of GLOBAL-DETECTOR is therefore knowledge-based. To make things easier this part will be called an expert system[6], because it's a computer program which uses the knowledge of one or more experts to solve problems in a specific field (e.g. Hayes-Roth et al., 1983). Since Evans et al. (1989) provide a fine overview of the structure and working of expert systems in an agricultural economics journal, this will therefore not be reviewed here.

Knowledge acquisition with IMAGINE

The analysis part was in the first instance used as a tool for acquiring knowledge. The expert consulted this part on 14 farms and wrote down his conclusions for each of them. These findings formed the basis for the development and application of a specific method for knowledge acquisition from experts: IMAGINE (Independent Method for Acquisition by Graphs and Implementation and Notification of Expertise).

Hennen (1991a) described and compared a dozen techniques for knowledge acquisition. This was done with special reference to agricultural economics. However, none could be used to handle combinatorial explosion, which seems to be a characteristic problem of the economic domain. This problem vanished with the application of IMAGINE.

The expert is asked to concentrate on a certain problem or conclusion (i.e. strong or weak aspect or advice) which may occur on an imaginative farm. After he has formed an image of this problem in his mind ("imagine"), he is requested to fill in a form which looks like a bar-graph. On this form he has to write down the data or variables which are needed to infer if that particular problem exists. For each variable the level of importance and some boundaries have to

---

[6] The authors are acquainted with the different definitions and the fact that the diagnosis part doesn't fit in some of them. Therefore the remarks of Evans et al (1989) are supported in full by the authors: "The term 'expert system' is often abused by those impressed with the implication of the phrase. In reality, seldom does a system reach a level of competence that is deserving of the title 'expert'. In this paper, in accordance with most of the available literature, the name most often used will be 'expert system'".

be indicated. These boundaries may be used to support, adjust and/or reject the strength of the conclusion. A score can be calculated for each variable, based on the level of importance, the values of the boundaries and the actual farm's value of that variable. The average score of all variables give the score or strength of that particular conclusion.
These forms may be filled in independent from the knowledge engineer (i.e. the builder of an expert system). The data on the form can very easily be stored in the knowledge base of GLOBAL-DETECTOR. Software has been developed by the LEI to present the expert's knowledge to the user, in combination with the relevant explanation and the way the conclusions are drawn.

It appeared during the development, that in this domain IMAGINE is a very useful method for knowledge acquisition. A more detailed description of IMAGINE will be presented in detail by Hennen (1991b).

Results from the diagnosis part

Still being in GLOBAL-DETECTOR, the user may skip from the analysis part to the diagnosis part, simply by chosing from the menu. The relevant conclusions, i.e. strong and weak aspects and advices, appear on the screen (Fig. 5). As can be seen, each of these performance judgements are summarized in only a mere handful of remarks. Each judgement is quantified in a score or strength, and that enables to discriminate between judgements. All conclusions are presented on their importance. The most important, having the highest score, is displayed first. Each conclusion is additionally be accompanied with it's certainty factor.

Conclusions which may be less obvious, as well as irrelevant findings, are displayed separately. Extensive information about how the expert has reached to this conclusions can be retrieved by the user. The displays show the user the necessary information. One part of the information is an easy readable text about how the expert generally came to such conclusion. This serves as background information. The other part of this information, which the user also gets displayed on the screen, is a bar-graph (Fig. 6) which is almost identical with the form the expert has filled in during knowledge acquisition. The only difference is the supplementing with farm-data and the calculated score of the conclusion. In Fig. 6 this explanation is presented. The conclusion, in this case an advice, is provided with a moderate to high positive score. This means that there is evidence for it's truth on this farm. According to the expert, two variables determine the strength of that advice: the deviation between actual and standard value for cattle-credits and the deviation between the actual and the standard value for total amount of purchased feed. Both deviations (-176 and 72.5 respectively) support the advice since they are on the right side of the bar-graph. After calculation, the scores for cattle-credits and purchased feed seem to be +3.5 and +1.2 respectively, resulting in an average score of 2.35 for the advice.

```
DETECTOR (L.E.I.)
     P R E S E N T A T I O N   o f   C O N C L U S I O N S        SCORE  CF

NR.       RELEVANT STRONG-/WEAK ASPECTS, ADVICES

12   Improve the feed and grasland management                      2.35   58
27   Improve the returns from cattle-credits                       2.3    57
10   Improve genetic potential; milk yield may then increase       1.28   29
0    Decrease the manuring with nitrogen                           1.05   22
```

Fig. 5. The most important conclusions from a particular farm. Output from GLOBAL-DETECTOR.

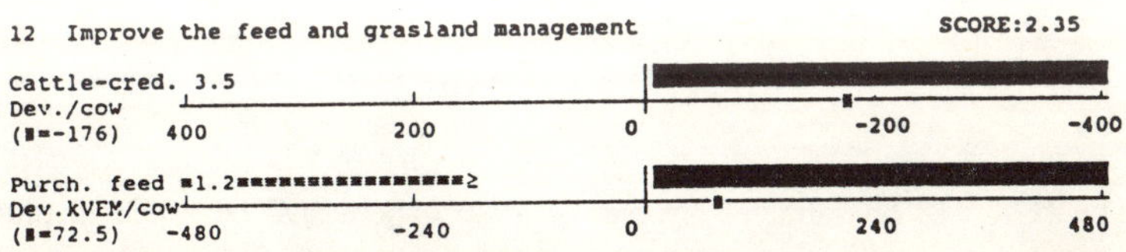

Fig. 6. Presentation of an advice with the IMAGINE method. Output from GLOBAL-DETECTOR.

The user may retrieve more detailed information of this method by means of a programmed help-facility.

Due to the global feature, many advices from GLOBAL-DETECTOR have a medium- or long-term characteristic, e.g. increase milk production, improve commercial management or purchase of land with a high milk quota. They mainly support tactical decisions of a farmer. Implementation of these advices can take considerable time and may have a medium- or long-term effect on the farm's structure and management, eventually - and hopefully - resulting in an inrease in income or profitability. In this perspective, the advice part may support management with an economic goal of the farmer.

EVALUATION OF GLOBAL-DETECTOR

A paper of De Gier (1990) describes in detail the favourable changes on a Dutch farm due to right managerial decisions over a couple of years. The data from this farm were also analysed by GLOBAL-DETECTOR, and it was striking to see that comparable advises were given by GLOBAL-DETECTOR (Hennen and De Hoop, 1991). From this comparison, Hennen and De Hoop conclude that this computer program can signal main striking points and give directions for improving the farm-performance in the future. The farmer, with or without his advisor, can use this outcome as a starting point for further detailed analysis to detect the main causes and to take the necessary actions.

At the moment the system is being tested in some accounting-offices to be able to find out whether the system can be used in their organisation. No test-results are available yet, but members of these offices voiced the need of such a system.

GLOBAL-DETECTOR will also be placed on the microcomputers in a couple of farms in January 1991. At the same time, this system will be integrated with the Farm Accounting Data Network (FADN) of the LEI.

FURTHER RESEARCH

GLOBAL-DETECTOR will be validated by one or more experts and be tested in practice. After that, a further (detailed) elaboration of the conclusions may be executed and implemented in the system. A perspective is also an extension with the fixed costs and an analysis and diagnosis of the financial structure. With these augmentations, we wish to hand the dairy farmer a system for supporting integral management.

The system's objective is also to serve research purposes, in particular the investigation of differences in management in relation to the farmer's income. Especially self-criticism is a major point of view, since ".... the farmer's willingness to criticize his own decisions and actions and to continue learning are fundamental in keeping the enterprise profitable." (Zachariasse, 1974). This research will be done after the system has been validated and thoroughly tested.

The interaction with other systems (e.g. causal networks, tactical planning systems, systems for optimization, neural networks, etc.) will also be an objective for the future in order to develop more integrated management information systems for Dutch dairy farms.

DISCUSSION

GLOBAL-DETECTOR is a knowledge-based computer system for supporting management on dairy farms. However, on dairy farms there are not only differences in farm-structure, but also manager's differences in information and decision behaviour (Bemelmans, 1987). This is mainly caused by a distinction in the farmer's goals and his willingness to criticize and learn (Zachariasse, 1990a). Farmers possess numerous goals, like maximize profit or return, increase net worth, avoid losses, increase leisure time, have a neat and well-kept farmstead, etc., and these goals may change over the life cycle of the individual (Boehlje and Eidman, 1984).
Due to differences in information, decision behaviour and goals, each individual farmer has a specific need for information (De Hoop et al., 1988) and this individuality will certainly result in various levels of appreciation and use of the system. Roep et al. (1991) came to such conclusions, after interviewing 104 dairy farmers who use a program for analysing feeding costs (DELAR).
Each farmer has specific wishes and demands and it is therefore a difficult task to develop management information systems that will be used on large scale (De Hoop et al., 1988). It should be obvious that Dutch farms are too small (as contrasted with industries) to develop an information system for each or for a small group. So it is an arduous task to supply them with systems which match their individual goals completely and as a result support their individual management satisfactory. It should therefore not be too surprising to see that GLOBAL-DETECTOR does not match up with the individual wishes and demands. However, an optional framework has been implemented in GLOBAL-DETECTOR to meet this problem halfway. Further investigations will show if the optional approach is preferabe. Due to the global character of the system and as a result mere indications of good or bad performance, individual differences in management mainly play a role in the detailed analyses on the farm itself done by the farmer and/or his advisor. GLOBAL-DETECTOR may therefore be more general. The very flexible programming environment which has been used during the development of GLOBAL-DETECTOR (muLISP), allows rapid modifications when this seems necessary. Specific wishes can then be met rather easy.

GLOBAL-DETECTOR obtains data from the LEI-database, without a manual data entry. When integrating the system with databases from other organisations or with a farmer's database, the same data should be used. In the Netherlands, Information Models were being developed for all branches of agriculture (Poppe, 1991b; Zachariasse, 1990b). In these models data-definitions were harmonised and described. Although Information Models seem to have a positive impact on the adoption of information technology in Dutch agriculture, the use of uniform data by the different organisations has not been fulfilled yet. Integration of GLOBAL-DETECTOR with other databases requires therefore a thorough investigation of the available data from these databases. After knowing how the data are defined, some precalculations and a number of adjustments of the system might be necessary before installation.

The knowledge-based approach is inevitable in the diagnosis part, as indicated before. By means of proper explanation facilities, the farmer may have access to the knowledge which might be new to him. This possibility makes computerized expert system beneficial (Webster and Amos, 1987). The extension service may use such a systems for their specialists as an aid or as an intelligent assistant, to increase the knowledge in complex areas, and to give uniform advice (Hennen, 1989). On the other hand, the knowledge and skill available from dairy extension specialists may be used for developing expert systems that evaluate dairy herd and farm management data. There exists significant opportunities for this approach in the US (Smith, 1989).

The way conclusions are inferred in GLOBAL-DETECTOR are quite simple and easy to explain to the user. Due to this simplicity, the reliability of the outcome may be less than one should wish. In general, it should be clear that by increasing the reliability of a system, the acceptance by the user will also increase (Fig. 7).
The reliability may increase when taking into account probabilities, dependencies, certainties etc. or performing some kind of corrections. However, in this situation the expert may have too many difficulties to verbalize his knowledge. Even if this would be possible, the outcome should also be clear to the user. If too many corrections etc. are carried out in a such very reliable system, it may be too difficult for the user to understand. Decrease in understanding will lead to a decrease in confidence and undoubtedly lead to a decrease in acceptance. This is especially true for unstructured problems. Refering to Fig. 7, it must be our goal to have a system with such a great reliability that the acceptance will be maximal. With thorough explanations and/or very good support, the acceptance will be higher. A complexer - and through that a more reliable - system is then possible (dotted line in Fig. 7). This illustrates the importance of implementing explanation facilities in management information systems, which is also emphasized by Evans et al. (1989) who remark: "Without such an ability user confidence in a system will be understandably fleeting and the system simply will not be used.".

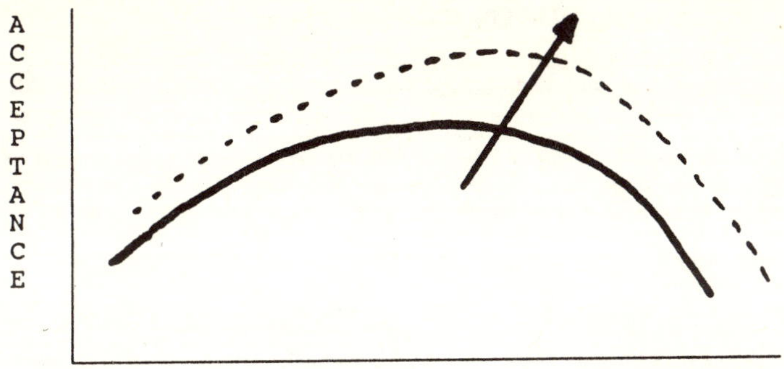

Fig. 7. The influence of reliability on acceptance for unstructured problems.

The drawing of conclusions of the performance was not only done in a very simple way, but also very shallowly or globally. The farm-data used were restricted to the most important data found in the bookkeeping database, comparable with the "quick and easy" approach in the expert system FinARS (Boggess et al., 1989). This limitation can lead to wrong judgements, because we don't possess all the necessary and detailed information to be highly accurate. However, it is our objective to be as reliable as possible with only a few data at our disposal. A larger amount of data might lead to an unmanagable domain. It should be clear in the presentation that the drawn conclusions are strong evidences, but no absolute truths. It is the farmer's task, with or without an advisor, to take notice of the relevant conclusions. These can act as important signals to take the necessary actions, or as a starting point to carry out further detailed investigations with or without an advisor or computerprogram. Farmers don't expect that information systems give the ultimate answer, but want to use these systems for support, that is gaining more insight in the aspects of decision-making, in the rationale of algorithms and in the direction of the outcome (De Hoop et al., 1988). This should stimulate the dairy farmers in their creativity. A system which is prescriptive instead of informative is therefore not desirable. The farmer must take the ultimate decisions, and it's our task to provide the appropriate tools to support these decisions.

REFERENCES

Alleblas, J.T.W. Management in de glastuinbouw, een zaak van passen en meten. Thesis. Den Haag, LEI, 1988. (English summary).

Batte, M.T., G.D. Schnitkey and E. Jones. "Sources and uses of farm management information findings from the Ohio State University survey." In: R.P. King ed.: Future directions for farm information systems research. St. Paul, Agricultural Experiment Station University of Minnesota, 1990b.

Bemelmans, T.M.A. Bestuurlijke informatiesystemen en automatisering. Leiden, Stenfert Kroese, 1987.

Boehlje M.D. and V.R. Eidman. Farm Management. New York, etc., John Wiley & Sons, 1984

Boggess, W.G., P.J. van Blokland and S.D. Moss. FinARS: A Financial Analysis Review Expert System. Agr. Systems 31(1989), pp 19-34.

Brand, A., J.H.M. Verheijden, D.S. Brée, J.F. Schreinemakers, J.A. Renkema and L.C. Zachariasse. ANIMAL FARM. An intelligent knowledge-based computer system for integral management in animal husbandry. Rotterdam, Erasmus University, Management Report Serie No. 11, 1986.

Brée, D.S. and W.H.G.J. Hennen. "The use of expert systems for the interpretation of technical and economical performance of dairy farms." In: G. Schiefer ed.: Expertensysteme in der Agrarwirtschaft: Entwicklung, Erfahrung, Perspektiven. BRD, Vauk Kiel, 1989.

Daatselaar, C.H.G. De invloed van de melkgift op het saldo per ha. Den Haag, LEI, 1988.

Dobbins, C.L. A review of farm business analysis research. USA, University of Minnesota, Draft 2.2, 1988.

Dobbins, C.L. and R.P. King. An expert system for interpreting the year-end business summary of crop-hog farms. USA, University of Minnesota, Draft 2, 1988.

Evans, M., R. Mondor and D. Flaten. Expert Systems and Farm Management. Can. J. Agr. Ec. 37(1989), pp 639-666.

Gier, J.J. de. Eight years Nitrogen Pilot Farm A.A.W. Theunissen. Meststoffen 3, 1990.

Haan, T. de. Het ontwikkelen van bedrijfsspecifieke vergelijkingsmaatstaven voor de analyse van het bedrijfsresultaat op melkveebedrijven. Den Haag, LEI, 1991. (submitted).

Harsh, S.B., R. Brook, R. Harmon. "AIMS - Agricultural Integrated Management Software." Proceedings of the 3rd international DLG-Congress for computer technology on Integrated Decision Support Systems in Agriculture. BRD, Frankfurt a.M., 1990.

Hayes-Roth, F., D.A. Waterman and D.B. Lenat [eds]: Building Expert Systems. Wokingham, England etc., Addison-Wesley Publishing Company, 1983.

Hennen, W.H.G.J. De methode voor het bouwen van expert systemen. Getest voor de analyse van de omzet op melkveebedrijven. LEI, Den Haag, 1989.

Hennen, W.H.G.J. Elicitatie-technieken. Mogelijkheden en beperkingen voor de ontwikkeling van de GLOBAL-DETECTOR en de modules van het MPP-project. Den Haag, LEI, 1991a. (in preparation).

Hennen, W.H.G.J. IMAGINE: Acquisition, representation and presentation of economical performance knowledge. Den Haag, LEI, 1991b. (in preparation).

Hennen, W.H.G.J. and D.W. de Hoop. Een computermatige kijk op het stikstofproefbedrijf van A.A.W. Theunissen. Meststoffen, 1991 (?) (submitted).

Hoop, D.W. de, J. Engelsma, G.J. Wisselink. De tactische boer; het management en de informatiebehoefte van melkveehouders. Den Haag, LEI, 1988.

James, S.C. and E. Stoneberg. Farm Accounting and Business Analysis. Ames: Iowa State University Press, 1986.

King, R.P. and S.T. Sonka. "Management Problems of Farms and Agricultural Firms." In: R.J. Hildreth, K.L. Lipton, K.C. Clayton, C.C. O'Connor [eds]: Agriculture and rural areas approaching the twenty-first century; Challenges for Agricultural Economics. Iowa, Iowa State University Press, 1988.

King, R.P., S.B. Harsh and C.L. Dobbins. Farm information systems: farmer needs and system design strategies. TSL, 5(1990)1, pp 34-59.

LEI/VLB. Gedetaileerd informatiemodel "analyse en diagnose". Den Haag/Leiden, LEI/VLB, 1989.

Longchamp, J.Y., J.P. Nicoletti and L. Lescar. "A Coherent set of Decision Support Software for Farm Management." Proceedings of the 3rd international DLG-Congress for computer technology on Integrated Decision Support Systems in Agriculture. BRD, Frankfurt a.M., 1990.

McGrann, J.M., K. Karkosh and C. Osborne. Agricultural Financial Analysis Expert Systems: Software Description. Can. J. Agr. Ec. 37(1989), pp 695-708.

Morahan, A.G., D.J. Ruane and M. Butler. "The development and evaluation of a microcomputer based management information system for a dairying enterprise." In: Dodd and Grace [eds]: Land and Water Use. Balkema, Rotterdam, 1989.

Phillips, J.J. and S.B. Harsh. "An Expert System Application to the Financial Analysis of Lender Case Farm Records." Paper presented at AAEA annual meeting. Lansing, Michigan, 1987.

Poppe, K.J. Van bedrijfsuitkomsten tot financiële positie (BEF). Samenvattend overzicht van landbouwbedrijven tot en met 1984/1985. Den Haag, LEI, 1986.

Poppe, K.J. "Using farm accounts: a survey and recommendations for further research." In: K.J. Poppe ed.: Information needs and accounting in agriculture. Den Haag, LEI, 1991a. (in press).

Poppe, K.J. "Determining farmers' financial information requirements." In: K.J. Poppe ed.: Information needs and accounting in agriculture. Den Haag, LEI, 1991b. (in press).

Roep, D., J.D. van der Ploeg and C. Leeuwis. Zicht op duurzaamheid en kontinuïteit, bedrijfsstijlen in de Achterhoek. LUW, vakgr. Agr. Ontwikkelingssociologie, Wageningen, 1991.

Smith, T.R. The Potential Application of Expert Systems in Dairy Extension Education. J. Dairy Sci 72(1989), pp 2760-2766.

Steele, G.L. Jr. Common LISP: The Language. USA, Digital Press, 1984.

Waterman, D.A. A guide to Expert Systems. Reading, etc., Addison-Wesley Publishing Company, 1985.

Webster, J.P.G. and J.J. Amos. Expert systems for agricultural management. Farm Management 24, 1987

Zachariasse, L.C. Farmer and Farm returns. An analysis of causes of differences in profitability of similar arable farms in the North-East-Polder. Thesis, Wageningen, 1974. (English summary).

Zachariasse, L.C. Managementcapaciteiten: elementen en beïnvloeding. In: Bureau PHLO [eds]: Achtergrond en gebruik van economische modellen en expertsystemen ter ondersteuning van management-beslissingen op melkvee- en varkensbedrijven. PHLO, Wageningen, 1990a.

Zachariasse, L.C. "Farm management information systems planning and development in the Netherlands." In: R.P. King ed.: Future directions for farm information systems research, St. Paul, Agricultural Experiment Station University of Minnesota, 1990b.

An Optimisation Model for Setting Pressure Controllers to Minimise Leakage in Pipe Networks *

K. S. Hindi
Decision Technologies Group
Computation Department
University of Manchester Institute of Science and Technology
(UMIST)
P.O.Box 88, Manchester M60 1QD,Britain

Y. M. Hamam
Ecole Superieure d'Ingenieurs en Electrotechnique et Electronique,
2 Boulevard Blaise Pascal
B.P.99, 93160 Noisy-Le-Grand, France

Abstract

The issue of minimising leakage in pipe networks by appropriate control of the settings of pressure-control elements (valves in water networks and governors in gas networks) is addressed. The problem is first formulated as a non-linear, non-convex optimisation problem. The limitations of iterative linearisation are then discussed. An alternative linearised model, based on separable programming, is presented. Results of computational studies to assess the efficacy and efficiency of the proposed model are presented and discussed.

---

*This work was carried out under contract for the Water Research Centre,P.O.Box 85, Swindon, England

List of principal symbols

$\mathcal{A}$	=	set of pipe arcs
$\mathcal{V}$	=	set of arcs representing valves
$\mathcal{D}$	=	set of all nodes excluding source nodes
C_d	=	arc-node incidence matrix for all nodes $\in \mathcal{D}$ with
c_{ij}	=	$\begin{cases} +1 & \text{if flow in arc } j \text{ leaves node } i \\ -1 & \text{if flow in arc } j \text{ enters node } i \\ 0 & \text{if arc } j \text{ is not incident on node } i \end{cases}$
p_i	=	pressure at node i
q_a	=	flow in arc a
Q	=	vector of arc flows
D	=	vector of demands
p_a^s	=	head (pressure) at sending (initial) endpoint of arc a
p_a^t	=	head (pressure) at receiving (terminal) endpoint of arc a
p_i^{min}	=	minimum head (pressure) required at demand node i

1 Introduction

Losses through leakage from pipe (water or gas supply) networks can be significant. For example, they are estimated to vary in Britain between 10% and 50% of the total supply of various water authorities, with an average of the order of 25% [1].

Several factors affect leakage such as the state and quality of pipes and fittings and the characteristics of the soil in which they are laid. In particular, the higher the pressure is, the higher is the rate of leakage [1, 2, 3]. Hence, it is advantageous to reduce pressures as far as possible, particularly that pressure is the only factor among those affecting leakage that can be easily controlled in an existing network. On the other hand, it is necessary to maintain, throughout the network, pressures sufficient to meet consumer demands. There is, thus, a need for compromise between these two conflicting objectives. To this end, use is made of pressure-control elements.

The objective of this work is to develop a mathematical model and computational techniques to determine the settings of these elements, given a set of demands and the pressures at the sources, in order to minimise leakage while maintaining the security of supply.

Very little work seems to have been carried out on mathematically modelling this problem within an optimisation framework. The only two works the authors know of are those of Sterling and Bargiela [8], Germanopoulos [4] and [6], which will be discussed in section 3.

2 Problem Formulation

Let each pressure control element be represented by an arc v. The problem can then be stated as:

Problem P1

$$\min \sum_{i \in \mathcal{D}} f(p_i) \tag{2.1}$$

subject to

$$C_d Q = -D \tag{2.2}$$

$$p_a^s - p_a^t = f(q_a) \qquad \forall a \in \mathcal{A} \tag{2.3}$$

$$p_v^t \leq p_v^s \qquad \forall v \in \mathcal{V} \tag{2.4}$$

$$p_i \geq p_i^{min} \qquad \forall i \in \mathcal{D} \tag{2.5}$$

$$q_a \text{ unrestricted} \qquad \forall a \in \mathcal{A} \tag{2.6}$$

$$q_v \geq 0 \qquad \forall v \in \mathcal{V} \tag{2.7}$$

The pressures are specified for source nodes; unknown for all others.

The objective function (2.1) is to minimise leakage as a function of pressure at demand nodes. The exact nature of this function is still subject to debate. In the present work, it is assumed that, in the absence of agreed, experimentally substantiated results, a linear relationship is as good as any. The linear relationship employed is:

$$f(p_i) = w_i p_i$$

where w_i is a weighting factor. Thus it is assumed that total leakage is equal to the weighted sum of pressures at demand nodes. The weights are considered as input parameters to be supplied by the users reflecting their estimation of the extent of leakage at each demand node.

Constraints (2.2) represent the nodal balance equations. Constraints (2.3) represent the pressure-flow relationships, which are of the form:

$$f(q_a) = k_a \mid q_a \mid^{\alpha-1} q_a$$

where $1 \leq \alpha \leq 2$ and is usually taken to be 1.85 for water networks and 2 for gas networks.

Constraints (2.4) ensure that the pressure at the outlet of each pressure reducing valve is less than or equal to the pressure at the inlet. Constraints (2.5) ensure that the pressure at each demand node is greater than a specified minimum.

The nature of the pressure-flow relations and the fact that the flow variables are free (unrestricted in sign, since flow in an arc can be in either direction) render the problem nonlinear and non-convex. This, in addition to the large scale of the networks involved, is the major source of difficulty. Lack of convexity means that any solution to the problem, when formulated as a nonlinear programming problem, will be a local optimum. This does not mean, necessarily, that the global optimum will not be achieved; rather that if and when it is achieved, it will not be possible to ascertain that it is indeed so. Therefore, the realistic objective is to produce 'good' solutions, whose 'goodness' is established by steady-state simulation.

3 Limitations of Iterative Linearisation

The most natural approach to solving problem (P1) is to attempt iterative sequential linearisation. Unfortunately, this approach suffers severe limitations. In this section, we discuss why.

Starting with an initial estimate of the flows, the pressure-flow relationship can be linearised from one iteration n to the next iteration $n+1$, such that:

$$\Delta p_a^{n+1} = k_a \mid q_a^n \mid^{\alpha-1} q_a^{n+1}$$

Thus at iteration $n+1$, the following linear programming problem is solved:

Problem P2
$\min \sum_{i \in \mathcal{D}} w_i p_i$
subject to (2.2), (2.4), (2.5), (2.6), (2.7) and

$$p_a^s - p_a^t = k_a \mid q_a^n \mid^{\alpha-1} q_a \qquad \forall a \in \mathcal{A}$$

However, such iterative linearisation will fail to converge. The reason is that the solution of the linear programming (LP) (by the variants of the Simplex method) proceeds by moving from one corner of the feasible region to an adjacent corner. For the solution of a nonlinear programming problem by iterative linearisation to succeed, the LP solution from one iteration to the next would have to move between nearby corners. However, in the present case, non-convexity means that LP solutions oscillate between opposite corners. This is manifested by the flow in some arcs changing direction from one iteration to the next.

Thus iterative linearisation will fail, unless the network being modelled is nearly radial. For, in the latter case, the direction of the flow is virtually predetermined and the problem is therefore convex. Sterling and Bargiela [8] employ iterative linearisation. However, to avert the possibility of oscillation, they formulate the problem in terms of finding pressure settings as near as possible to a known desirable profile, which in effect amounts to linearisation around a predetermined operating point.

In [4] and [6] ensuring convergence is sought by calculating q_a^* from:

$$\Delta p_a^{n+1} = k_a \mid q_a^n \mid^{\alpha-1} q_a^*$$

and taking:

$$q_a^{n+1} = 0.5(q_a^n + q_a^*)$$

But although this scheme may aid convergence in some cases, it does not rule out oscillation and failure to converge, as flow in some arcs can still change direction from one iteration to the next continually.

4 Solution by Separable Programming

One alternative for solving some non-linear programming problems is separable programming [9, 10], whereby non-linear relations are approximated by piece-wise linear separable functions, thus transforming the non-linear programming problem in hand to an approximately equivalent linear programming problem.

The pressure-flow relationship is linearised as shown in figure 1, with F_a and the slopes of the line segments chosen judiciously (as explained below). Thus for each arc:

$$\left.\begin{array}{l} p_a^s - p_a^t = -\gamma_{a1}q_{a1} + \gamma_{a2}q_{a2} + \gamma_{a1}q_{a3} - R_a \\ q_{a1} \geq 0 \\ 0 \leq q_{a2} \leq 2F_a \\ q_{a3} \geq 0 \\ q_{a1} \neq 0 \text{ iff } q_{a2} = 0 \\ q_{a3} \neq 0 \text{ iff } q_{a2} = 2F_a \end{array}\right\} \forall a \in \mathcal{A} \tag{4.8}$$

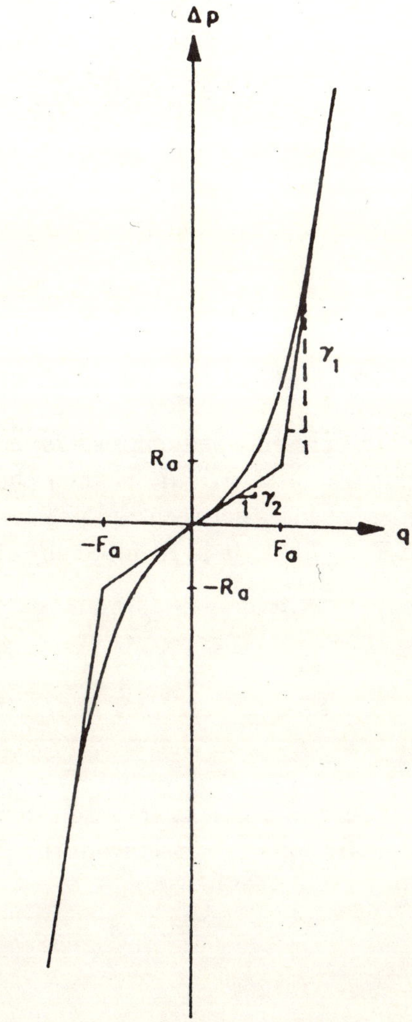

Figure 1 Separable Linearisation of Head-Flow Curve

Employing this model leads to the following linear program:

Problem P3

$\min \sum_{i \in \mathcal{D}} w_i p_i$

subject to (2.2), (2.4), (2.5), (2.6), (2.7) and (4.8).

Q in (2.2) is now the vector of flows, whose elements are: $q_a = -F_a - q_{a1} + q_{a2} + q_{a3} \quad \forall a \in \mathcal{A}$ and $q_v \quad \forall v \in \mathcal{V}$

The above linear program can be solved by the Revised Simplex algorithm, modified to take account of the conditions relating the variables q_{ai} to each other. In a manner similar to that suggested by [7], this can be implemented, at each Simplex step, by identifying from among the q variables not currently in the basis those eligible for entry into it. Eligibility can be determined in the following way:

For each set of q variables, $q_{ai}, i = 1 \ldots 3$, do
begin
  If q_{a1} is not in the basis and $q_{a2} = 0$ then q_{a1} is eligible
  If q_{a2} is not in the basis and $q_{a1} = q_{a3} = 0$ then q_{a2} is eligible
  If q_{a3} is not in the basis and q_{a2} is at its upper limit then q_{a3} is eligible
end

Naturally, the parameters of linearisation have to be chosen carefully to ensure an acceptable accuracy for the approximation. F_a was chosen as follows: a network analysis is carried out with all valves shorted and F_a is taken to be equal to the resulting flow in arc a. The rationale is that the flow in most pipes will, when the pressure-reducing valves are activated, likely be of the same order of magnitude as F_a. R_a is then chosen to minimise the deviation, in a least squares sense, between the pressure-flow curve and the line segment $(0,0)$–(F_a, R_a). Thus, it is required to minimise, with respect to R_a:

$$F = \int_0^{F_a} (q_a^\alpha - \frac{R_a q_a}{F_a})^2 dq_a$$

which yields:

$$R_a = \frac{3}{\alpha + 2} F_a^\alpha$$

The parameters of the second segment are also calculated to to minimise the deviation, again in a least squares sense, from the pressure-flow curve.

5 Case Studies and Computational Considerations

A number of case studies have been carried out to determine both the efficacy and the computational efficiency of the proposed model and optimisation technique.

In each case study, the solution given by the separable programming scheme described above was tested by steady-state simulation [5]. The simulation was run with the indicated valve settings and the results examined to ascertain that the minimum nodal pressure is indeed equal to the prescribed limit. In every case, this was so to within 2%. Thus the solutions given by the algorithms are indeed feasible. The question of optimality is, however, more difficult. As discussed earlier, the fact that the overall problem is non-convex means that overall optimality can not be guaranteed. Nevertheless, the solutions achieved were judged by experienced analysts to be good, if not optimal.

In principle, a search for the optimal solution could be carried out by associating zero-one integer variables with the segments of the linearised pressure-flow relationships and solving the resulting mixed integer programming model. However, the resulting problem would be intractable computationally for all but very small networks, due to the large number of integer variables introduced.

nodes	pipe arcs	valves	discrepancy from specified minimum pressure %	solution time minutes
18	20	3	-0.65	0.16
56	79	5	1.18	2.83
93	122	8	1.32	12.94

Table 1: Results of three case studies

Table 1 gives the results of three representative cases solved employing the piecewise linearised model on a microcomputer with a 16 MHz 30386 CPU and a 30387 Mathematics co-processor. The minimum pressure discrepancy is calculated in the following manner: a simulation using the valve-pressure settings indicated by the solution of the separable programming model is carried out and the difference between the minimum pressure thus observed and the specified minimum pressure is calculated as a percentage of the latter. The results attest to the efficacy of the model as well as to its good computational efficiency.

6 Conclusions

Problems of steady-state optimisation of pipe networks are complex. The difficulty stems from the fact that they are invariably large-scale problems, due to the size of the networks involved, as well as being non-linear and non-convex due to the nature of the pressure-flow relationships. Attempts to solve such problems by iterative linearisation face severe limitations, even if devices to aid convergence are employed.

In this paper, an alternative linearisation approach, based on the idea of separable programming has been presented, with particular reference to the economically and environmentally important problem of minimising leakage in pipe networks. A model has been developed and a software package implementing it has been used in several case studies. These confirmed both the efficacy and computational efficiency of the model. The experience thus gained indicates that the separable programming approach would be effective in solving other steady-state optimisation problems in both the water industry and the gas industry.

Acknowledgement

The authors are grateful to Mr J. Creasey of the Water Research Centre for his help and guidance throughout the work on this project, as well as for many fruitful technical discussions. They are also grateful to their colleague, Dr A. Osiadacz, for his help and suggestions.

References

[1] Water Authorities Association, *Leakage control policy and practice*, 1985.

[2] Bessey, S G 'Progress in pressure control', Aqua, No. 6, 1985, pp. 325–3330.

[3] Bessey, S G 'Some developments in pressure reduction', Journal of the Institution of water Engineers and Scientists, Vol. 39, No. 6, 1985, pp. 501–505.

[4] Germanopoulos and Jowitt, P. J. (1989) Leakage reduction by excess pressure minimization in water supply networks, Proceedings of the Institution of Civil Engineers, Vol. 87, pp. 195–214.

[5] Hamam, Y M and Hindi, K S 'Steady-state solution of pipe networks: a new efficient optimisation-based algorithm', DTG Report, Computation Department, UMIST, 1989.

[6] Jowitt, P. J. and Xu C. (1990) Optimal valve control in water distribution networks, ASCE Journal of water Resources Planning and Management, Vol. 116, No. 4, pp. 445–473.

[7] Miller, C E 'The simplex method for local separable programming', in Graves, R L and Wolfe, P (Eds), *Recent Advances in Mathematical Programming*, McGraw-Hill, 1963, pp. 89–110.

[8] Sterling, M J H and Bargiela, A 'Leakage reduction by optimised control of valves in water networks', Trans. Inst. of Measurement and Control, Vol. 6, No. 6, 1984, pp. 293–298.

[9] Murtagh, A B *Advanced Linear Programming: Computation and Practice*, McGraw-Hill, 1981.

[10] Williams, H P *Model Building in Mathematical Programming*, Wiley, 1989.

Optimal decisionmaking or optimal trouble-shooting?

G.J. Hofstede & A.J.M. Beulens
Wageningen Agricultural University, the Netherlands
Dept. of Computer Science
e-mail hofstede@rcl.wau.nl
fax (+31)8370.84731

Abstract

The aim of this paper is to view the notion of optimal decision support from the practical perspective of a user - manager. Using this perspective forces one to conclude that optimization techniques in the classical OR sense do not necessarily lead to improved, let alone optimal, decision support. The organizational and environmental contingencies determine what kind of DSS, if any, are feasible to support decisionmaking in a given situation.

For the area of tactical / operational planning decisions, we propose a simple assessment tool to judge which type of DSS could be appropriate. The tool investigates eight aspects from both the context and the object system in a qualitative manner. The possibilities of the tool are demonstrated for two cases: cultivation planning in potted plant nurseries, and physical distribution in a large production company. The present status of the tool is tentative. The tool predicts that in most planning situations highly interactive planning systems, in which the planner has primacy over the automated system, are called for.

Introduction

This Conference bears the title "Optimization-based Computer-Aided Modelling and Design". The present paper deals with the notion of optimization in the context of Decision Support Systems. It is written from the point of view of a manager using a DSS for a real-world planning problem situation. The types of problem situations considered are tactical or operational: repeatedly occurring problems with a marked combinatorial aspect. What does optimality mean for the user, that is, the planner or manager? Is it attainable, and what does it consist of? For instance, optimality from the user's viewpoint requires at the very least that the decision reached with help of the DSS can actually be implemented, and that it fits with related decisions. In our experience organizational decisionmaking is usually not a neatly partitioned activity. On the contrary, it is more like a whirlpool: no decision can be singled out, and it is very hard to grasp how and why decisions are arrived at. More often than not, *ad hoc trouble-shooting* is what planners do, rather than *optimizing isolated decision-making processes*. Our experience with the cases of production planning in potted plant nurseries and of physical distribution in a large organization is that optimality in an organizational context is something quite different from the mathematical notion of optimality familiar to Operations Researchers. If DSS designers intend to strive for optimal decision support they have to be aware of the environmental and organizational context in which their systems will be used. The result may well be a system which is childishly simple from a designer's point of view, but which fits into the organization and its decision processes, and satisfies performance requirements, rather than a sophisticated optimizing system which is not accepted and cannot be integrated into existing decision making practices.

In the next sections we shall elaborate on our views about organizational decisionmaking and DSS, concentrating on tactical / operational planning decisions. We shall mention some DSS literature in support of our view that the context of a planning situation is of paramount importance when designing a DSS. Then we present the tentative tool for assessing DSS feasibility in a given situation. We illustrate the use of the tool for potted plant production planning and for physical distribution in a large company. Finally a discussion about the merits of the tool and directions for further research concludes the paper.

Optimal organizational decisionmaking

Prescriptive and descriptive

Theories of organizational decisionmaking come in two orientations: *pre*scriptive and *de*scriptive. Either implicitly or explicitly all such theories contain a mix of these two orientations.

The prescriptive or normative theories stress that partitioning activities and predefining a goal structure should act as a basis for decisionmaking, and such theories even define procedures, models and algorithms to be applied for decisionmaking (e.g. Anthony 1965, Kampfraath & Marcelis 1981, Lindley 1985).

Descriptive approaches stress the mess which is present in organizations: decisions interact, work is fragmented, goals are never made explicit and are of a qualitative and/or quantitative nature, or they are invented after the fact to justify decisions. In other words, the conditions under which formal methods such as mathematical optimization are of value may not be met, at least when considering organizational decisionmaking as a whole (e.g. Cyert & March 1963, Lindblom 1959, March & Olsen 1976, Mintzberg 1973).

In accordance with the descriptive approaches we define *organizational decisionmaking* as a *complex of interrelated activities in which decisions do not stand by themselves*. As such many decisions defy attempts at exhaustive formal modelling, for instance in a DSS. However, structuring these activities in the sense of the prescriptive theories is generally desirable and DSS can play a role in this. We define a decision as the outcome of a decision problem. A *decision problem* is a *conceptual entity abstracted from the organizational processes*. A decision problem has goals and variables and operates on an object system (OS). To indicate a decision problem which is not yet clearly conceptualized, together with its organizational context we use the term *decision situation*.

DSS and unstructuredness

Many authors of DSS papers, see van Dissel et al.(1990), seem to agree on a few key characteristics of DSS. DSS are supposed to support decision makers, rather than replace them. Further DSS are supposed to be concerned with support to solve semi- and unstructured problems. Unstructuredness of the problem may be defined as the degree of incompleteness of the knowledge of the decisionmaker of one or more of the following:

- the demarcation of the object system from its relevant environment, as well as the demarcation between relevant and irrelevant environment.
- the initial state of the object system, including available resources,
- the goals to be attained and the attributes of relevance attached to these goals,
- decision alternatives and their expected consequences as generated by a (set of) model(s) of the OS.
- procedures and methods to obtain necessary information, to specify goal attributes and to generate and evaluate decision alternatives using available MIS and DSS.

This enumeration shows that unstructuredness can reside in various aspects of a decision problem. In fact, since a decision problem is a conceptualization, by definition *unstructuredness resides in the mind of the conceptualizer*. If a problem owner and a DSS designer both contemplate a problem situation they may arrive at different conceptualizations. As a problem owner learns about his problem the problem becomes more structured, and this is entirely a conceptual learning process which does not affect the problem situation as it would be perceived by a third person. It follows that a good DSS is most likely amongst others an 'LSS', or learning support system, for the problem owner. By analogy the design process of a DSS is also a learning process, gone through by designer and problem owner, which hopefully results in a shared conceptualization.

DSS and improved decisionmaking

DSS are intended to improve decisionmaking. This means that, to begin with, they must be used. It is not realistic to expect organizational decisionmaking, which is rooted in human social behaviour and cognitive limitations, to change overnight in order to accommodate a DSS. Rather a DSS must fit into the existing pattern or demand modest changes, depending on the will to adopt it (see e.g. Beulens & Hofstede 1990). It is then that organizational decisionmaking can be 'optimized', or rather, improved.

Frequently there are very low-brow practical impediments to improved decisionmaking. Beulens (1990) sums up a number of these impediments. Basically they come down to the fact that in many cases, practical functional and performance requirements for DSS have not been properly defined. Such requirements are the yardstick for measuring quality, or if you will optimality, of the DSS. They can be derived from aspects such as the organizational and environmental context, the tasks and relative priority of these of the user, the way in which these tasks are being performed and interact (fragmented decision making processes), the problem and systems knowledge of the user, the information sytems that are to be interfaced with. The *decision* itself as a modelled abstraction from the organizational whirlpool plays no more than a modest role.

Organizational contingencies

The nature of an organization's decisionmaking processes sets conditions for DSS development and DSS use. The people, procedures, and production processes in an organization, its culture and its environment all play a role. If an organization strongly adheres to prescriptive management theory, e.g. decisions are explicitly defined, procedures to solve them are explicit, high-quality data are collected, and the like, then optimization in the mathematical sense may be feasible. If, on the other hand, decisionmaking is informal, fragmented, lacking accurate data, then mathematical optimization is most definitely not feasible. Most cases will be intermediate and ask for interactive, dynamically robust DSS.

Reports from practitioners who have developed DSS frequently make mention of organizational factors which have impeded use of the system, or of downward adjustment of the sophistication of a system during the implementation phase (e.g. Institution of Electrical Engineers 1990). In many cases this can be attributed to incorrect or incomplete assessments of the kinds of functional and performance requirement previously indicated. Users, on the other hand, are typically content when at least clerical tasks are taken off their hands by a DSS but are often distrustful of the outcome of model-based reasoning or computations generated by a DSS. They are certainly not content if (clerical) tasks are to be performed when using a system when no real benefit is perceived.

Example of school timetabling

For example, take the case of Verbraeck (1990). This author has developed and successfully marketed a lesson-planning system for large schools. His experience when working with planners in schools made him aware of the misfit which can occur between a human planner and an automated DSS. On p. 209 Verbraeck remarks:

> "Manual lesson-planning has a number of advantages over automated planning. The planner has a clear understanding of the planning situation. Difficulties can be tackled in parallel. The planner knows where the initial information can be altered without creating trouble. The planner is able to identify partial problems, blocking lessons, and small puzzles that can be solved apart. The time it takes to make a schedule can be controlled by the planner. The criteria the schedule has to meet can be changed when the process threatens to take longer than expected."

The keywords behind this enumeration seem to be *flexibility* and *problem expertise*. However manual planning also has severe drawbacks such as inconsistencies and errors, excessive time consumption. In his planning system Verbraeck has attained the benefits of automation without losing too much flexibility by designing an algorithm with the following properties (p.209):

- The planner is able to edit the schedule manually. The algorithm does not affect manually created plan parts.
- The search time is limited and under control of the planner.
- In the allotted time a schedule is always presented whether all lessons are included or not.
- With growing search time, the quality of the schedule increases.
- The algorithm works even if there are inconsistencies in the input data.

Summarizing we can say that Verbraeck's system is very much a satisficing rather than an optimizing system, and that it leaves the planner in full control of his planning strategy. These are obviously important assets in an environment which is as unpredictable as a school and in which constraints are so manifold but hard to quantify.

Example of Job-Shop scheduling

A strong viewpoint about the misfit between many automated planning systems and actual planning practice in organizations is expressed by McKay et al. (1989). These authors carried out an investigation among over 300 practitioners of job-shob scheduling and found that *not one* of the planning situations in which these persons worked contained *any* of the following properties:

- well-known and stable manufacturing process
- simple goals not affected by hidden agendas
- predictable and reliable setup and processing times
- relatively short cycle times to allow most work to start and complete without interruptions
- accurate and complete drawings, routings, and bills of materials
- reliable, stable, and accurate product demand forecast
- known material quality, quantity, and arrival times.

Obviously these 300 planning situations are ill-suited to formal modelling and full automation. McKay et al. remark (p.172):

> "In general, the world of scheduling remains as it was in the fifties and sixties. Neither Operations Research nor Artificial Intelligence has made a significant impact on how scheduling is done in the real world."

Any conference on DSS, OR or AI can serve to illustrate this remark. For instance at the first specialized IFORS Conference on DSS held in March 1991, it was remarked in keynote speeches that OR had drifted from solving real problems to finding solutions looking for problems. Recently, the concept of DSS has provoked a renewed interest in OR. Getting or keeping the OR research community in touch with organizational needs was perceived as a major challenge. At present the situation is not ideal; as J. Sviokla mentioned in a panel session the ratio between research prototype systems to beta-test versions to organizationally implemented systems is about 100 to 10 to 1.

An assessment tool for DSS in planning

It is our conviction that a large majority of tactical / operational planning situations of very diverse nature will remain intractable for models without assistance by human planners. At the same time, given flexible, incremental models and an awareness of the importance of organizational contingencies, much improvement should be possible.

We have attempted to operationalize the above description of organizational decisionmaking, generating a tentative tool which can be used during a quick scan to assess chances for DSS development in a given decision situation. In fact the tool was born out of frustration of one of us who unsuccessfully tried to get potted plant growers to accept normative support. The tool investigates contingency factors that have to be taken into account when specifying functional and performance requirements for DSS. Given a decision area of concern in the area of tactical and operational planning we propose to rate eight aspects of the problem context. Aspects that concern the organization, the environment of the organization, and the direct decision making context are grouped in the category "context characteristics", aspects that are related directly to the object system to be controlled are grouped in the category "object system characteristics".

Context characteristics

1 How large is the organization?

In a very small organization the tactical level is not separated from the strategic and operational levels, because the same person or group of persons attend to all levels. This means strong 'contagion' of the decision by almost all other decisions. Plans tend to be informal or even absent. If on the other hand the organization is large then the planning process becomes more detached from other organizational decisions and there may exist formal organizational planning procedures.

2 Is there a specialized planner?

In the absence of a specialized planner, planning is often done by someone with many other obligations. It may be done in a quick-and-dirty, ad hoc way, especially if the other responsabilities of the person who does the planning are perceived as more important or more fun. If there is a person or group of persons specifically concerned with the planning situation - which often occurs in larger organizations - then usually the planner is an expert, spends much time on planning, likes to do a good planning job, and has an interest in automated support (but perhaps also fear to be chased from his job by a computer).

3 How dynamic is the environment?

In a sector where the environment (in a broad sense) is dynamic and unpredictible, decisionmaking has to be highly responsive to external signals. If the environment is comparatively stable, there is more to gain by an orientation towards improving the efficiency of internal operations. Often an organization is to some extent free in defining its environment, as in the case of a potted plant grower choosing to sell through private channels or via the auction.

4 What is the frequency of the decisionmaking process?

Tactical and operational planning decisions they are by definition recurrent. But the point is still relevant if formulated differently: how often does the decision making process occur before a decision situation changes so much that it must be considered to be different from the current decision problem? In most organizations changes are fairly frequent. For instance, if a planning decision is taken yearly and major organizational changes occur once every three years, then developing a DSS to support the generation of these plans may not be cost-effective.

Object system characteristics

5 How predictable is the object system?

The better an OS can be predicted, the better an automated model of the OS can function as a means to generate decision alternatives and expected consequences thereof. An OS can be considered predictable when a planner accepts a model of the OS and its forecasts within a specified context. In fact when the OS is not predictable this can mean one of two things: either it is known that there are limits to predictability, as with the weather influencing crop growth, or the complexity is such that there currently is no predictive model but it remains open whether a predictive model will be found. Although in both cases a simulation model can be of great value, the potential predictive benefits of a model are larger in the latter situation.

6 Are people concerned?

This point is no more than a special case of the previous one but so important that it deserves special mention. As soon as people's interests are affected by a plan then a variety of constraints come into play. Both during plan generation and during plan execution there will be soft constraints related to persons. Especially if planner and planned have some relationship then interpersonal considerations will play an important part.

7 How controllable is the object system?

To some extent, adaptive control measures can counteract unpredictability, thus making planning feasible. An important assumption to make model-based DSSs feasible is that planners using the DSS are able to generate plans that can actually be realized. For instance, in potted plant culture one can counteract unfavourable radiation circumstances by artificial lighting.

8 Are reliable data available?

However predictable and controllable a process, if data needed by a model are not available, not reliable, or too expensive, then the output of a DSS based on this model is of limited value. This point directly relates to the availability and accessibility of information primarily contained in operational information systems (OIS). Besides it is important to mention here that there may exist an actuality and relevancy gap between the DSS and the systems to be interfaced with. By *actuality gap* we refer to the fact that in many cases OIS are up to date to for instance T0, the current time is Tc and the DSS requires data up to T1 with T1>Tc>T0. With *relevancy gap* we refer to incompatibilities that may exist between the data models of OIS and DSS.

Operationalizing the scales of the tool

The assesment tool can be applied by scoring each of the eight characteristics on an ordinal scale from 1 to 5. The following table shows what real-world properties may be associated with the extreme scale values.

feature	situation with rating 1	situation with rating 5
1 org. size	1 to 5 people. At most one allround boss.	Over 100 people. Formally defined, clear function separation
2 planner	Boss does the planning among many other tasks.	Specialized planner or team; does nothing else.
3 environment	Not all relevant variables are known. There are major changes in external conditions on each repetition of the decision making process.	All variables are accepted to be known. The conceptualization can cope with the changes of external conditions (markets, prices, laws, ...).
4 frequency of decisionmaking process	Unique decision	Decision process repeated unchanged many times for subsequent planning periods
5 predictability of OS	No accepted model of the OS and/or essential variables are unpredictable within 50%.	Accepted model of OS and all variables are assumed sufficiently predictable within allowed %.
6 people	People are being scheduled. Their wishes are very important.	No interests of people are assumed to be affected by the plan in any way.
7 controllability of OS	Process not controllable.	Process controllable.
8 data quality	Data are of unknown quality, often unquantified rumours, hunches, expectations.	Data are quantitative, accurate, complete, up to date, reliable.

Table 1: operationalized assessment tool for DSS feasibility

For the time being this assessment tool is in need of empirical validation. A specific point is that some of the elements are probably highly correlated and should therefore be joined. Another point is that some characteristics may be of more importance than others. However, our conviction is that by using the tool critically it can evolve into a valuable and empirically sound instrument for assessing DSS chances. The following examples show how the tool can be applied.

The case of a potted plant nursery

The first case is production planning in potted plant culture under glass, which has some special properties: small firms with poorly partitioned decisionmaking, unpredictable weather entailing an unpredictable primary process, and unpredictable markets, a dynamic environment all work together to create conditions unfavourable for optimization-based decision support. Because glasshouse space is expensive high space occupation is important. Potted plants typically need to be spaced several times during cultivation, and transport is also expensive. So, to simplify somewhat, there is a conflict between space occupation and labour cost, added to the uncertainties mentioned above. A more elaborate description of this planning problem can be found in Hofstede (1990).

We have tried an approach based on user-manipulatable heuristics, and found that even that was too ambitious. An evolutionary approach to DSS, starting with low-brow support, working closely together with users, turned out to be succesful in this case.

As an instance we take the case of a modern, innovative potted plant nursery in the Dutch Westland region, grower R. Grower R. wishes to go quite far in automated support of production planning; in fact they have been experimenting with Linear Programming-based DSS.

The scores for grower R are as follows:

1 Organization: 50 persons, in the process of specializing. Entire management meets weekly. Score 2, going towards 3.

2 Planning: would-be specialized planner, much needed for other work. Score 3.

3 Environment: Highly dynamic. Markets, technology, products subject to yearly changes, i.e. conditions differ each planning cycle. Score 1.

4 Frequency: Each year has a different greenhouse asssortment, objectives. Yet principle constant over time. Score 2.

5 Predictability: Growth unpredictable due to weather, quality of basic material. Fluctuations up to some 25% of cultivation time. Furthermore, unexpected events or opportunities may arise. Score 2.

6 People: Planning has some, but not severe, consequences for labour, especially at peaks. Relation between management and labourers is valuable, so labour conditions are important. Score 4.

7 Controllability: growth conditions can be controlled by extra lighting, heating, chemical treatment and other means, but costs are considerable. Also, new cultivars tend to show unpredictable reactions to treatments, e.g. ugly flowers in some Spathiphyllum varieties. Practically speaking the process is hard to control and only within tight constraints. Score 2.

8 Data quality: Registration of production data is automated and suficiently detailed, namely to the individual production batch. But the automated system does not generate the desired reports. Price data are not specific enough, e.g. differences between growers can be significant but are not found in the statistics coming from the auction. Score 2.

There are many low scores of 2. If the innovations desired by R. are realized, some scores can rise a few points, but not drastically. On this basis we predict that the planner must be very cautious about automating cultivation planning. Optimization should be used with care, because its preconditions do not hold. There are too many factors which are unpredictable, or unknown, or unquantified, or have to be decided ad hoc. A modest approach, aimed at generating feasible and robust plans, possibly at *what if*-exploration of given plans, seems the highest level of support which fits. Coupling between a planning DSS and actual plan realization data is essential because it saves a lot of clerical work. Currently the only automated support system used in production planning by grower R is a spreadsheet application built by the planner himself. By the way, most of the characteristics of grower R are fairly generic to potted plant nurseries. A smaller or less innovative nursery than R would have had even a much lower rating. At a nursery similar to R. we implemented a simple planning system which basically consists of a Gantt-chart-like interface with interactive editing facilities.

The case of physical distribution

The second case is of a large manufacturing firm, with some planning situations for which data accepted to be controllable and high-quality are available. The problem area is physical distribution. One operational physical distribution planning problem is to effectively allocate and dispatch finished products to client-warehouses throughout Europe on a daily basis. The stocks available at the factory warehouses have to be allocated to client-warehouses. Subsequently the allocated products must be assigned to trucks under stacking, volume, and weight constraints. The allocation is based on up-to-date sales forecasts and stock data and aims at equal expected service levels per product over all depots. Over time the logistics managers developed a good insight in the way in which this problem can be dealt with. This does not mean that they developed a perfect optimizing model. It does mean they developed a set of models and solution procedures that are accepted to adequately represent the main quantitative aspects of the problem. It also means that organizational procedures have been developed for parties (factories, country sales-units and warehouses) concerned, which are being accepted and adhered to, for the accurate and timely administration of sales forecasts, actual sales and stock data. Over time for this type of problem a sequence of DSS have been developed and implemented. Versions of these DSS have evolved over time such that the task distribution over planner/user and system has dramatically changed, the level of integration with other physical distribution systems has changed through the use of a shared database, the roles of the planners have changed, etc. In short we may say that over time the scope of functions provided by successive systems increased, and that the way in which specific tasks are being performed have evolved into more sophisticated functions. The sophistication resides in the fact that models, used for the allocation of finished goods to client warehouses and the optimal loading and stacking of these goods into trucks, can generate practical feasible truck-loads that are frequently accepted and dispatched without further planner intervention. The last version of the DSS has been effectively used during a number of years to generate decision scenarios which the users/planners could further refine at a qualitative level. The system has provided the users with structured working knowledge of optimization models and their restrictions. They accept the models and their results as valid in the problem situation and claim that the effective execution of their tasks requires the use of the system. If we look at the context and object system characteristics of the problem situation just depicted it is easy to see that the score for all eight characteristics is high (4 to 5). Within tight organizational constraints the problems and solution procedures have been made structured and are accepted by the planners to be so. Thus there has been a joint process of organizational change and of learning, thanks to which a sophisticated DSS offering model-based support with little planner intervention has been developed and implemented and is being used.

Discussion

The assessment tool and DSS interactivity

The evidence from these two cases suggests that the assessment tool does have a relation with DSS chances and especially with the opportunities for model-based DSS.

At the cost of some oversimplification, the eight characteristics could be projected onto a single support dimension. This dimension concerns the *interactivity* of a DSS. Interactivity can compensate deficiencies in an automated model, inasmuch as it allows the user to bring in *ad hoc* elements during a planning session (see Hofstede 1991).Note that our definition of interactivity is stronger than is often the case in papers by OR practitioners. We define *full interactivity* as the condition in which the DSS user can both monitor and overrule the activities of the automated system during the entire planning session. In other words, if the system contains one or more models these models themselves must be interactive. A planning session is defined as the period(s) from entering the planning system till leaving it, associated with one organizational planning cycle and with the generation of one or more distinct plans for the problem instance at hand. *No interactivity* exists when the user's role is limited to manipulating the input and output of the planning session. In the potted plants case, full interactivity with no normative support was the only acceptable situation for the user. In the physical distribution case, a fully automated model with no interactivity was accepted but only after a learning process and a series of incremental additions to the DSS. We believe that some growth to normative support can also be expected in the potted plant case.

Limitations of the tool

A *caveat* about this assessment tool is appropriate. The tool tells us something about the feasibility of a DSS for a given case, about contingency factors to be taken into account when specifying functional and performance requirements for a DSS, about the type of DSS that could be appropriate, but not about the actual opportunities for getting a DSS built and used! For example, it does not take into account preconditions for DSS success such as innovativity of the organization, or personal acquaintance of the DSS designer within the organization, or the attitude of those who have to pay for the development.

Possibilities of the tool

By applying the tool to the two cases we illustrated its usefulness. We believe that given more empirical validation it can grow into a valuable aid for *a priori* assessing chances of DSS development.

A different possible use of the tool is to diagnosticize a given decision situation not with a view to build a DSS but rather to alter the situation itself, e.g. by taking measures to improve the score on one of the aspects.

Whatever the objective of using the tool, the insight to be gained by user and designer of a prospective DSS by considering the planning situation in the light of the tool is valuable. It may be a help in starting the learning process mentioned earlier through which user and designer must go together.

Final words

Our experiences with design and implementation of DSS as well as our viewpoint on organizational decisionmaking in general lead us to make a plea for interactive, dynamically robust DSSs for most planning situations. Such DSS will allow the user to improve decisionmaking even in situations that do not allow the use of formal models. They allow incremental development of more sophisticated DSS in situations that do allow the use of formal models. The assessment tool presented in this paper can give an indication which type of models and interfaces are appropriate for a given planning situation.

We hope that the first effect of the tool proposed here is to generate a fruitful exchange of ideas among DSS researchers and practitioners. Perhaps the perspective on decision support to which the paper's title refers is even more important than the assessment tool itself.

References

Anthony R.N. (1965)
Planning and Control Systems, a Framework for Analysis, Harvard University, Boston.

Beulens A.J.M. (1990)
More powerful and user-friendly DSS by incorporating ES technology? in: D. Ehrenberg, H. Krullmann & B. Rieger (eds), *Wissensbasierte Systeme in der Betriebswirtschaft*, Ehrig Schmidt Verlag, Berlin.

Beulens A.J.M. en Hofstede (1990)
Information Systems and DSS in Agriculture: Current status and future possibilities, in: W.H.G.J. Hennen et al. (eds), *Informatica-toepassingen in de Agrarische Sector*, voordrachten VIAS-Symposium 1990, Agro-Informatica-reeks no 4, pp. 87-94 (in Dutch, English abstract).

Cyert R.M. & J.G. March (1963)
A behavioral theory of the firm, Prentice-Hall, Englewood Cliffs, New Jersey.

Dissel H.G. van, H.P. Borgman & A.J.M. Beulens (1990)
Task-Allocation between DSS and Problem Owner: The example of Box & Jenkins Time Series Analysis, *Decision Support Systems* 6, pp 339-345.

Hofstede G.J. (1990)
Interactive Planning System design, a model and an application, *Proc. first Int. Conf. on Expert Planning Systems, IEE Conference Publ. 322*, the Institution of Electrical Engineers, London, pp. 175-180.

Hofstede G.J. (1991)
Interactive Heuristics, paper presented at the first IFORS-SPC on DSS, Bruges, March 26-29, submitted for publication.

Institution of Electrical Engineers (1990)
Proc. 1st IEE Conf. on Expert Planning Systems, IEE Publ. 322, the Institution of Electrical Engineers, London.

Kampfraath A.A. & W.J. Marcelis (1981)
Besturen en organiseren, Kluwer, Deventer.

Lindblom C. E. (1959)
The Science of Muddling Through, *Public Administration Review*, 19, 79-88.

Lindley D.V. (1985)
Making Decisions, 2nd ed., Wiley, London.

March J.G. & J.P. Olsen (1976)
Ambiguity and Choice in Organizations, Universitetsforlaget, Bergen, Norway.

McKay K., J.A. Buzacott, F.R. Safayeni (1989)
The scheduler's knowledge of uncertainty: the missing link, in J. Browne (ed.), *Knowledge Based Production Management Systems*, Elsevier Amsterdam.

Mintzberg H. (1973)
The Nature of Managerial Work, Harper & Row, New York.

Verbraeck A. (1990)
A Decision Support System for timetable construction: automated lesson planning using a special timetabling algorithm, *Proc. first Int. Conf. on Expert Planning Systems, IEE Conference Publ. 322*, the Institution of Electrical Engineers, London, pp. 207-211.

SLP-IOR: A MODEL MANAGEMENT SYSTEM FOR STOCHASTIC LINEAR PROGRAMMING - SYSTEM DESIGN -

P. Kall and J. Mayer*
Institute for Operations Research, University of Zurich

1. INTRODUCTION

Bridging the gap between mathematical programming model-, algorithm-, and software-development on one side and decision makers on the other side became recently one of the central problems in operations research.

On the decision makers' side the rapid evolution of decision support systems (DSS) has created an environment in which decision makers became accustomed to using personal computers and simple but powerful modeling tools such as electronic spreadsheets. On the mathematical programming side much effort has been concentrated for supporting the work of OR-practitioners through the development of modeling languages or in a more general setting model management systems to improve the usually very time-consuming modeling process. Integrating these model management systems with the model base- and model-manipulation subsystems of decision support systems seems to be one possible way for closing the gap mentioned above.

In the field of stochastic programming the models as they appear in the modeling process are frequently to be transformed into a different form (e.g. into a linear-, mixed-variable linear- or into a nonlinear programming problem) for the solvers. This transformation may also involve restructuring of the model and depends on the model type, on the probability distribution of random variables in the model and on the particular solver selected. The usual problem of different solvers having different input/output data-formats appears as an additional complication here. The resulting numerical models are typically quite complex and difficult from the computational point of view (e.g. very large-scale LP problems or hard nonlinear programming problems). This implies that solution algorithms are fairly intricate; using them usually requires specialized knowledge in the field of stochastic programming. Existing solver software is mostly located at academic institutions. These circumstances make it difficult for OR-practitioners to include the stochastic programming approach into their modeling activity.

The purpose of this paper is to outline the main features of the stochastic programming model management system SLP-IOR, the development of which is currently in progress at the Institute for OR of the University of Zurich.

2. MAIN FEATURES OF SYSTEM DESIGN.

Stochastic programming models are apart the deterministic parts typically formulated in terms of integrals (representing e.g. expected value or a probability distribution function). In many cases it is possible to reformulate the problem as a mathematical programming problem given in terms of algebraic expressions. Under such circumstances solving the original model means solving this equivalent problem either by employing a general optimization package or

* On leave from the Computer and Automation Institute, Hungarian Academy of Sciences.

by using specialized solvers which utilize the structure of the problem. Another solution approach builds on a sequence of approximating mathematical programming problems of the algebraic type. A third approach keeps the integrals and evaluates or approximates them during the solution procedure. A family of algorithms is based on stochastic quasigradients and stochastic decomposition. The selection of the appropriate model-transformation and solver presupposes expert knowledge in the field of solution algorithms of stochastic programming.

The central idea of the system design is to build a model management system for stochastic linear programming around an existing general-purpose modeling system for mathematical programming. Model representation and model management have to account for the original stochastic programming model, for the different model-transformations, for different types of mathematical programming models resulting from the transformations and for a great variety of solvers. To provide a uniform and at the same time flexible framework for representing and solving models a modeling system is being utilized. From the spectrum of well-developed modeling languages and systems (see e.g. [3], [6], [15], [23], [51], [52], [53]) the modeling system GAMS [6] has been chosen for the following reasons. This system incorporates besides linear programming also nonlinear and mixed-variable models and offers easy access to powerful solvers for these model-classes. The important aspect of linking new solvers with GAMS is also well-supported.

GAMS is an algebraic modeling system which means that all functions appearing in the model must be algebraic expressions. This being true for the deterministic parts of the stochastic programming models these parts can entirely be represented and handled by GAMS. Except of the special case of deterministic linear programming stochastic linear programming models cannot directly be represented and manipulated by GAMS in their entirety however. In the case when algebraic equivalents exist these can very well be represented by GAMS. In the general case when considering the stochastic part of the model then GAMS serves for documenting distribution parameters, transmitting them to the appropriate solvers and for handling regression coefficients. To include these facilities appropriate representation conventions are to be developed for random variables and probability distributions in the modeling language of GAMS. SLP-IOR extends the capabilities of GAMS to stochastic linear programming by superimposing the appropriate model manipulation machinery on it. GAMS accepts models written in the GAMS modeling language and stored in a text-file. This text-file is automatically written by SLP-IOR. In the case when an algebraic equivalent exists it would be possible that the user supplies this file. As the formulation of the algebraic equivalent is beyond the modeling activities and much more part of the solution procedure we decided to keep it completely under the control of SLP-IOR.
Regarding the various possible goals for a stochastic programming model management system the following purposes have been taken into account in the design phase.

(1) *Serving as a model management system with a dialog management subsystem for OR practitioners.* To achieve the goal of providing OR-modelers with a facility of utilizing the stochastic linear programming modeling approach the requirements listed below should certainly be met by the system.

(1.1) All of the main SLP model-types should be built in, including LP, two-stage (multistage) problems with various recourse types, chance-constrained problems with separate and with joint chance-constraints, alternative goal settings (multicriteria models).

(1.2) General OR knowledge including also basic facts on stochastic programming, and modeling experience should be sufficient to use the system. (e.g. no technical knowledge should be required concerning SLP solvers). This goal will be achieved by an extensive context-dependent help-system, and by incorporating rules (knowledge) concerning SLP models and available solvers for the individual model types. For each model type depending on its particular specification a solver will be recommended. This choice of solver can be overridden by the user.

(1.3) Large-scale models should be enabled with respect to the deterministic part of the models. If large-scale is in the stochastic part (many random variables) then appropriate methods (e.g. stochastic quasigradient algorithms, see [14] or [19]) could help to deliver at least rough solutions; support for experimenting with scenarios will be incorporated (simulation, computing bounds and approximations). Large-scale is a hardware-dependent notion implying that portability of the system is in this respect an important feature. The present version is developed on a PS/2®* Model 70 computer with 4MB storage capacity. As programming language in the development phase Turbo PASCAL®** 5.5 has been chosen, but for achieving portability a C (or C++) version will also be developed.

(2) *Educational purposes*. The education of SLP-modeling will be supported (help-system, rules). For teaching solution algorithms special care should be taken by allowing for a stepwise running mode of the solvers; this feature will not be included in the present version.

(3) *Usage as a workbench for research in SLP*. Standard test problems (see [36]) and solvers will be available in an easily accessible fashion. Connecting new solvers to the system inevitably means to carry out the standard procedure necessary to make available new solvers with GAMS. For the integration into the model manipulation part of the system software support will be provided. Special attention will be given to discrete approximation methods for two-stage problems by including a subsystem which supports building of algorithms of this kind.

(4) *Serving as the model-base management subsystem of a decision support system*. Extending the system to a DSS for some specific application domain would mean that the appropriate database management and dialog generation and management subsystems would have to be developed and integrated with the present system. This goal is supported by the design of the model management system which follows the usual lines and fulfills most of the requirements of the model-base management subsystem of a DSS (see [5], [54]). Clearly specified interfaces and a thorough technical reference manual will support this activity.

(5) *Serving as a basis for an intelligent model-management system*. The object-oriented model manipulation component will also contain rules but in an integrated manner. The usual approach would require the development of a separate knowledge base and inference engine (see e.g. [43]). This is not planned in the present version.

3. FUNCTIONAL REQUIREMENTS

This section is devoted to the discussion of functional requirements for the model management system SLP-IOR. A general overview of functional requirements for model management systems in operations research can be found in Dolk [10]. The main issues which will be addressed here are model description and model manipulation. The third important aspect of functional requirements, model control, will only moderately be present in the first version of the system, just in the form of a backup facility. Dolk [10] recommends Geoffrion's Structured Modeling [20], [38] for model description. He has considered a model management system for the whole spectrum of OR models which certainly necessitates the generality inherent in Geoffrion's system. In our case we concentrate on a relatively narrow subclass of OR-models for which GAMS augmented with a facility for representing random

---

* PS/2 is a registered trademark of International Business Machines Corporation.

** Turbo PASCAL is a registered trademark of Borland International, Inc.

variables and distributions is a very well suited means of model representation. A great advantage of GAMS is the availability of a well-tested, widely used implementation, with powerful solvers attached to it. We completely agree with Dolk's proposal in [10] of using object-oriented techniques for model-manipulation; in fact this approach is being implemented in SLP-IOR. He recommends to build a language for model manipulation, in our case a menu-driven user interface will do the job. For the purposes of model control Dolk suggests using relational databases.

For model management systems in the field of mathematical programming see also [9], [11], [42], [51].

3.1. Model description

Relying on the modeling language GAMS results in a uniform, consistent and robust model representation ensuring also the relative independence of model structure and underlying data. The database-part, the matrix-generator part, the symbolic model-part as well as the solver-activation and the report-generator parts of a GAMS input file will be separately handled and used as building-blocks for numerical models. Model integrity will be checked prior to transforming the model into GAMS input-format by SLP-IOR through utilizing rules which ensure that the model is well-specified.

Regarding multiple views the mathematical view is clearly well-supported by GAMS. The natural language view will only be moderately supported by the model representation through allowing for user-selected names in the model and by comments in the GAMS input file. SLP-IOR itself will contain an extensive context-dependent help-system, a hotkey for a modeling status report, error and warning messages and messages containing advices. Some graphical facilities will also be included (e.g. for showing various matrix-patterns).

3.2. Model manipulation.

Model manipulation will involve operators acting on models such as retrieve, update, store, document, generate, show, evaluate, optimize, check sensitivity, report, restructure.

Independence of model description from solution operators will be achieved by relying consistently on the GAMS-format of model-description and by building interfaces for all solvers to this model-representation form. For the solvers the same kind of interfaces will be built as those connecting GAMS to the GAMS-solvers, see [12]. As mentioned earlier stochastic linear programming necessitates the availability of an extensive library of solvers.

Internally the models will be represented by a hierarchy of objects corresponding to the various stochastic linear programming model types. The objects in this hierarchy will contain rules implemented in the form of polymorphic Boolean functions for checking model consistency and integrity. Solvers will also be represented by an object-hierarchy with rules for checking whether a solver is appropriate for a model instance. The object-oriented programming style allows for easy extension and modification in both hierarchies.

4. STOCHASTIC LINEAR PROGRAMMING MODELS

In this section a brief summary will be given on the stochastic linear programming models which will be incorporated into SLP-IOR. Our single objective in this section being the specification of the scope of SLP-IOR we restrict ourselves to the formal description of the models. This means that we do not discuss here under what conditions these problems are well-defined, or what properties the individual models have, etc. For a detailed presentation the interested reader is invited to consult e.g. Kall [25]. For each model-type a short reference will be made concerning the solvers which will be included into the system.

Let us consider a linear programming problem in the following form.

$$\begin{array}{rrl} & \min\ c^T x & \\ & Ax & = b \\ & Tx & = h \\ l \ \leq & x & \leq u \end{array} \tag{4.1}$$

If some of the coefficients are just formally replaced by random variables then the resulting formulation becomes meaningless:

$$\begin{array}{lrl} \text{"min"} & c(\omega)^T x & \\ & A\,x & = b \\ & T(\omega)\,x & = h(\omega) \\ l \leq & x & \leq u, \end{array} \tag{4.2}$$

where (Ω,F,P_ω) is a probability space, $\omega \in \Omega$. There exist various approaches for getting a meaningful model in this modeling situation (for a general framework see Kall (1976)), the two main model classes comprise the two-stage- (or recourse-) models and the chance-constrained models.

4.1. Two-stage models.

$$\min\ [\ c^T x + E_\omega Q(x,\omega)\ ]$$

$$\begin{array}{rrl} & Ax & (\text{rel})\ b \\ l \leq & x & \leq\ u, \end{array} \tag{4.3}$$

where (rel) means that in the rows of this system of relations any one of the symbols =, ≥ or ≤ is permitted and the function $Q(x,\omega)$ is defined as follows:

$$\begin{array}{ll} Q(x,\omega) = \min q^T y & \\ & W\,y = h(\omega) - T(\omega)\,x \\ & y \geq 0 \end{array} \tag{4.4}$$

for every fixed pair x, ω; i.e. $Q(x,\omega)$ is also a random variable for every fixed x. Problem (4.4) is called the second-stage problem (or recourse problem) and may represent e.g. compensation for violating the constraints $T(\omega)x = h(\omega)$; the matrix W is called the recourse matrix of the problem. In the special case $W=(I,-I)$ with I being an identity matrix the problem is called a simple recourse problem.

In the case of a finite discrete probability distribution the solvers included in the system will either be relying on decomposition [26], [50], [55], or on approximation [16], [18]. For continuous distributions discrete-approximation methods will be used [1], [16], [17], [18], [24], [25], [28], [31], [32], [33], [34]. Most of these methods are based on the close relation between computing bounds and solving moment problems [27], [29], [30]. Stochastic quasigradient

methods [14], [19] and methods based on stochastic decomposition [21], [22] and importance sampling [7] will also be included.
For the simple-recourse case see [59], [60]; and for an overview on algorithms [1], [25], [26], [31], [32], [34].

4.2. Chance-constrained models, separate chance constraints.

$$\begin{array}{llll} \min & E_\omega c(\omega)^T x & & \\ & P_\omega(\{\omega \mid t_i(\omega)\, x \geq h_i(\omega)\}) & \geq \alpha_i & i=1,\dots,s \\ & Ax & (\mathrm{rel})\ b & \\ l \leq & x & \leq u, & \end{array} \tag{4.5}$$

where $t_i(\omega)$ denotes the i-th row of matrix $T(\omega)$, $h_i(\omega)$ denotes the i-th component of $h(\omega)$ and α_i, $i=1,\dots,s$, are prescribed probability (reliability) levels for the fulfillment of the individual constraints $t_i(\omega)x \geq h_i(\omega)$ $i=1,\dots,s,$.

Solvers for this model class will mainly be GAMS-MINOS for linear- and nonlinear programming algebraic equivalents and GAMS-ZOOM for mixed-integer equivalent models, [6].

4.3. Chance-constrained models, joint chance constraint.

$$\begin{array}{llll} \min & E_\omega c(\omega)^T x & & \\ & P_\omega(\{\omega \mid T\, x \geq h(\omega)\}) \geq & \alpha & \\ & Ax & (\mathrm{rel})\ b & \\ l \leq & x & \leq u, & \end{array} \tag{4.6}$$

where α is a prescribed probability level for the joint fulfillment of the constraints $Tx \geq h(\omega)$. Notice that $T(\omega)$ has been replaced by T meaning that a random technology matrix will not be permitted.

The solvers used in this case will be those published in: [37], [40], [41], [47], [48], [58]. For an overview of methods see [32], [49].

For the computation of distribution functions procedures based on Monte-Carlo integration will be included, see [8] for an overview, and [57].

4.4. Modeling the random variables.

The careful modeling of the random elements in stochastic programming models plays a crucial role from the point of view of the numerical solution. Assume that (T,h,q) contains altogether 50 independent random variables each of them only having 2 realizations. This would mount in 2^{50} realizations of the joint distribution, which except of some special cases results in numerically intractable stochastic programming problems. It was observed early (see e.g. [24], [25]) that in most practical problems utilizing mathematical statistics a significantly lower amount of random variables $\xi_1(\omega),\dots,\xi_r(\omega)$ can be found with regression coefficients $q_0,\dots,q_r$; $h_0,\dots,h_r$; $T_0,\dots,T_r$; such that the relations below hold:

$$q(\omega) = q_0 + q_1\,\xi_1(\omega) + \ldots + q_r\,\xi_r(\omega),$$

$$h(\omega) = h_0 + h_1\,\xi_1(\omega) + \ldots + h_r\,\xi_r(\omega), \qquad (4.7)$$

$$T(\omega) = T_0 + T_1\,\xi_1(\omega) + \ldots + T_r\,\xi_r(\omega).$$

This approach yields often problems of a size which can be solved by today's technology.

5. OVERVIEW OF THE SYSTEM

In this section an outline of the essential features of the system will be given. For the main system-constituents see Figure 1.

5.1. The dialog management system.

The user interface is menu-driven with the following main characteristics. The user will communicate with the system via the keyboard or by using a mouse. Function keys will also be available for getting help, or getting information concerning modeling status or using a notebook. The interface being menu driven the communication will be based on pop-up and pull-down menus, with data entry occurring via matrix-editor format. For entering nonlinear functions a formula-editor will be available. The display will mainly be used in text-mode. The modeling process will be guided by a context-dependent help system and by the rules concerning the models and solvers which present themselves for the user in the form of warning or guiding messages. A User's Guide will also aid the modeling process.

According to the user actions the dialog management system sends messages to the model-manipulation system and communicates the response to the user. The main menu contains the following items: Specification of type and stochastic parts of the model; manipulation of random variables and their distribution; input/output of model data (including randomly generated problems); operations related to the model- and solver-library; solution activities (e.g. starting solvers).

5.2. The model manipulation system.

The model-manipulation subsystem plays a central role in the overall system by governing all of the main activities. The subsystem is being built in object-oriented programming style. The main object-hierarchies (classes) will be addressed in the next section, here we confine ourselves to discuss some functional issues. From the functional point of view the main activities are as follows.

--- *Processing the messages from the dialog management system.* This activity essentially means sending the appropriate messages to various instances of objects in the class-hierarchies.

--- *Controlling I/O of model data.* Source of model data can be the following.
   --- Data communicated through the user interface;
   --- data stored on a floppy in one of the following formats:
      --- MPS-format, (For the underlying LP-problem, or for two-stage problems the equivalent block-angular LP);
      --- data in BDGGKW* data format;

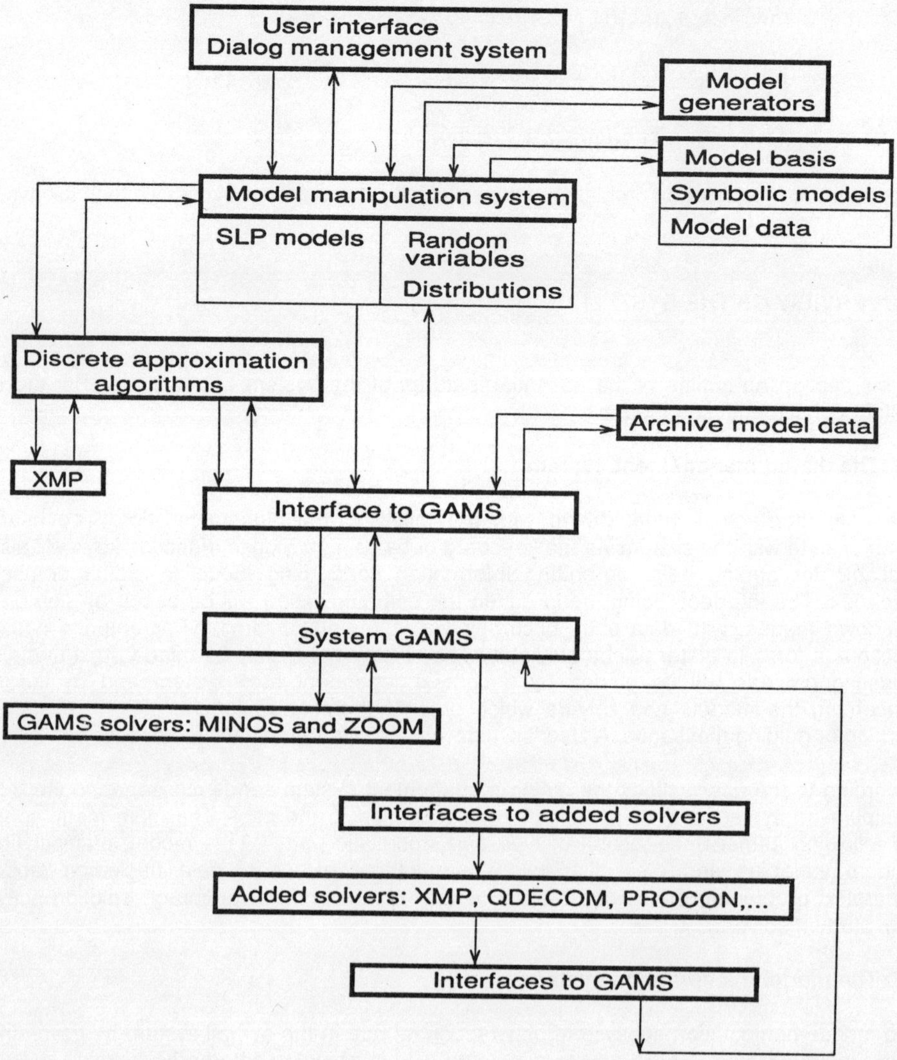

Figure 1. *Schematic overview of the system.*

--- model given as a GAMS input-file, stored on a floppy;
--- on-line data in the model-base, stored in the system's internal data format;
--- data in GAMS input-file format in the model-base;
--- archive data in GAMS-format in the model archive of the system;
--- symbolic data in the model-base, stored according to GAMS-syntax;
--- transformation formulas needed to generate the arrays for the various models (e.g. corresponding to the block-angular structure for two-stage problems with discrete distributions). These serve as the matrix-generator parts of the GAMS-input file.
    --- The model-equations specifying the model;
    --- commands for starting the various solvers;
    --- transformation formulas needed to communicate data and results. These serve as the report generation parts of the GAMS input-file.

--- *Identifying the model, checking for integrity.* This means determining the model-type; identifying what kind of data are needed; starting the appropriate processes for getting these data; checking if the data are appropriate (i.e. checking a covariance-matrix for positive definiteness). The process is accompanied by the retrieval of the corresponding symbolic data from the model-base.

--- *Identifying the solver.* This activity includes the selection of a solver to be recommended to the user on the basis of the particular model-specification. It means retrieving data describing solver-capabilities from the solver-base; and performing the selection using appropriate rules. For a user-selected solver it will be checked if it is well-suited for the current model.

--- *Sending the model to the GAMS-interface.* Symbolic and numeric data are sent for processing to the GAMS-interface along with a specification of activities to be performed on the model (e.g. optimization).

--- *Sending the model to the discrete approximation subsystem.* The same type of data as before are sent to the subsystem which implements a discrete-approximation scheme in an iterative-refinement manner.

--- *Processing results.* Results can e.g. either be optimal solutions, or the information that the model possesses no optimal solution, or retrieved archive data (archive data are in GAMS-format, retrieving them means that GAMS has been activated to get these data in the system's internal format). After some analysis of the modeling situation an appropriate response is being sent to the dialog management system for initiating a user interaction.

5.3. Interface to GAMS.

This part of the system performs the tasks of transforming the model into a GAMS-format (GAMS input file), and vice versa, transforming the results available in a GAMS listing file to the internal data representation of the system. After producing a GAMS input -file control will be passed to system GAMS, which returns control to the model management system after its termination.

5.4. System GAMS.

GAMS is included into the system without any modification the sole exception being the modification of the algorithm-capability table for the new solvers (see [6], [12].

---

* data format proposed by Birge, Dempster, Gassmann, Gunn, King and Wallace, see [2].

5.5. Adding new solvers to GAMS.

In the case of stochastic linear programming several new solvers are to be connected to GAMS. This for each individual solver mainly means the development of two computer-codes performing data-transformation. One of them transforms model data as they appear on the output-side of GAMS into the specific format required by the solver, the other transforms solver-results back to the format acceptable for GAMS for processing the results. In building these interfaces the same methodology will be used as by interfacing GAMS with its own solvers GAMS-MINOS and GAMS-ZOOM, see [12].

5.6. Discrete approximation methods.

These methods require invoking GAMS in an iterative manner. The model-management system will pass control to this subsystem which performs the iterations in an autonomous manner and passes control and results back to the model manipulation system after termination. The methods implemented in the subsystem will work on the basis of successive refinement of discretization, each refinement requiring the solution of the discretized problem by invoking GAMS, and possibly also the solution of the diagonal linear programming subproblems. For the solution of these LP's (which are usually quite numerous) a direct access to XMP (see [39]) will be built in.

5.7. Model generators.

Two model generators will be included.

--- GENSLP [35] for producing randomly generated complete-recourse test problems;

--- a test problem generator for chance-constrained problems.

5.8. Model base.

Models are stored in the model base as follows:

--- Model data stored in the system's internal data format in binary form to have quick access. This part of the model base might be called the on-line part, because retrieving a model from here means immediate access to the model-data according to their modeling status (partially specified models can also be stored here; they are stored along with an appropriate description of the modeling status). Optionally models and distributions can be stored separately thus facilitating the building of models with various distributions or vice versa building various models using the same distribution;

--- various parts of a GAMS input-file as text-files, serving as building blocks to be sent to the GAMS interface;

    --- the database part containing numerical data;
    --- the symbolic matrix-generator part of a model-type;
    --- the symbolic model-equations part;
    --- the symbolic report-generator part.

5.9. Solver base.

This database contains the symbolic solver-initiating part for a GAMS input file. Besides this for each solver it contains information of the type outlined below:

--- List of model-classes for which the solver is an appropriate choice along with information how well-suited the solver is for the particular model-type;
--- ramifications concerning e.g. model dimensionalities;
--- parameter-settings (if any);
--- recommendations of usage.

5.10. Archive models.

This database serves for keeping a collection of test-problems and models not currently in use. The content of this database is as follows.

--- Database parts of the GAMS input files for models;
--- completely documented models in GAMS-format.

6. THE MODEL MANIPULATION SUBSYSTEM

This section is devoted to present a brief summary of the main features of the model manipulation subsystem. The subsystem is being built in object oriented style making extensive use of polymorphic objects and methods.

6.1. Basic components.

The basic constituents of the subsystem are the ModelManager, the ModelLibraryManager, the SolverLibraryManager and a hierarchy of objects representing models. The main part of the model-hierarchy is the following (hierarchy levels are denoted using indentation):

```
---- BaseModel
        ---- Matrix
        ---- RandomVariable
        ---- Distribution
        ---- MathematicalProgrammingModel
                ---- LPModel
                ---- SLPModel
                ----  ...
```

and the hierarchy is continued downwards according to the various stochastic programming model-types as shown in Figure 2. In the object hierarchy BaseModel is an abstract polymorphic object establishing the standardized communication protocol for the hierarchy. The main standard messages are the following:
Init, *Done* for constructing and destructing objects;
ReceiveDimensions, *ReturnDimensions* for model dimensions;
Read, *Write* for I/O in text-mode;
Load, *Store* for binary I/O;
WriteGAMSForm for writing the object in GAMS-syntax;
Edit for invoking a matrix-editor;
Show for showing model-pattern;
Consistent for consistency-checking;
Complete for checking completeness.

- Models
  - Deterministic models
  - Stochastic models
    - Two–stage models
      - Linear recourse models
        - Fixed–recourse models
          - Incomplete recourse
          - Complete recourse
            - Simple recourse
        - Random–recourse models
      - Nonlinear recourse models
    - Chance–constrained models
      - Separate chance constraints
        - Single objective
        - Multiobjective
      - Joint chance constraints

Figure 2. *Class hierarchy of models.*

The Distribution entry in the hierarchy above is implemented in the form of a class-hierarchy of specific distributions.

Most of the objects are of a composite nature. So e.g. the SLPModel object contains (in the form of pointers) an LPModel object and a RandomVariable object. The various arrays in the LPModel object are included as pointers to the Matrix object and similarly the RandomVariable object includes Distribution objects.

6.2. Control flows.

A message sent to an object frequently induces a series of further messages (like a chain reaction). Let us consider e.g. the message Read sent by the ModelManager to an instance of the SLPModel. According to the Read method in the SLPModel class some basic data corresponding to this model will be read and afterwards the Read message will be sent to the constituent objects LPModel and RandomVariable. The LPModel object will send further Read messages to its constituent Matrix objects and similarly RandomVariables sends the Read message to Distribution objects.

The Optimize message which is part of the protocol of objects from the LPModel "downwards" in the model hierarchy may deserve a short discussion. When an object receives this message then after performing a check for consistency and completeness it will send the Select message to the SolverLibraryManager. This message carries the signature of the model-instance which is a string comprising the main characteristics of the model. The SolverLibraryManager when receiving this message sends the message called Appropriate to the solver objects in turn. (For each solver an object is implemented for the purpose of taking part in the selection procedure). The individual solver objects perform a check whether they are appropriate for solving the model. To make this decision they possibly need further information (e.g. number of nonzero entries in some model-matrix) which they acquire by sending the appropriate message directly to the model-object. This way the SolverLibraryManager gets a list of appropriate solvers which in the first version of the system will be presented to the user for selecting a solver. The identifier of the selected solver will be sent back to the model object. The Optimize method continues afterwards by issuing the ReadGAMSForm message followed by starting system GAMS and retrieving the results.

6.3. Rules.

Rules will be implemented in the form of polymorphic PASCAL Boolean functions which employ if-then conditional statements for the rules. (AI analogy: production rules). The encapsulation is extended in this respect for encapsulating also the rules. (AI analogy: frames-containing-rules). This construction results in a system of rules accompanying the model hierarchies. Reasoning is strictly determined by the hierarchy but in return for this drawback it is rather quick.

Examples for such polymorphic rule-functions are the messages Consistent, Complete or Appropriate.

Surprisingly enough due to polymorphism the outlined construct for incorporating rules has some flexibility. Extending the rule-system by a new rule just means to introduce a descendant object at the appropriate location in the hierarchy which contains a redefiniton of one of the Boolean functions to incorporate the new rule. Similarly changing of rules can be accomplished by inserting an object into the hierarchy, and in this object the function containing the rule can be overridden.

6.4. Methods.

In this subsection an overview of those methods (messages) will be given which are contained in the communication protocol of individual objects or are valid only for some parts of an object-hierarchy. Messages already discussed will not be listed again here.

<u>ModelManager</u>

--- *Restructure.* Transforming the problem from two-stage to chance-constrained structure, or vice versa.

--- *Build.* This means e.g. assembling models using various separately stored distributions or deterministic parts.

--- *Validate.* This will be performed by invoking alternative solvers, or by computing the reliability of a two-stage solution or discrepancy of a chance-constrained solution.

--- *Create and evaluate alternatives*, e.g. computing solutions using other distributions with the same expected value, or for an originally dependent case computing a solution with independent random variables.

Mathematical programming objects.

The class-hierarchy of stochastic linear programming model-types serves as the backbone of the model manipulation subsystem, for the hierarchy see Figure 2. Deterministic LP models have been incorporated as well, thus allowing e.g. for solving the underlying deterministic LP problem. The class hierarchy contains also those models for which presently no solution method is known. This is in accordance with the general goal of the system being also a workbench for research in SLP; the system architecture supports the inclusion of new solvers.

--- *Optimize.* Activate an optimizer. The following optimizers will be available.
- --- For two-stage problems:
  - --- GAMS-MINOS [6],
  - --- GAMS-ZOOM [6],
  - --- XMP [39],
  - --- MINOS [44],
  - --- QDECOM [50],
  - --- TWOSTAGE [55], [56],
  - --- Discrete approximation methods for the complete recourse case: Kall-Stoyan [33] and Frauendorfer [17] methods,
  - --- Wets [60] and Kall-Stoyan [33] methods for simple recourse problems,
  - --- Stochastic quasigradient methods [14], [19],
  - --- Stochastic decomposition, Higle-Sen [21], [22],
  - --- Importance sampling, Dantzig-Glynn [7].
- --- For separate chance constraints:
  - --- GAMS-MINOS [6],
  - --- GAMS-ZOOM [6],
  - --- XMP [39],
  - --- MINOS [44], [45].
- --- For joint chance-constraints:
  - --- Szántai's method, [58],
  - --- PROCON [41],
  - --- Prékopa-Deák method, [48],
  - --- Komáromi method. [37].

--- *Document.* If the model itself is to be documented the GAMS-form of the model will serve as a documentation. This means generating a GAMS input file. If solution information is also needed, the GAMS listing file for a solution run will serve as a base for the documentation.

--- *Generate.* This means the invoking of a random test-problem generator.

--- *Evaluate.* These methods serve as tools for generating scenarios to evaluate the model if some parts of the variables, or distributions are fixed making the problem easily solvable. Examples: Solve the two-stage problem with a fixed realization (LP), or with fixed first-stage variables (decomposable LP); evaluate the reliability of a given feasible solution; evaluate alternative objectives at a given point; compute possible compensation costs for a solution of a chance-constrained model.

--- *Compute sensitivity.* Either usual sensitivity analysis concerning deterministic parts or some experimental sensitivity computations concerning the distributions or the stochastic parts will be built in. This means activating the optimizers from the previous solution with perturbed data.

Matrix

--- *Rank.* Computes the rank of a matrix.
--- *CompleteRec.* Checks whether W is a complete recourse matrix.

RandomVariable

--- *Generate the joint discrete distribution.*

Distribution

This class-hierarchy supports the manipulation of probability distributions. Two kinds of distributions will be considered: Finite discrete distributions and absolutely continuous distributions (i.e. distributions with a density function). The hierarchy follows the usual classification scheme for distributions; most well-known distributions will be available.

--- *Generate sample.*
--- *Determine approximate support.*
--- *Compute distribution function.*
--- *Compute gradient of distribution function.*
--- *Compute moments.*

REFERENCES

[1] BIRGE, J. R., WETS, R. J.-B.: "Designing approximation schemes for stochastic optimization problems, in particular for stochastic programs with recourse", *Math. Programming Stud.* 27 (1986) 54-102.

[2] BIRGE, J. R., DEMPSTER, M. A. H., GASSMANN, H., GUNN, E., KING, A. J., WALLACE, S. W.: "A standard input format for multiperiod stochastic linear programs", *IIASA Working Paper* WP-87-118 (1987).

[3] BISSCHOP, J., MEERAUS, A.: "On the development of a general algebraic modeling system in a strategic planning environment", *Math. Programming Stud.* 20 (1982) 1-29.

[4] BORELL, C.: "Convex set-functions in d-space", *Periodica Math. Hungarica* 6 (1975) 111-136.

[5] BONCZEK, R.H., HOLSAPPLE, C. W., WHINSTON, A. B.: "Foundations of decision support systems", *Academic Press* (1981).

[6] BROOKE, A., KENDRICK, D., MEERAUS, A.: "GAMS. A User's Guide", *The Scientific Press*, (1988).

[7] DANTZIG, G. B., GLYNN, P.W.: "Parallel processors for planning under uncertainty", *Technical Report* SOL 88-8R, Department of Operations Research, Stanford University, (1989).

[8] DEÁK, I.: "Multidimensional integration and stochastic programming", in Ermoliev, Y., Wets, R., J.-B., (eds.) *Numerical Techniques for Stochastic Optimization, Springer-Verlag*, Berlin (1988) 187-200.

[9] DOLK, D. R.: "A generalized model management system for mathematical programming", *ACM Transactions on Mathematical Software* 12 (1986) 92-125.

[10] DOLK, D.R.: "Model management systems for operations research: A prospectus", in *Mathematical Methods for Decision Support*, ed. G. Mitra, *Springer* (1988) 347-373.

[11] DOLK, D. R., KONSYNSKI, B. R.: "Knowledge representation for model management", *IEEE Transactions on Software Engineering* SE-10 (1984) 619-627.

[12] DRUD, A. S.: "Interfaces between modeling systems and solution algorithms" in *Mathematical Methods for Decision Support*, ed. G. Mitra, *Springer* (1988) 187-196.

[13] EDWARDS, J.: "A proposed standard input format for computer codes which solve stochastic programs with recourse", in Ermoliev, Y., Wets, R., J.-B., (eds.) *Numerical Techniques for Stochastic Optimization, Springer-Verlag*, Berlin (1988) 215-227.

[14] ERMOLIEV, Y.: "Stochastic quasigradient methods and their application to systems optimization", *Stochastics* 9 (1983) 1-36.

[15] FOURER, R., GAY, D. M., KERNIGHAN, B. W.: "A modeling language for mathematical programming", *Management Science* 36 (1990) 519-554.

[16] FRAUENDORFER, K.: "Solving SLP recourse problems with arbitrary multivariate distributions - The dependent case", *Mathematics of Op. Res.* 13 (1988) 377-394.

[17] FRAUENDORFER, K.: "A simplicial approximation scheme for convex two-stage stochastic programming problems", *Manuscript, IOR University of Zürich* (1989).

[18] FRAUENDORFER, K., KALL, P.: "A solution method for SLP recourse problems with arbitrary multivariate distributions - The independent case", *Probl. Control & Inform. Th.* 17 (1988) 177-205.

[19] GAIVORONSKI, A.: "Interactive program SQG-PC for solving stochastic programming problems on IBM/XT/AT compatibles-User Guide", *IIASA Working Paper* WP-88-11, (1988).

[20] GEOFFRION, A.M.: "An introduction to structured modeling", *Management Science* 33 (1987) 547-588.

[21] HIGLE, J.L., SEN, S.: "Stochastic decomposition: an algorithm for two-stage linear programs with recourse", SIE Technical Report 87-7, University of Arizona , Tucson (1988).

[22] HIGLE, J.L., SEN, S.: "Statistical verification of optimality conditions", SIE Technical Report, University of Arizona , Tucson (1988).

[23] HUERLIMANN, T., KOHLAS, J.: "LPL: A structured language for linear programming modeling", OR Spectrum 10 (1988) 55-63.

[24] KALL, P.: "Approximations to stochastic programs with complete fixed recourse", *Numer. Math.* 22 (1974) 333-339.

[25] KALL, P.: "Stochastic linear programming", *Springer-Verlag*, Berlin, (1976).

[26] KALL, P.: "Computational methods for solving two-stage stochastic linear programming problems", *ZAMP* 30 (1979) 261-271.

[27] KALL, P.: "Stochastic programs with recourse: An upper bound and the related moment problem", *ZOR* 31 (1987) A119-A141.

[28] KALL, P.: "On approximation and stability in stochastic programming", in Guddat, J. et al. (eds.) *Parametric Optimization and Related Topics, Akademie-Verlag,* Berlin (1987) 387-407.

[29] KALL, P.: "Stochastic programming with recourse: Upper bounds and moment problems", in Guddat, J. et al. (eds.) *Advances in Mathematical Optimization, Akademie-Verlag,* Berlin (1988) 86-103.

[30] KALL, P.: "An upper bound for SLP using first and total second moments", *Preprint, IOR University of Zürich* (1989).

[31] KALL, P.: "A review on approximations in stochastic programming", *Preprint, IOR University of Zürich* (1989).

[32] KALL, P.: "Solution methods in stochastic programming - A review-", *Preprint, IOR University of Zurich* (1990).

[33] KALL, P., STOYAN, D.: Solving stochastic programming problems with recourse including error bounds", *Math. Operationsforsch. Statist., Ser. Optimization* 13 (1982) 431-447.

[34] KALL, P., RUSZCZYNSKI, A., FRAUENDORFER, K.: "Approximation techniques in stochastic programming", in Ermoliev, Y., Wets, R., J.-B., (eds.) *Numerical Techniques for Stochastic Optimization, Springer-Verlag,* Berlin (1988) 33-64.

[35] KELLER, E.: "GENSLP: A program for generating input for stochastic linear programs with complete fixed recourse", *Manuscript, IOR University of Zürich* (1984).

[36] KING, A., J.: "Stochastic programming problems: Examples from the literature",in Ermoliev, Y., Wets, R., J.-B., (eds.) *Numerical Techniques for Stochastic Optimization, Springer-Verlag,* Berlin (1988) 543-567.

[37] KOMÁROMI, É.: "A dual method for probabilistic constrained problems", *Math. Programming Stud.* 28 (1986) 94-112.

[38] LENARD, M. L.: "Structured model management", in *Mathematical Methods for Decision Support*, ed. G. Mitra, *Springer* (1988) 375-391.

[39] MARSTEN, R. E.: The design of the XMP linear programming library", *ACM Transactions on Mathematical Software* 7 (1981) 481-497.

[40] MAYER, J.: "A nonlinear programming method for the solution of a stochastic programming model of A. Prékopa", in Prékopa, A. (ed.) *Survey of Mathematical Programming, North-Holland,* Vol. 2 (1979) 129-139.

[41] MAYER, J.: "Probabilistic constrained programming: A reduced gradient algorithm implemented on PC", *IIASA Working Paper* WP-88-39 (1988).

[42] McALLISTER, P. H., STONE, J. C., DANTZIG, G.B.: "An interactive model management system: User interface and system design", *Systems Optimization Laboratory, Stanford University, Technical Report* SOL 90-3 (1990)

[43] MITRA, G.: "Models for decision making: An overview of problems, tools and major issues", in *Mathematical Methods for Decision Support*, ed. G. Mitra, *Springer* (1988) 17-53.

[44] MURTAGH, B. A., SAUNDERS, M. A.: "Large scale linearly constrained optimization", *Math. Programming* 14 (1978) 41-72.

[45] MURTAGH, B. A., SAUNDERS, M. A.: "A projected Lagrangian algorithm and its implementation for sparse nonlinear constraints", *Math. Progr.Study* 16 (1982) 84-117.

[46] PRÉKOPA, A.: "Logarithmic concave measures with application to stochastic programming", *Acta. Sci. Math.* 32 (1971) 301-316.

[47] PRÉKOPA, A.: "Eine Erweiterung der sogenannten Methode der zulässigen Richtungen der nichtlinearen Optimierung auf den Fall quasikonkaver Restriktionen", *Math. Operationsforsch. Statist., Ser. Optimization* 5 (1974) 281-293.

[48] PRÉKOPA, A., GANCZER, S., DEÁK, I., PATYI, K.: "The STABIL stochastic programming model and its experimental application to the electricity production in Hungary", in Dempster, M.A.H. (ed.): *Stochastic Programming, Academic Press,* London (1980) 369-385.

[49] PRÉKOPA, A.: "Numerical solution of probabilistic constrained programming problems", in Ermoliev, Y., Wets, R., J.-B., (eds.) *Numerical Techniques for Stochastic Optimization, Springer-Verlag*, Berlin (1988) 123-139.

[50] RUSZCZYNSKI, A.: "A regularized decomposition method for minimizing a sum of polyhedral functions", *Math. Programming* 35 (1986) 309-333.

[51] SCHITTKOWSKI, K.: "EMP: An expert system for mathematical programming", Mathematisches Institut, Universität Bayreuth, (1987).

[52] SCHRAGE, L., CUNNINGHAM, K.: "Demo LINGO/PC: **L**anguage for **IN**teractive **G**eneral **O**ptimization, version 1.04a", *LINDO Systems Inc.,* Chicago (1988).

[53] SIMONS, R.: "Mathematical programming modeling using MGG", *IMA Journal of Mathematics in Management* 1 (1987) 267-276.

[54] SPRAGUE, R.H., CARLSON, E. D.: "Building effective decision support systems", *Prentice-Hall* (1982)

[55] STRAZICKY, B.: "On an algorithm for solution of the two-stage stochastic programming problem", *Methods. Oper. Res.* 19 (1974) 142-156.

[56] STRAZICKY, B.: "TWOSTAGE: A code of a basis decomposition method for stochastic programming", *IIASA Working Paper* WP-87-? (1987).

[57] SZÁNTAI, T.: "Calculation of the multivariate distribution function values and their gradient vectors", *IIASA Working Paper* WP-87-82 (1987).

[58] SZÁNTAI, T.: "A computer code for solution of probabilistic-constrained stochastic programming problems", in Ermoliev, Y., Wets, R., J.-B., (eds.) *Numerical Techniques for Stochastic Optimization, Springer-Verlag*, Berlin (1988) 229-235.

[59] WETS, R. J-B.: "Solving stochastic programs with simple recourse I", *Department of Mathematics, University of Kentucky, Lexington* (1974).

[60] WETS, R. J-B.: "Solving stochastic programs with simple recourse", *Stochastics* 10 (1983) 219-242.

OPTIMIZATION PROBLEMS OF GNOSTICS

P. Kovanic

Institute of Information Theory and Automation,
Czechoslovak Academy of Sciences
182 08 Prague 8, Czechoslovakia

1. Summary

Data processing algorithms based on the gnostical theory of uncertain data possess high robustness with respect to both outlying data and changes of their statistical characteristics. However, application of this new powerful technique gives rise to interesting optimization problems resulting from the complicated nature of extremized functions. Effectiveness of the solution of this new problem is demonstrated by examples connected with the estimation of probability distribution functions of data in the random quality control.

2. Gnostical theory of uncertain data

Development of computers enabled mass applications of statistical methods to practical problems. Such a confrontation of statistical models with the reality resulted in doubts on practical applicability of statistics to analysis of small samples of real data contaminated by gross observation errors, to investigations of real (nonrepetitive, nonstationary) processes especially under a limited access to data caused by their high price, insufficient observation time and other reasons such as a small number of objects under analysis and similar. There exist real processes, too, statistical modelling of which is not reasonable at all. Although the recent development of robust statistics weakened some of assumptions on statistical models and improved partly the applicability of statistical methods, it was still not able to justify theoretically the operations on small data samples. Importance of existing problems in modelling the uncertain reality motivated the development of methods based on the fuzzy set theory. However, this approach is also dependent on subjective assumptions on the uncertainty which do not result from the features of the analyzed data samples.

A fundamentally new approach to mathematical modelling of the uncertainty represents the gnostical theory of uncertain data ('GT', 'gnostics'). It has been developed as an original alternative of the mathematical statistics, as a new theoretical basis for both efficient and robust analysis of small samples of considerably dispersed data. The basic ideas have been exposed in [1] . In contrast to other theories of uncertainty, the gnostical theory of data samples is based on an axiomatic theory of an *individual* uncertain datum and on a data composition axiom. All three axioms of this theory are strongly motivated by objective features of the real world. The **first** axiom reflects the experience of the secular activity of the mankind in measuring some real quantities. The **second** axiom assumes a natural symmetry of functions modelling the influence of the uncertainty on data in a mathematical way. These axioms have been proved to result in two particular geometries over the structure of gnostical events and in important variational principles making it possible to design an ideal closed cycle of gnostical transformations (actual quantity - datum - actual quantity). This cycle is a theoretical model of an optimum treatment of a datum, because the loss of information and entropy drop (caused by uncertainty of an individual datum) are proved to be extremized along its path. The **third** gnostical axiom (the gnostical composition law) has also an objective motivation - it is shown to be a theoretically justified analogy of the relativistic law of momentum and energy conservation. The main consequence of this axiom (distinguishing this theory from the others) consists in a high robustness of all gnostical characteristics of data samples which is an inherent, natural feature of the theory and not anything added as a supplement to the basic non-robust theory. (Under *robustness* we understand here a substantially reduced sensitivity of results of data treatment to gross errors of data and their full independence on some statistical assumptions on the data model.) This is why programs extremizing gnostical characteristics (such as information loss or entropy drop) in application to estimation, decision-making and model identification leads to excellent results even under hard conditions of praxis.

3. Available gnostical algorithms

The following gnostical procedures have already been developed relevant for both general and special (control) applications:

- gnostical process monitors (treating time series, performing robust filtering of the process level, its trend and acceleration, including robust diagnostics of the process);
- gnostical predictors for robust forecasting of disturbed processes;
- gnostical analysers of small data samples (for a detailed analysis of important data, such as estimating of probability of rare events, emergency limits for process control, random control of production quality, reliability studies, testing of homogeneity of objects and of their behaviour);
- gnostical identifiers of models (for robust identification of mathematical models of a process or object from disturbed observations);
- several ways of robustifying control systems by means of gnostical procedures:

1) PID-control using gnostical filters to get robustly filtered proportional, integral and derivative signals;

z_i). It is worth mention that for a given fixed datum z_i and for extremum values of z (going to zero or to infinity) the irrelevance reaches its limit +1 or −1 and the fidelity falls to zero. The monotonously rising function

$$l_i(z,s) = (1 + h_i(z,s))/2 \tag{5}$$

can be then interpreted as the normalized distribution function of the individual datum z_i, i.e. as the distribution function of the expectation of the event 'the unknown true value of the datum observed as z_i is z'.

Introduce now the arithmetical means

$$f(\bar{z},s) = \sum_{i=1}^{i=n} f_i(z,s)/n \tag{6}$$

and $\bar{h}(z,s)$, analogously. The expression

$$w(z,s) = \sqrt{[\bar{f}(z,s)]^2 + [\bar{h}(z,s)]^2} \tag{7}$$

is then the gnostical weight of the data sample corresponding to the point z. The *local* distribution function (l.d.f.) of the data sample under consideration is then

$$L(z,s) = (1 + \bar{h}(z,s))/2, \tag{8}$$

while the *global* distribution function (g.d.f.) being

$$G(z,s) = (1 + h(z,s)/w(z,s))/2. \tag{9}$$

Take for the moment the scale parameter s being a fixed given number. In case of its very small value (a weak influence of the uncertainty on the data, small errors of data) both d.d.f. $L(z,s)$ and $G(z,s)$ differ only in a negligible extent because of convergency of the $w(z,s)$ to n. However, the behaviour of both d.d.f.'s in case of gross errors of data will be quite different. This is not a bad but a desirable feature, it make them very usefull for applications to analyses of data samples of quite different kind. It is only necessary to know which d.d.f. should be used in a particular situation.

5. Local distribution function

In the sense of being a monotonous function for an arbitrary data sample, the l.d.f. $L(z,s)$ (8) exists always. In a special case of reasonability of a statistical interpretation of data, the l.d.f. can be shown to be an asymptotically consistent kernel estimate of the probability distribution function, the function l_i (7) being a proper kernel of Parzen's type. In such a particular case, the gnostical theory is used only as a source of a theoretically justified kernel (7) which generates remarkably nice and smooth density curves even for small data sample. But in a much more general case of data samples not allowing a statistical interpretation, formula (8) still has a good meaning as a continous model of distribution of the expectation that a 'new' datum of the same nature

as the 'old' ones will have a certain value. It can be shown that for a scale parametr s converging to zero, the l.d.f. convergs to the e.d.f. giving rise to local maxima of data density in each of observed data values. The scale parameter s plays thus a role of 'smoothing' factor of the l.d.f.
The l.d.f. is 'locally robust' in the sense that the form of l.d.f. corresponding to a subinterval of data range does not influence its form over an another subinterval. This is due to the steep descent of the kernel (7) for data moving away from the value z_i defining the particular kernel.

6. Global distribution function

Unlike the l.d.f., the g.d.f. $G(z, s)$ (9) has a theoretical support only for special data samples of s.c. *homogeneous* type. Such samples are supposed to have an unimodal curve of the data density function. When applied the formula (9) to a nonhomogeneous data sample, the function $G(z, s)$ may lose the fundamental feature of a distribution function, its monotony. (This fact enables to perform efficient tests of homogeneity of data samples.) Behaviour of the g.d.f. under decreasing scale parameter s is also surprising: There exists a minimum of the absolute value of maximum difference between g.l.f. and e.l.f. Howevever, the most distinct is the g.d.f. in that it is *globally robust* in the sense of a weak sensitivity of its form with respect to 'outlying' data as well as to whole 'peripheral' subclusters of data. This leads to unique reliability of estimation of the expectation of rare events (of values of the g.d.f. for very small or very great values of the variable z. Such tasks appear often on practice in connection with the random quality control, with studies of life–times a.s.o. This type of gnostical distribution function has no known statistical analogy.

7. Mutual benefits of gnostics and optimization

Important point in data processing is the evaluation of the quality of results. Within the framework of the gnostical theory there are functions of data available which quantify the information loss and entropy gap caused by uncertainty of individual data. Another important objects are gnostical data distribution and density functions mentoned above. All these characteristics are complicated functions of data. Efficient numerical methods of extremization of such criterial functions are necessary to be applied, but it is worth doing because of the high quality of the final results. These methods include the extremization of nonsmooth functions (see Example 1 below), as well as unconstrained and constrained extremization of functions of vector parameters. It is clear now how important benefit is gnostics obtaining from the optimization theory and its techniques. But there is also benefit which could optimization get from gnostics: There are different criteria of goodness of approximations and of fits in optimization techniques. What about using the gnostical criterial functions measuring the entropy and information losses caused by 'errors'? A better robustness of results could be then expected. There exist another ways to improvement of optimization techniques. Example 2 below demonstrates a particular case of mutual benefits of optimization and gnostics.

Example 1: Robust estimation of scale parameters

Using the features of the both gnostical distribution functions explained above, one can take as a 'best' estimate of the scale parameter s such its value which

- minimizes the maximum absolute difference between values of the e.d.f. and of the g. gnostical d.f.;
- sets the maximum absolute difference between values of the e.d.f. and of the l.d.f. to equal a certain 'critical' value of a nonparametric test of a good agreement of both distribution functions.

Because of the 'staircase' character of e.d.f., the estimation of the scale parameter represents the extremization of nonsmooth functions in both mentioned cases. It can be shown that the usage of distribution functions of gnostical types maximizes the information. This results in a high quality of the estimates of the expectation (or probability) even in application to small samples of bad data.

Let us consider two particular samples of real data: Given two 10-couples of data having the form x_i and y_i, where $= 1, ..., 10$. Values of x_i (of y_i, resp.) represent quality of products randomly chosen from a mass production process during two working days (the first one being represented by the x's, the second one by the y's). The values were:

Day 1. (x's): 723, 728, 721, 726, 728, 725, 719, 722, 728, 717.

Day 2. (y's): 714, 698, 713, 719, 707, 716, 714, 713, 717, 702.

An additional information is given that only values from the interval (200, 2000) can be actual results of the measuring of the quality. It is required to compare the quality of productions of both working days in terms of distributions functions.

This problem has been solved in following steps:

1. Transformations of data having the limited support (200, 2000) into an unlimited interval (0, inf) satisfying the requirements of the gnostical theory.
2. Estimating the scale parameters ensuring the best agreement of g.d.f.'s of both data samples with corresponding e.d.f.'s.
3. Test of homogeneity of both data samples (by unimodality of their g.d.f.'s and l.d.f.'s).
4. Decision on the adequate distribution function of each of the samples.
5. Taking conclusions on the quality of the production of both days.

The first day production is illustrated in Fig.1 by the empirical distribution function, by the global distribution function and by its density. (Both gnostical functions have been calculated over the unlimited interval and then retransformed back to be shown over the original support, the horizontal scale being logarithmic). Both g.d.f. (shown in Fig.1) and l.d.f. (not shown, but differring from the l.d.f. only negligibly) have unimodal density curve. Hence, the first sample is taken as unimodal and the g.d.f. should be used to get good estimates of expectations (probability) even for extremal quantiles to evaluate the wastage of the production.

Analogical analysis of the production of the second day leads to different conclusions as illustrated in Fig.2 (showing the g.d.f. and its density) and in Fig.3 (the l.d.f. and its density). The letter distribution function has a distinctly bimodal density rejecting thus the hypothesis on homogeneity of the second day production. It is interesting now to move the density function in Fig.2 horizontally to ensure coincidence of the location of its maximum with that of density in Fig.1. It will appear that forms of both densities differ only very slightly although the second data sample contains a couple of outliers. This example supports the statement on high robustness of the global distribution function with respect to outliers: its form in Fig.2 has been determined by the main ('inner') cluster of data.

We can now conclude from the comparison of all three distribution functions the following:

1. mean production quality of the second day was significantly lower;
2. production process of the second day was inhomogeneous (two of ten randomly chosen products were rejects);
3. the relative random fluctuations of the 'main' clusters of products of both days were unchanged (the appearence of two rejects on the second day cannot be thus explained by the 'usual' randomness).

Example 2: A model of surviving

This example is related to the identification of a model of surviving of some individuals based on observations of their life-times. Such problem arises not only in the living nature but also in reliability aspects of engineering. There are often two models to be identified, the dependence of the life-time on some observable parameters and a model of the randomness of the observed life-times. The letter problem is complicated by the necessity to make use of two categories of data, the 'ordinary' (the actual, the whole life-times actually observed) and the 'cenzored' ones (related to the individuals still surviving at the moment of observation). A gnostical approach to such a model building includes the nonparametric estimation of the model of the uncertainty (using the *global* d.f.) and a multidimensional optimization procedure which eventually includes given constrains on parameters and the nonsmoothness related to the scale parameter. There is a good experience with this approach especially due to its robustness and to its independence on some a priori assumptions related to the nature of uncertainty.

8. Optimization enviroment

An important role in realization of gnostical procedures is played by the optimization enviroment (called OPTIA) developed in the Institute of Information Theory and Automation of Cz.Ac.of Sci. (Prague). It makes it possible to prepare procedures computing functions to be extremized separately and to test different optimization methods flexibly within the frame-work of the OPTIA.

References

[1] Kovanic P.: A new theoretical and algorithmical basis for estimation, identification and control, Automatica IFAC, **22**, 6 (1986), 657-674

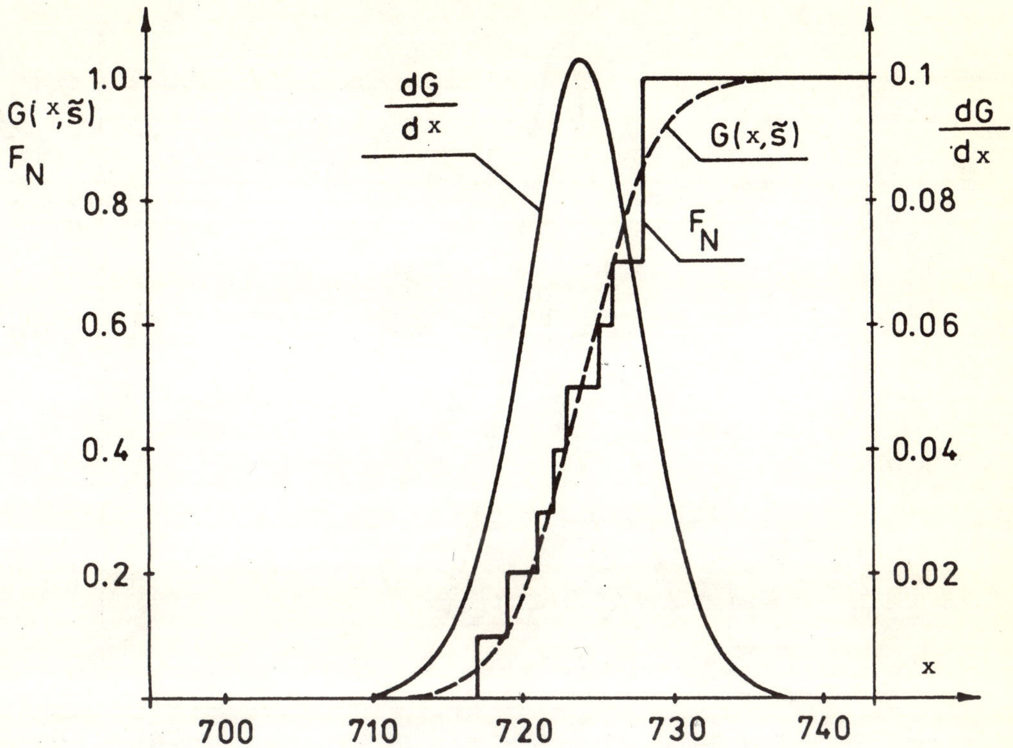

FIG. 1: GLOBAL DISTRIBUTION FUNCTION AND DENSITY FOR THE FIRST DAY PRODUCTION

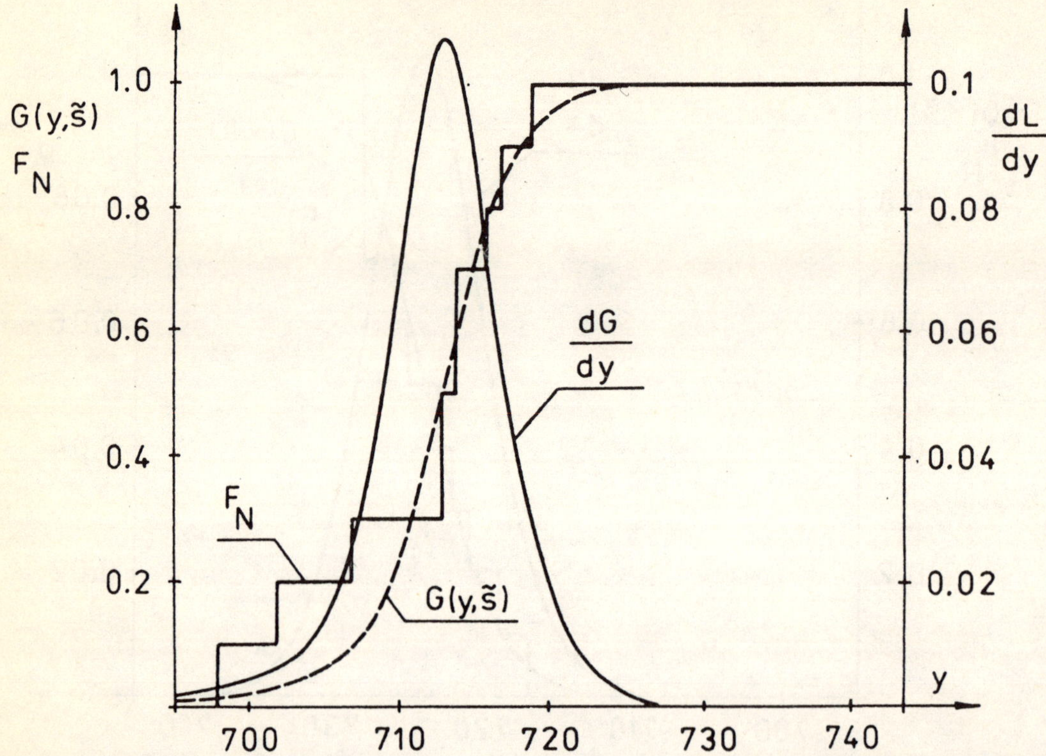

FIG. 2: GLOBAL DISTRIBUTION FUNCTION AND DENSITY FOR THE SECOND DAY PRODUCTION

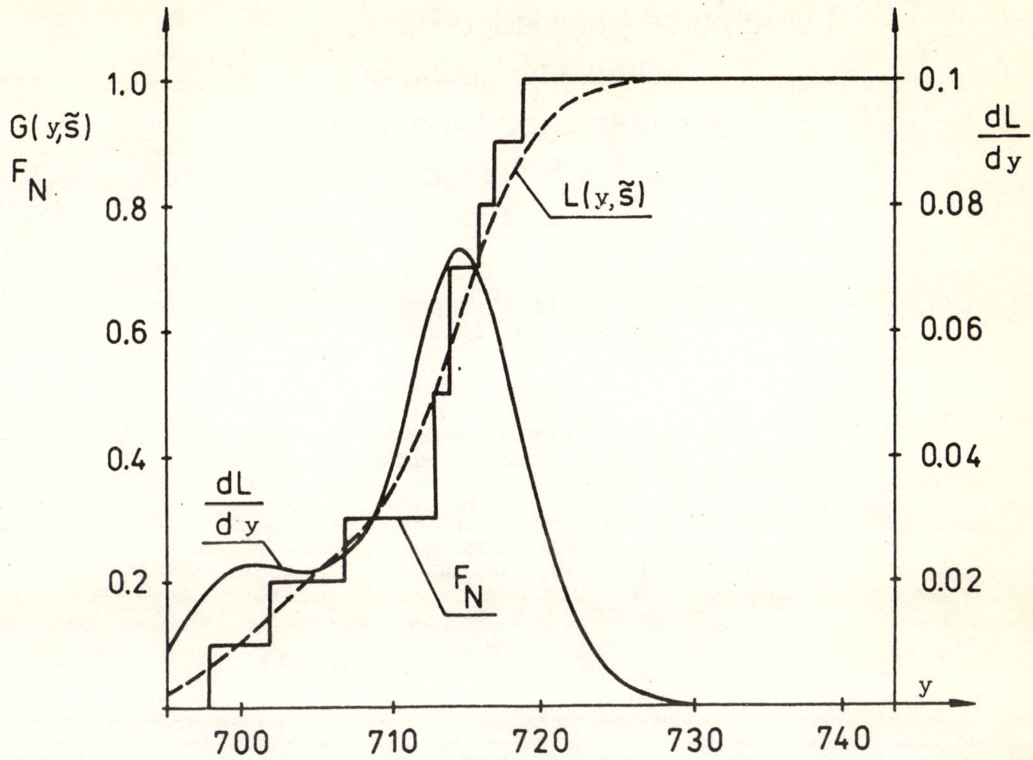

FIG. 3: LOCAL DISTRIBUTION FUNCTION AND DENSITY FOR THE SECOND DAY PRODUCTION

A Distributed Knowledge-Based System for Implementation of Manufacturing-Programs on the Shop Floor

Prof. Dr. H. Krallmann
Dipl.-Inform. S. Albayrak

TU-Berlin
Fachbereich Informatik
Institut für Quantitative Methoden
Fachgebiet Systemanalyse und EDV
Sekr. FR 6-7
Franklinstr. 28/29
D-1000 Berlin 10
Tel: +49 30 -314 73 260
Fax: +49 30 - 314 21 103

Introduction

Manufacturing control is becoming a more and more central part of companies, being the `heart´ of the manufacturing process. The objectives of high accuracy in meeting delivery dates, minimized lead time, and production with small stocks can not be met using conventional methods. New concepts have to be developed, which rely increasingly on the methods of artificial intelligence (AI) in order to clear away the weaknesses of the conventional methods.
The problems in using conventional methods for accomplishing tasks in manufacturing are described at length in /Albayrak90a/, together with an account of the advantages of using ai-based methods.
The subtasks of implementing the manufacturing program (scheduling and detailed planning, detection of conflicts, consistency-maintenance, fault-management) are also dealt with in /Albayrak90b/. There it is shown that the subtasks are of such a high complexity that they nearly prohibit the use of conventional approaches. The following description of scheduling, as given by Fox, should suffice to give an example of the complexity at this point,:

"But in a single factory having 85 orders, 10 operations, and only one substitutable maschine, we could create over 10^{880} alternative schedules. Therefore, while this style of search is theoretically interesting, it is impractical because too many alternatives must be considered. Search must be smarter; in fact, search must be structured such that the search space is reduced from 10^{880} to something much smaller and more manageable."/Fox90/

In addition, the knowledge needed for accomplishing the single subtasks is distributed among several people.

Intense and functional communication takes place between the agents (experts) dealing with the solution to problems arising in manufacturing. Modelling of this procedure in a single-agent system (expert system) is not just difficult but unsuitable. Adequate modelling of problem solving processes in manufacturing calls for a multi-agent system, which also allows for modelling the communication of the agents.

Thus, concepts from the area of distributed problem solving, especially distributed artificial intelligence (DAI), and their implementation in manufacturing control have to be analyzed.

In the following chapters, the problem situation in manufacturing will be briefly described. Based upon that, a flexible and intelligent approach to solving those problems is introduced. The fault management knowledge source will be described at length in a separate chapter.

2 Problem situation in manufacturing

Manufacturing control consists of all the decision-making and activities done before, during, and after execution of the manufacturing program given by manufacturing planning and control which are necessary for a smooth-running, on-schedule, and economical manufacturing process. So, the central task of manufacturing control is the realization of the manufacturing program. All realization-tasks aim at realizing given plans. The tasks are therefore in particular connected with present activities, short-term planning and controlling activities in manufacturing. In this context, the sub-tasks of planning, consistency-controlling and fault management can be differentiated (see fig. 2.1). These sub-tasks are strongly interconnected, in particular planning and controlling-tasks often interact.

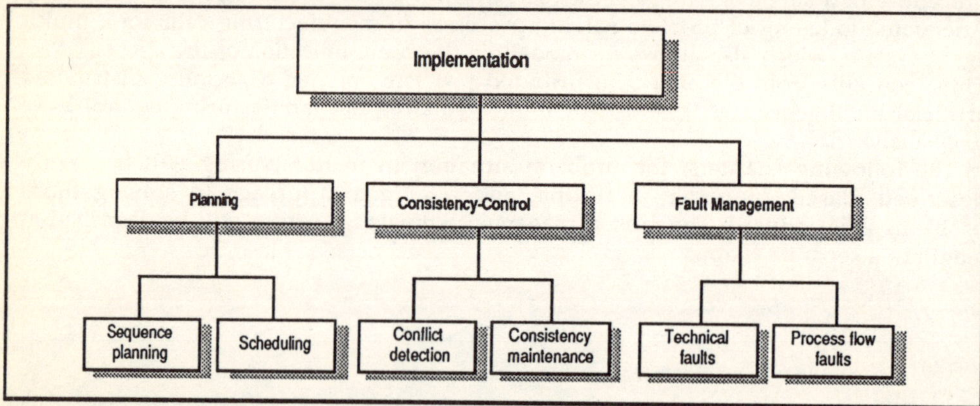

Figure 2.1: Task-profile of manufacturing control

Planning can be divided into sequence- and detailed-planning. Sequence planning states the sequence of work shop orders connected with the manufacturing program. The number of different sequences is J! (J being the number of work shop orders), if no constraints are to be met. The number of sequences for 10 work shop orders is 3,628,800.

Thus, the complexity of sequence planning grows combinatoric with the number of work shop orders.

The detailed planning department on the one hand determines the allocation of available machines and resource units for the single operations in work shop orders, on the other hand the order of operations (with respect to time) of different work shop orders has to be assigned. The complexity of this task surpasses that of sequence planning by far. Detailed planning or resource sequencing planning belongs to the class of NP-complete problems. A simple example will show this complexity. Given 5 work shop orders with 5 operations each, which could be run in any sequence on any one of 5 different machines, approximately $24.8 * 10^9$ different resource sequence plans can be configured. The solution space grows according to the formula $(J!)^M$ (M being the number of operations).

In addition to resource planning for work shop orders, re-planning has to be done in detailed planning. In particular, this is to be done if faults arise in the manufacturing process or critical discrepancies are observed.

The consistency-control-subtask can be divided into two phases. One phase is that of detecting discrepancies by evaluating incoming reports on work progress (conflict detection); the other is that of reaction upon the discrepancy by adapting the actual data to the planned data and/or the planned data to the actual data (consistency maintenance). A multitude of constraints is to be observed in this context.
A discrepancy is to be understood as an observed difference between planned and actual situation. Therefore, discrepancies can arise in two ways:

- work progress is less than expected; a delay is at issue.
- work progress is more than expected; an acceleration is at issue.

When such a conflict was detected, an interpretation is needed in order to determine consequences to other orders. Depending on the discrepancy with respect to time and quantity the conflict can be classified as "irrelevant" or "critical". With small discrepancies, or if the conflict resolves itself within short time, plans do not have to be revised. A discrepancy classified "critical", which means it can not be compensated for, leads to revision of the (by then) inconsistent plan.
In real life it is a problem that work progress reports come in on an irregular basis and that the decision making person is often not capable of evaluating discrepancies with respect to their consequences on other orders. Again, this shows the high complexity of this field.
The third area to be worked in is fault management. Faults can be grouped as technical and process flow faults. Technical faults imply the breakdown of a resource unit or machine. A technical fault always leads to cancellation of a planned resource. Consequences of such a breakdown depend on the duration of the breakdown and on the size of the buffer following that resource.
A technical fault with long duration can lead to a process flow fault. Two alternatives are possible:

- A resource following the defected machine in process flow runs out of parts due to an empty parts-buffer.
- The parts-buffer of a resource in front of the defective machine in process flow grows.

In order to compensate such process flow faults, precautions have to be taken to restrict consequences. The following example is to show that this type of fault management is distributed amongst several cooperating people (see also fig. 2.2).
If, on the machine level, a technical fault arises, the expert responsible for the setting-up and well-functioning of the machine is called. He tries to locate the reason for the fault and determine its scope. The expert decides, whether he can repair the machine and how long that would take, or if the manufacturer of the machine has to be called. The expert gives all this information to his superior, commonly the shop floor manager. The shop floor manager, in turn, evaluates the consequences on other orders in his work shop unit, depending on the duration of the breakdown and takes adaptive measures, possibly after consulting manufacturing planning and control. On the level of MP&C the breakdown is evaluated and, once delivery dates are checked and other departments are consulted, orders connected with the breakdown are assigned new priorities and - if necessary - put in a different order, which implies re-planning on the work shop level.

The knowledge necessary for problem solving in realization of the manufacturing process is distributed amongst various experts, as shown in the example above. In order to realize a computer-based solution for this group of tasks, it is necessary to model the individual agents who are working on the problem and there cooperation with one another.

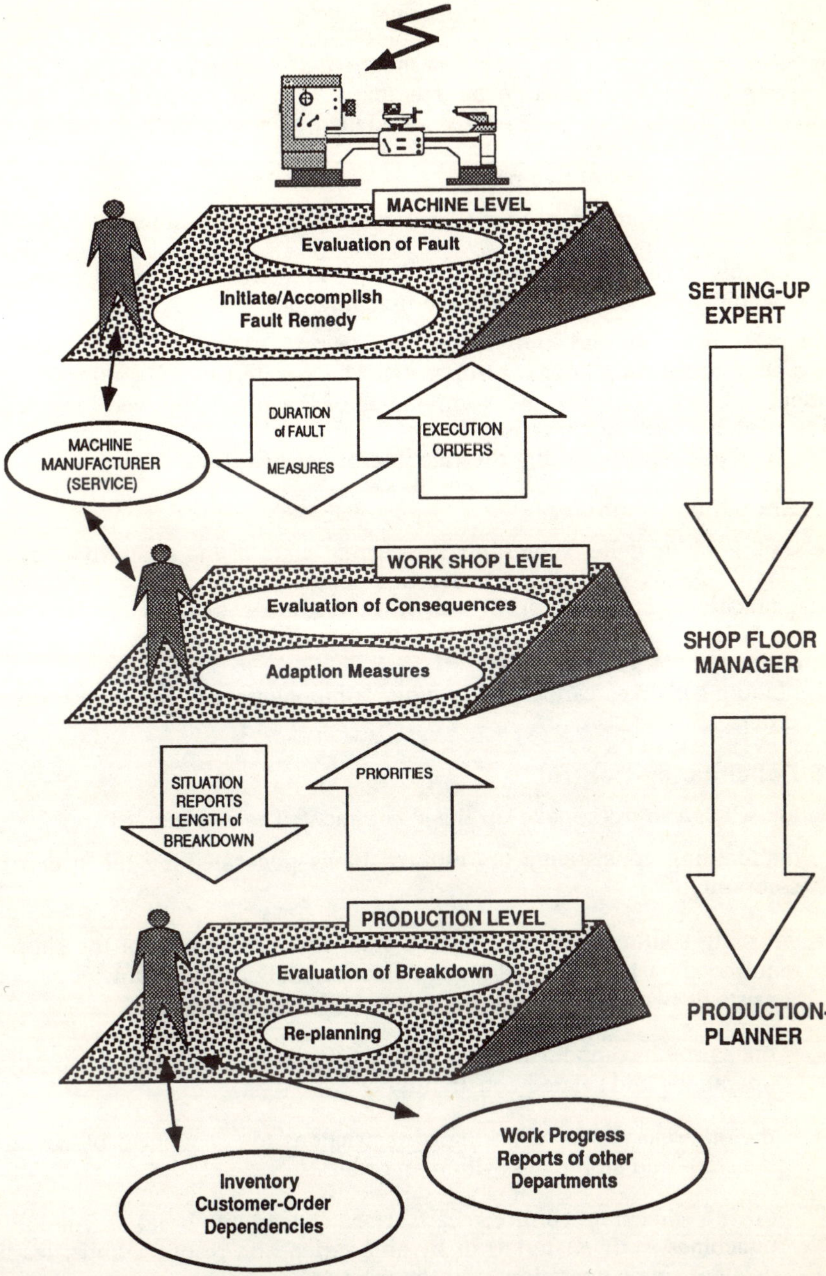

above.

Figure 2.2: Structure of problem solution in fault management

3 Approach for distributed problem solving in shop floor control

An approach for solving the problems described in the previous chapter was developed in a research project at Technical University of Berlin.
For solution of each of the problems mentioned in chapter 2 (see fig. 2.1, *subtasks of implementation*) a knowledge source (expert system) is realized. The process of problem solving is, as required above, modelled on a cooperative base; the cooperation is realized via blackboards.
The approach consists of two parts:

- the user interface; it supports "manual planning" (possible) and
- a knowledge-based approach to fault management, detailed planning and re-planning. It is combined with the user interface.

Both parts use a shared knowledge base. Figure 3.1 shows the architecture of the knowledge-based shop floor control center. The architecture is based on the blackboard model /Nii86a/, /Nii86b/. All components of the prototype were developed in Lisp using the tool **GBB** /Johnson88/, except for the fault management knowledge source, which was implemented using the rule interpreter **Foxglove** /Foxglove90/.

3.1 Shop floor modeler

The shop floor modeller represents the current state of the shop floor on the domain blackboard. To accomplish this task, this component receives data about resource-units, machines, staff, material and other resources (e.g. tools) periodically from control MDE[1]. According to these data the current shop floor model is then updated on the domain blackboard.
This component takes care that the other components are provided with actual and correct data.

3.2 Consistency-Control

Two knowledge sources make up this component. Their objectives are:

- maintaining consistency of resource plans generated by the user or planning component.
- detecting conflicts between desired state and actual state of the shop floor. The required data is sent by the shop floor modeller. This knowledge source itself consists of two components:
    - one is a sub-component for updating the planning database (states of resources, operations and related constraints);
    - the other serves for checking of restrictions (on sequences of operations, plus the start- and stop-dates within an order).

    during checking conflicts can arise, caused by breakdowns of resources (machines, staff, material) or by an overload on resource-units, leading to the delay of single operations and the production order.

1 Machine Data Equipment Units

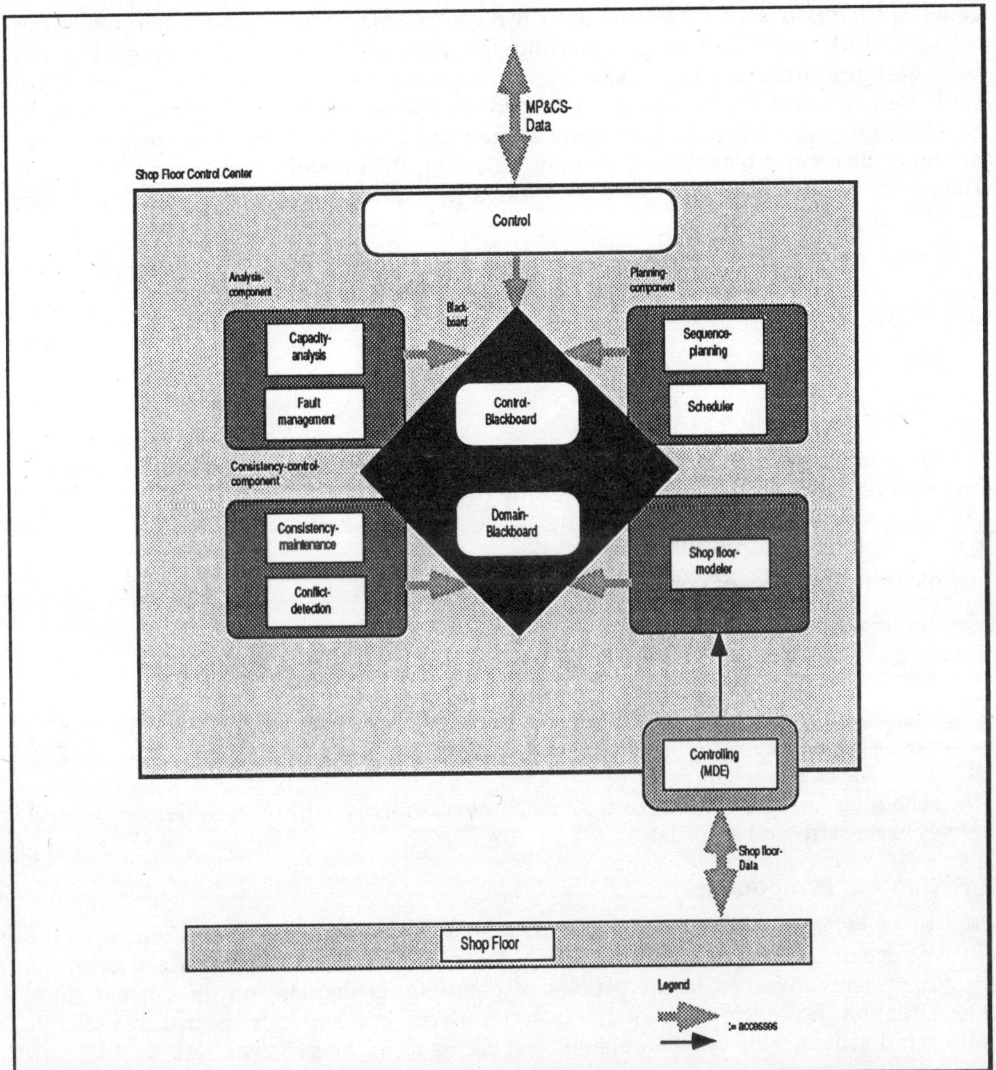

Figure 3.1: Architecture of the knowledge-based shop floor control center

3.3 Analysis component

The analysis component consists of two knowledge sources:

- capacity analysis and
- fault management.

The capacity analysis compares available resource-units (capacities) and the respective load by manufacturing orders. Overloaded as well as under-loaded resource-units are identified, which could effect the planning component because inadequately loaded and bottleneck resources are detected. The knowledge source capacity analysis generates heuristics that are put onto the control blackboard. These heuristics can cause a different scheduling, resulting for example in generally observing the bottleneck-resources at scheduling.

Fault management examines conflicts and proposes methods for plan revisioning which should solve all or at least some of the considered conflicts. These proposals are put onto the control blackboard, thereby activating the planning component.

The conflicts examined are caused by failures (machines, staff, missing material); plan revision approaches are:

- switching to alternate capacities (alternate machines, manual production, etc.),
- changing order sequences,
- shifting operations and orders,
- changing operation sequences.

The fault management knowledge source can be used stand-alone, as well. A detailed description of that knowledge source will be presented in chapter 4.

3.4 Planning component

The planning component consists of two knowledge sources:

- sequence planning and
- scheduling.

Sequence planning defines the sequence of operations. This component is called at capacity failures, for example. In that case a new sequence of operations is generated, taking the breakdown into account.

The scheduler assigns operations to machine resources within resource units and defines exact start- and stop-dates.

3.5 Control component

Control knowledge is needed to coordinate all system components and will warrant efficient use of all components. The control knowledge is used to control activation of the sub-systems involved in the process of planning. Dependent on the current shop floor situation the control knowledge is accumulated in a superior control knowledge source and activates the one component that seems to fit the problem best.

3.6 Blackboards

Two distinct blackboards exist in the system, the domain blackboard and the control blackboard. In the following we will list exemplary the data on each blackboard:

Domain Blackboard

- model of the shop floor
- capacity-entities (possibly defect)
- which operation is presently in what state (manufactured partial products, numbers of pieces, queues, ...)
- existence and state of materials and tools
- transport systems
- actual schedule; what operations are to be put on which capacities ("*Plantafel*"[1])

Control Blackboard

- problem descritiptions, objectives (meeting set dates, capacity-load optimization, ...)
- strategies, heuristics
- memorandum of possible steps in planning
- chosen steps in planning (protocol of problem solution)

1 Planning device tool

4 The fault management knowledge source

4.1 Problem situation

The task of manufacturing control is to clear off orders on time and with no extra costs. In real-life production processes, interruptions of the production flow often emerge, caused by machine breakdowns, personal on sick-leave, and missing material. The emerging of interruptions calls for quick reaction, that means decisions have to be made on how to continue. Usually a decision is made by a person with adequate competence and responsibility. Should the decision maker, amidst the decision making process, realize that the scope of his competence is surpassed, the process is shifted to the next higher level. The required decision is then made cooperatively, if needed further carriers of information or decision-makers are incorporated.
It can be seen in real-life that decision making crossing different levels and employing several people takes even more time, because the competent people are not available within short time and therefore more time has to be reserved for communication. The longer it takes to react, the more severe the consequences resulting from a fault turn out. Sometimes auxiliary decisions are made for problems that have to be dealt with in short time; within a larger context it might turn out that this decision made the actual decision even more complex.
The knowledge about time-consuming decision making processes leads to keeping buffers on each level, in order to ease consequences during the decision making.
The problem situation is therefore characterized by the following peculiar features:

- The correct measure to deal with an interruption is, next to the duration of the interruption, highly dependent on the current level-specific surroundings of the present decision maker (high contextual relevance).

- For evaluation of the scope of an interruption and selection of the resulting measures, information and decision making knowledge is needed which is distributed amongst several people, often even in several functional departments and on different hierarchical levels (decentralized, distributed information- and decision-categories).

- The span of time between emergence of an interruption and putting a reactive measure to action is relevant to the consequences (breakdown length, costs, etc.) resulting from that interruption (time-critical process).

This makes obvious that the economic objectives in manufacturing e.g.

- high balance of capacity and

- small intermediate inventory with

- high accuracy in meeting delivery dates

can only be met if quick reaction to production flow interruptions can be guaranteed.

4.2 Objectives of knowledge-based fault management

On work shop level objectives referring to time are most important. In addition to meeting the top-objective "meeting the set finishing date", the shop floor manager tries to work his resources and staff to capacity. If possible, he tries to keep intermediate inventory small. Explicit objectives with respect to costs are not to be found here, they are rather to be found in production planning. Manufacturing planning and control is on the next level up. Here, the main objective is meeting the deadline for a product ready for selling. Possibilities for adaption are the building-up and decreasing of intermediate stocks between printed circuit board production and final assembly.

Should, for example, an interruption arise at the bottleneck resource unit SMD-mounting (e.g. parts are too large), the shop floor manager will order material of better quality from the stock. If the required material is unavailable, or not available in the required quantity, it has to be checked whether alternative or better (higher quality) material can be used. This information has to be obtained from the production planning or even from the research and development department. Depending on the quantity of different materials costs per produced unit will rise. Production planning can give information about what quantity and type of alternative material could be used economically. If the interrupted production is part of an important order of a customer, the production has to continue in spite of higher costs per part, since, more costly damage (decrease in orders) has to be avoided. The same is true if cancellation of an order would bring up problems in final assembly, possibly leading to the breakdown of final assembly.

This example makes it obvious that for an economically sensible decision making the cooperation of different carriers of information and decision makers is required. A tremendous synergetic effect can be obtained if the knowledge scattered throughout the company is concentrated in one system.

Knowledge-based methods are the adequate instrument for this problem situation. The knowledge necessary for decision making, which is distributed amongst several decision making experts can be written down in general and special rules which are interconnected by coordination. This comprises a model of the decision making potential in a knowledge-based system.

Examplary rules are:
General Rule:

```
IF  type_of_interruption = material
  THEN   (1)    IF          right_to_order_material
                AND   material_in_stock
                AND   material_not_yet_assigned
         THEN   order_material

   (2)   IF           (1)_not_successful
                BECAUSE no_right_to_order_material
                AND   material_in_stock
                AND   material_not_yet_assigned
         THEN   initiate_additional_material_order
                AND   inform_mp&c

   (3)   IF           (1)_and_(2)_not_successful
         THEN   see_if_alternative_material_possible

   (4)   IF           (3)_successful
                AND   alternative_material_in_stock
                AND   alternative_material_not_yet_assigned
         THEN   order_alternative_material

   (5)   IF           (3)_not_successful
                AND   follow_up_order_for_respective_
                            printed_circuit_board_available
                AND   material_for_follow_up_order_in_stock
                AND   mp&cs_gives_ok
         THEN   order_material_assigned_to_
                            follow_up_order
```

Special Rule:

```
IF  fault = smd_mounting_machine_2
    AND    affected_order = board_x
    AND    follow_up_fault =
             missing_reserve_at_manual_mounting
    AND    missing_reserve_of_a_to_b_hours
    AND    no_reserve_of_different_boards
    AND    staff_at_manual_mounting_cannot_be_moved
    AND    one_day`s_supply_of_intermediate_product_
             board_x_mounted_in_stock
    AND    board_x_mounted_may_be_used (mp&c)
    AND    order_board_x_has_high_priority  (mp&c)

  THEN     call_board_x_mounted_from_stock
```

A system like that would be available independent of the human decision makers in a company. Therefore, urgent decisions to be made in reaction upon a fault - like during night shift - can be made fast and qualified. In daily routine such a system could ease the strain on the decision making experts, too, since the effort for communication between the affected persons will be reduced significantly by usage of the system. This is made possible by integration of the knowledge-based system into existing systems. The information requested for decision making (e.g. stock quantities, order priorities, intermediate stock quantities, basic data, follow-up orders, usage of alternative resources, etc.) can be obtained by utilizing data of adjacent systems that can be reached from the shop floor control center (MP&CS, stock inventory, material flow, etc.).

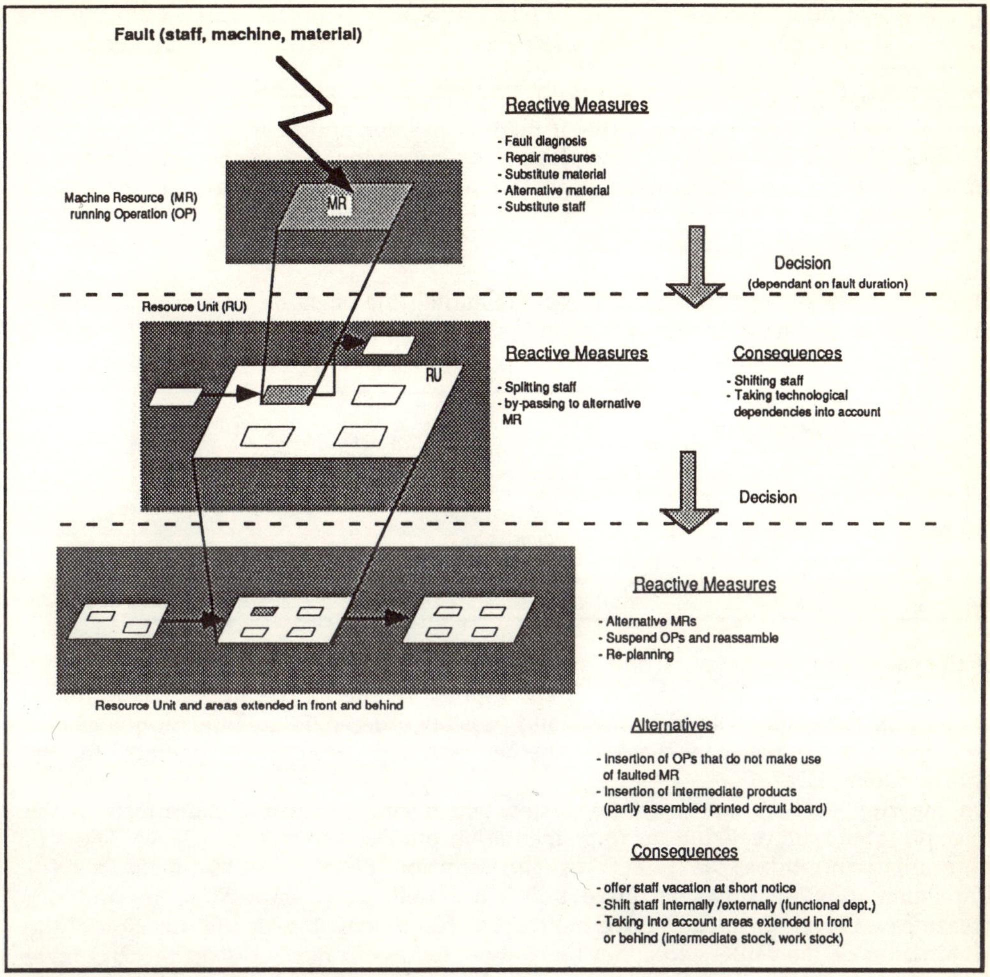

Figure 4.1: Concept of fault management

4.3 Concept of fault management

In order to generate fast reactions to occurring interruptions and to deduce measures, the follwing information is necessary:

- affected resource unit,
- affected machine resource,
- type of printed circuit board in process (order),
- fault category (human, machine, material),
- depending on the case: anticipated duration of interruption.

The steps of fault management are ordered into several levels which build on one another and are connected (see fig. 4.1). The objects with dark shading symbolize the view depending on the level.
The 1st level contains a so called implementational concept. The main task of this level is the fast elimination of faults. If there is an interruption at a machine resource, the system suggests measures, which lead to a local elimination of the fault depending on the type of fault[1]. Measures for the elimination of faults always refer to those possibilities, which compensate the cause of the interruption directly. So, if a machine is malfunctioning, fault diagnoses are performed and measures for repair are suggested.
If, for example, in the resource unit SMD-mounting the machine resource Panasonic 2 is put out of action because of a machine fault, the following rule could be used for a fast removal of the fault.

```
IF  fault = smd_mounting_machine_2
    AND    type_of_fault = machine
    AND    fault_observation = parts_are_placed_inexact
    AND    characteristic = many_lost_parts_in_
            centering_station

   THEN    remove_parts_from_centering_station
    AND    check_absorber_units_for_dirt_and
            clean_if_necessary
```

If the cause of the disruption lies within the area of material (e.g. missing or faulty material), it is checked whether material or possibly alternative material is available from stock and could/should be used, and possibly ordered. Is the interruption caused by missing personnel, it is checked whether qualified personnel is available for the corresponding task.
On the 2nd level measures are suggested which aim at limiting the effects of the disruption and/or realizing an implementation on the resource unit level. The aim here is to minimize the effects of a disruption or of possible measures for implementation on other resource units. If it had been impossible to find out measures on level 1, which remove the fault as fast as possible, or the duration of the elimination of the fault[2] exceeds a limit, local follow-up measures on the 2nd level and alternate possibilities have to be taken into consideration. Depending on the anticipated duration of the disruption on this level steps are suggested by the system, which on one hand take technological interdependencies into consideration and on the other hand smooth the resulting consequences. Steps like the following belong to this category:

- stopping of tasks that directly precede or follow other tasks in time-sequence if technological interdependencies have to be taken into account.
- re-shuffling of personnel.

A simple rule that takes interdependencies of this tasks into consideration is:

---

[1] human, machine, material
[2] duration of repair, transport time for material, etc.

```
IF  fault = smd_mounting
    AND    duration_greater_than_y_hours

  THEN     abort_preceeding_screen_printer
    AND    short_term_reshuffle_personnel
    AND    turn_off_succeeding_reflow_stove_after_
            reflow_of_last_mounted_board
```

Besides smoothing consequences, measures for implementation on the resource unit level are considered. For example, if a machine resource in a resource unit is running idle, one can switch over to it in case of machine fault. One has to take the expenditure of the switch-over, depending on the duration of the interruption, into consideration. A further measure of implementation is to get available intermediate parts (primary demand) from stock and to ensure the order by bypassing the source of the fault. If the cause for the disruption lies in missing personnel, the system checks whether a splitting of personnel is possible (one set-up expert for two machines).
If it is not possible to find a measure on this level which makes the implementation possible or if the extent of the fault is very large (long duration of disruption, no supply for succeeding resources) so that consequences for preceeding or succeeding manufacturing areas have to be taken into account, the problem is tackled on the 3rd level.
Here, measures for implementation are considered that have consequences on preceeding or following factory areas and possibly require changes of order plans. For example, it is checked whether other tasks can be interrupted, that run on this resource unit. The priorities of orders are taken into account. This is demonstrated in the following rule:

```
IF  fault = smd_mounting_machine_2
    AND    type_of_fault = machine
    AND    duration_of_disruption_greater_z_hours
    AND    affected_order = printed_circuit_board_x
    AND    priority_of_board_x_is_higher_than_priority_
            of_order_running_on_smd_mounting_machine_1
            (mp&c)

  THEN     cancel_order_on_smd_mounting_machine_1_and_set_up_
            for_board_x
```

It is also considered to switch to alternate resource units where again occurring conflicts have to be solved. Furthermore, it is checked whether consequences for preceeding or succeeding manufacturing areas have to be taken into consideration (increasing intermediate depots in front of the faulty machine resource, decreasing stock of parts in succeeding areas; see following special rule). This can, again, result in a new turn of fault management at the corresponding resource unit (follow-up interruption).
If it is not possible - even on the 3rd level - to find measures for implementation of the manufacturing program, the order is cancelled and it is checked whether other orders can be assigned with higher priority (no use of faulty machine resource) to ensure full use of the capacities. If such orders exist, their implementation is suggested.

On all levels information from adjacent systems is used, the demand of information being highest on the 3rd level.
The stepwise approach reflects the decision making process of a work shop manager, who first tries to eliminate a fault locally before more elaborate methods are applied, which require high tuning efforts.

5. Summary

Integrating knowledge-based fault management components in the work control center for printed circuit boards manufacturing extraordinarily increases the effective availability of the manufacturing capacity.
Another benefit is the conservation of very important distributed knowledge.

Bibliography

/Albayrak90a/ Albayrak, S.; Drewes, B.; Krallmann, H.: Wissensbasierter Fertigungsleitstand auf der Basis einer Blackboard-Architektur. In: Hübers, W. (Hrsg.): *Congressband VIII zur 13. Europäischen Congressmesse für Technische Kommunikation ONLINE `90*, Hamburg 1990, S. VIII.18.01-18.41.

/Albayrak90b/ Albayrak, S: Verteilte wissensbasierte Systeme in der Fertigung. In: Krallmann, H; Rieger, B. (Hrsg.): *Wissensbasierte Systeme in der Betriebswirtschaft*, Erich Schmidt Verlag, Berlin 1990.

/Fox90/ Fox, M.S.: AI and Expert System Myths, Legends, and Facts. In: *IEEE EXPERT* February 1990.

/Foxglove89/ *VAX Foxglove/VMS User`s Guide* [Guide to Version 4.0]. Digital Equipment Corporation, 1989.

/Johnson88/: Johnson, P.M., Gallagher, K.Q., Corkill, D.D.: *GBB Reference Manual, GBB Version 1.2*. COINS Technical Report 88-66, July 1988

/Nii86a/ Nii, P.: Blackboard Systems: The Blackboard Model of Problem Solving and the Evolution of Blackboard Architectures. In: *AI Magazine*, (38-53), Summer, 1986

/Nii86b/ Nii, P.: Blackboard Systems: Blackboard Application Systems, Blackboard Systems from a Knowledge Engineering Perspective. In: *AI Magazine*, (82-106), August, 1986

A Discrete–Event Process Analysis and Modelling

J. PIK

Institute of Information Theory and Automation of the
Czechoslovak Academy of Sciences, CS–182 08 Prague, Czechoslovakia

Abstract

A method of analysis and modelling of a complex discrete–event process represented by a sufficiently long sequence of events is considered. The corresponding model is based on sample path analysis and some ideas and techniques of structural pattern recognition are utilized. An application of the model for solving a problem of practical interest is mentioned.

1 Introduction

A growing need for analysis and modelling of systems and processes, whose terms correspond to logical or symbolic rather than numerical values, initiated a broad research of this field. A number of approaches to the analysis and the modelling of the discrete-event systems and processes have been proposed to reflect the different aspects of their behaviour and the many areas where these systems and processes arise. The different formalisms are utilized, e.g., finite state machines, Markov chains, Petri nets, calculus of communicating systems, communicating sequential processes, and finitely recursive processes belong to them, [7].

In the paper, a method of the analysis and the modelling of a complex discrete–event process represented by a sufficiently long sequence of events is considered. Using that, a formal representation of the process through an external or a black box type model is obtained. The proposed discrete–event process transformation model based on sample path analysis may be viewed as a structrural one as it does describe an event transition mechanism. To characterize the used formalism, algebraic linguistics and structural pattern recognition are utilized.

In Section 2 we summarize some basic concepts used in the process transformation model considered in Section 3. An application of the model for solving a problem of practical interest is illustrated in Section 4. It concerns the analysis and the modelling of a time series of formal symbols in the long–range weather forecasting.

2 Basic concepts

An alphabet is a finite nonempty set the elements of which we call symbols, events, or states. If Σ is an alphabet, then Σ^* denotes the set of all sequences of symbols of the alphabet Σ including the sequence λ consisting of no symbols. The length of a sequence X , written $|X|$, means the number of symbols in X when each symbol is counted as many times as it occurs, $|\lambda| = 0$. A sequence X is a subsequence of a sequence Y iff there are sequences X_1 and X_2 such that $Y = X_1XX_2$, where X_1XX_2 denotes the concatenation of the sequences X_1, X, and X_2.

A discrete-event system (DES) is defined as a 3-tuple

$$DES = (S, E, D),$$

where

$$\begin{array}{ll} S & \text{is an alphabet of states,} \\ E & \text{is an alphabet of events,} \\ D & \text{is a transition function,} \quad D : S \times E \rightarrow S \cup \{\lambda\}. \end{array}$$

Such DES is also called the untimed DES to distinguish it from the system where the event occurrence time is taken into account.

A sample path of the DES is given by an event sequence $e_1e_2 \ldots e_k \in E^*$.

The process transformation model presented here is based on the notion of similarity between two sequences. To determine it, a proper use of symbol–to–symbol operations is needed to change the one sequence into the other. The following operations are considered to transform a sequence X into a sequence Y, $X, Y \in \Sigma^*$:

1. deleting one symbol from X,
2. inserting one symbol into Y,
3. substituting one symbol of X for another single symbol.

The considered operations can be written as a pair of symbols $s = (a, b) \neq (\lambda, \lambda)$, $a, b \in \Sigma \cup \{\lambda\}$, where 1. $b = \lambda$, 2. $a = \lambda$, 3. $a, b \neq \lambda$, respectively.
A transformation is called length–preserving if it transforms X into Y and $|X| = |Y|$.

3 Model

Let a sufficiently long history of the system's behaviour be represented by the event sequence $e_1e_2 \ldots e_i$. Now, assuming the behaviour of the system in an interval $\langle i_1, i_2 \rangle$ represented by the event sequence $e_{i_1} \ldots e_{i_2}$, we require some description and/or characterization of the behaviour in the defined interval $\langle k_1, k_2 \rangle$.
An equidistant timing of the events may be considered and, moreover, a union of intervals instead of the interval $\langle i_1, i_2 \rangle$ is possible as well.

Let us consider an untimed $DES = (S, E, D)$ and let a sample path of the system be given by the event sequence $e_1e_2 \ldots e_i \in E^*$. More precisely, as follows from above, a simple timed sample path described by $(e_1, t_1)(e_2, t_2) \ldots (e_i, t_i)$, or, alternatively, $(e_1, v_1)(e_2, v_2) \ldots (e_i, v_i)$, where an inter-event time $t_{j+1} - t_j = v$, $v = const.$, can be considered.

Using a-priori defined event–to–event operations, the event sequence is transformed into a new one. To reflect a difference in the application of the operations, a nonnegative real number is associated with each event operation. Two modifications of the transformation are considered.

The former is based on a stochastic mapping $T : E \cup \{\lambda\} \rightarrow E \cup \{\lambda\}$, E is an alphabet of events, $T(a) = b$, $(a,b) \neq (\lambda, \lambda)$, with a probability $q(b/a)$ associated with each event–to–event operation $t = (a,b)$.
Assume at most one transformation of each event, the operation probabilities are consistent if $\Sigma_{b \in E \cup \{\lambda\}}\ q(b/a) = 1$ for all $a \in E \cup \{\lambda\}$. Following [3], the consistency of the multiple transformations model can be proved, therefore, $\Sigma_{\alpha \in E^*}\ q(\alpha/a) = 1$.
Supposing the independence assumption for the considered operations,
$q(b_1 b_2 \dots b_n / a_1 a_2 \dots a_n) = q(b_1/a_1) \dots q(b_n/a_n)$ for any sequences $a_1 a_2 \dots a_n \in E^*$, and $b_1 b_2 \dots b_n \in E^*$.
The probability of the transformation X into Y, $q(Y/X)$, $X = a_1 a_2 \dots a_n$, is defined by $q(Y/X) = max_{Y^k \in \tau}\ q(Y^k/X) = max_{Y^k \in \tau}\{\Pi_{j=1}^{n}\ q(\alpha_j^k/a_j)\}$, where τ is a set of all partitions of Y into n subsequences, $Y^k = \alpha_1^k \alpha_2^k \dots \alpha_n^k$, $\alpha_j^k \in E^*$, $j = 1, 2, \dots n$.
As follows from the definition of $q(Y/X)$, it corresponds to the most likely way of transforming X into Y.

The latter modification introduces the Levenshtein metric [2] for an optimal representation of the event sequences. A nonnegative real number $w(s)$ associated with each event operation is called a weight of the operation $s = (a,b)$. The notion of $w(s)$ is extended to a series of operations $S = s_1, s_2, \dots, s_m$ using
$w(S) = \Sigma_{i=1}^{m}\ w\ (s_i)$ and $w(S) = 0$ for $m = 0$.
The weighted distance $d_w(X,Y)$ from $X \in E^*$ to $Y \in E^*$ is defined by
$d_w(X,Y) = min_S\{w(S)\ :\ S$ is a transformation of Y from $X\ \}$.
The following conditions are added to obtain a metric in the ordinary sense (the Levenshtein metric) :

1. $d_w(X,Y) \geq 0$ and $d_w(X,Y) = 0$ iff $X = Y$,
2. $d_w(X,Y) = d_w(Y,X)$,
3. $d_w(X,Y) + d_w(Y,Z) \geq d_w(X,Z)$.

Procedures following Wagner and Fischer's algorithm [8] are commonly used for the computation of the weighted distance. In [8], dynamic programming is applied and the corresponding time complexity is $O(|X| \times |Y|)$.

Now, the numerically valued similarity between the event sequences is utilized to study structural properties of the given sample path corresponding to a process development. For an event subsequence, we look for all occurrences of the same or similar subsequences in the considered sample path. The next development of the found subsequences is extracted and a clustering based on the nearest neighbour rule ([4]) is used to get a partition of this set. The extracted subsequences clustered into the same partition classes are characterized by prototype subsequences and by associated absolute and relative frequencies corresponding to a probability space. As this characterization reflects the structural relations in the context of the process development, the results are utilized in the analysis and the modelling of the considered discrete–event process.

4 Application

The proposed model based on the length–preserving transformation of the event sequences is really utilized for the analysis and the modelling of the atmospherical circulation, [6]. It is a part of the computer–aided decision support for the long–range weather forecasting in the Czech Institute of Hydrometeorology.

In this application, the updated Hess and Brezowsky's standardization (GWL symbols) of the pressure field over the Atlantic–Europe region is considered,[1]. Twenty-nine well defined nonnumerical types of the daily configurations of the pressure fields are distinguished, moreover, another type is added to represent an exceptional configuration.

Starting from 1881 the considered time series contains about 40,000 symbols constituting a training set. There are attempts to utilize the standardization to the weather forecasting; e.g., [5], where the Markov chain theory is taken into account. States of the Markov chain are labelled using the alphabet of the GWL symbols and the corresponding transition matrix is computed. The obtained results are very briefly outlined and it is concluded that the considered Markov process is "...a first good approximation..., but a better approximation may be obtained often by fitting with a higher order autoregressive.", [5].

In our model, the set of event sequences of the given length over the alphabet of the GWL symbols Σ_{GWL} is reduced using the weighted distance. To compute it, we prepared two sets of the event–to–event operation weights. The weights of the former set follow a physical analogy of the pressure fields and are as follows
$\Sigma_{GWL} = \{C, S, W, A, B, H, V, X, Z, Y, T, R, J, I, F, E, M, O, N, D, 1, 2, 3, 4, 5, 6, 7, 8, 9, U\}$,
$\sigma_1 = \{C, S, W\}$, $\sigma_2 = \{A, B\}$, $\sigma_3 = \{H\}$, $\sigma_4 = \{V, X, Z, Y, T, R\}$, $\sigma_5 = \{J, I\}$,
$\sigma_6 = \{F, E, M, O\}$, $\sigma_7 = \{N, D\}$, $\sigma_8 = \{1, 2, 3, 4, 7, 9\}$, $\sigma_9 = \{5, 6, 8\}$, $\sigma_{10} = \{U\}$,
$w(a, b) = c_1$ iff $a, b \in \sigma_i$ for some $i \in \{1, 2, \ldots, 10\}$,
$w(a, b) = c_2$ iff $a \in \sigma_i$, $b \in \sigma_j$, $i, j \in \{1, 2, \ldots, 10\}$ and $i \neq j$, $c_1 < c_2$.

The latter set represents a more complex case as the weights depend on the correspondence between the weather and the standardization and, in effect, the twelve sets of the monthly weights are introduced.

References

[1] Hess P. and Brezowsky H.: Katalog der Grosswetterlagen Europas. Deutsch. Wetterd., Offenbach a.M., 1969.

[2] Levenshtein A.: Binary codes capable of correcting deletions, insertions and reversals. Sov. Phy. Dokl., Vol.10, 707–710, 1966.

[3] Lu S.Y. and Fu K.S.: Stochastic error-correcting syntax analysis for recognition of noisy patterns. IEEE Trans. on Computers, Vol.26, No.12, 1268–1276, 1977.

[4] Lu S.Y. and Fu K.S.: A sentence–to–sentence clustering procedure for pattern analysis. IEEE Trans. on Systems, Man, and Cybernetics, Vol.8, No.5, 381–389, 1978.

[5] Mares C. and Mares I.: Testing of the Markov dependence for certain meteorological parameters. Ninth Prague Conf. on Inf. Theory, Stat. Dec. Functions and Random Proc., Prague, 1982.

[6] Pik J. and Brůžek V: A pattern recognition model of a complex natural system. Wissenschaftliche Berichte der Technischen Hochshule Leipzig, Heft 6, 1989.

[7] Varaiya P. and Kurzhanski A.B. (Ed.): Discrete Event Systems : Models and Applications. IIASA Conf., Sopron, August 3-7, 1987, Lecture Notes in Control and Information Sciences, 103, Springer–Verlag, New York, 1988.

[8] Wagner R.A. and Fischer M.J.: The string–to–string correction problem. JACM, Vol.21, No.1, 168–173, 1974.

HEURISTIC REASONING WITH THE INTERACTIVE MATHEMATICAL PROGRAMMING SYSTEM EMP

K. Schittkowski
Mathematisches Institut
Universität Bayreuth
D - 8580 Bayreuth

Abstract: EMP is an interactive software system that supports the numerical solution of various mathematical programming problems, e.g. of nonlinear programming, data fitting, min-max programming, multicriteria optimization, non-smooth optimization, quadratic programming, or linear programming, subject to linear or nonlinear constraints. Nonlinear problem functions must be defined by sequences of FORTRAN statements assigning a numerical value to a user-provided name. The system writes complete FORTRAN source programs, which are linked and executed automatically. For each nonlinear programming model, program generators for several mathematical algorithms are available. The selection of a suitable code is supported by EMP heuristically depending on the requirements of the user. The system is capable to learn, i.e. to improve its own knowledge on the success of the algorithms, and to perform a rule-based error analysis in case of nonsuccessful termination. The paper describes the heuristic, knowledge-based options of the user interface.

1. General Information on EMP

EMP is an interactive programming system to support model building, numerical solution and data processing of constrained and unconstrained mathematical programming problems. Various options are available in EMP to facilitate the formulation of problem functions. The objective function e.g. may be a linear or quadratic function, a data fitting function, a sum or maximum of functions, or a general function without a structure that could be exploited. More precisely the following mathematical models are available for facilitating the formulation of objective or constraint functions and exploiting special structures numerically whenever possible:

- Linear programming
- Linear regression
- Quadratic programming
- Nonlinear L_1-data fitting
- Nonlinear L_2- or least squares data fitting
- Nonlinear maximum-norm data fitting
- Multicriteria optimization
- Min-max optimization
- Non-smooth optimization
- Global optimization
- General nonlinear programming

All problems may have bounds for the variables and linear or nonlinear constraints. Data fitting problems are either composed of a sequence of arbitrary nonlinear functions or of one model function, where the experimental data are provided separately.

For most optimization problems, many different algorithms are available. The present version of EMP contains mathematical methods of the following type:

- Sequential quadratic programming methods for nonlinear programming
- Bundle methods for non-smooth or ill-conditioned problems
- Stochastic global optimization methods
- Levenberg-Marquardt, Gauss-Newton, Newton, and quasi-Newton methods for nonlinear least squares problems
- Ellipsoid method for smooth and non-smooth optimization
- Dual and primal methods for quadratic programming
- Adapted sequential quadratic programming methods for constrained L_1-norm, L_2-norm, maximum-norm and min-max problems

EMP includes program generators for codes of the frequently used optimization libraries NAG and IMSL, and the algorithm base is extended step by step.

For objective function and constraints, the input of quadratic or linear functions reduces to definition of some vectors and matrices, respectively, where sparsity can be exploited. Gradients of nonlinear and nonquadratic functions are approximated numerically, but can also be provided by the user in analytical form. The input of 'simple' objective or constraint functions is facilitated, if they differ at most by an index.

Only the problem relevant data need to be provided by a user in an interactive way. General functions must be defined by sequences of FORTRAN statements addressing a numerical value to a user provided function name. All generated problems are stored in form of a data base system, so that they are easily retrieved, modified, or deleted on request. EMP proposes a suitable mathematical algorithm and writes a complete FORTRAN source program. The system executes this program and stores the numerical results in the data base, so that they are available for further processing. Since individual names for functions and variables can be provided by a user, it is possible to get a problem dependable output of the achieved solution.

The user will be asked whether he wants to link the generated FORTRAN program with some of his own files or whether he wants to insert additional subroutines, declaration and executable statements to formulate the problem. It is possible to generate the same programs automatically, that must be generated by 'hand' otherwise.

Alternatively it is possible to solve nonlinear programming and nonlinear least squares problems directly by an executable code without additional compilation and linking, if the problem functions can be described in form of analytical expressions. Then the nonlinear functions are evaluated by preprocessed interpretation, and gradients are calculated automatically, cf. Griewank (1989) and Liepelt, Schittkowski (1990).

In various ways the system is capable to learn and to store its own experience on the success of solution attempts. The proposals offered by EMP, will therefore become better and better with increasing knowledge on the numerical structure of the user provided models. A rule-based failure analysis explains some reasons for possible false terminations and proposes remedies to overcome numerical difficulties.

All actions of EMP are controlled by self-explained commands which are displayed in form of menues. Step by step the user will be informed how to supply new data. Whenever problem data are generated or altered, the corresponding information will be saved on a user provided file. Besides commands to generate, solve or edit a problem, there are others to transfer data from one problem to another, to delete a problem, to sort problems, to get a report on problem or solution data, to halt the system and to get some information on the system, the mathematical models and the available algorithms. It is even possible to insert arbitrary operating system commands without leaving EMP.

EMP is implemented in SUSY, cf. Schittkowski (1987), a language that was designed entirely for the generation of interactive problem solving systems like EMP with the additional feature to process heuristic knowledge and uncertainties. A corresponding interpreter was implemented by the author and must be available to start EMP, at present on VAX/VMS, HP-UNIX and MS-DOS computing environments.

The presented system to facilitate model building and numerical solutionof mathematical programming problems, is based on the host language FORTRAN and it is assumed, that a user is familar with this language. EMP was designed mainly for engineering applications, where we need a very flexible input procedure, since possible application problems are highly nonlinear. Since the generated programs can be used outside of the system, one could consider EMP also as a software development tool.

Although EMP can be used in form of a 'stand-alone' product, additional efforts can be undertaken to extend its knowledge base and to improve its intelligence. In particular a user may alter existing models and define new ones. In addition the system is implemented in a way to allow an extension of the existing algorithm base very easily, i.e. to scratch or add new algorithms for an existing model. The usage of the special system language SUSY allows an efficient alteration and adaption of the whole program to another situation. A complete documentation of SUSY is included in the system and it is possible to extract individual chapters interactively.

The following sections describe the mathematical models that can be formulated, the available numerical algorithms, and the knowledge-based features of the user interface, in particular the self-learning procedure, the heuristic proposal of a suitable numerical algorithm and the heuristic analysis of failures.

2. Mathematical Models

EMP is intended to formulate and solve nonlinear programming problems of the following general structure:

$$
\begin{array}{rll}
 & \min f(x) & \\
 & g_i(x) = 0 & ,i = 1, ..., m_e \\
x \in \Re^n : & g_i(x) \geq 0 & ,i = m_e + 1, ..., m \\
 & x_l \leq x \leq x_u &
\end{array}
$$

The used standard notation can be replaced by actual names for problem functions or variables and has the following meaning:

- n: Number of optimization variables.
- m_e: Number of equality constraints.
- m: Number of constraints without lower and upper bounds on the variables.
- x: Vector of n independent design variables
- $f(x)$: Real-valued objective function which is to be minimized. It is assumed that f depends on the n variables $x_1,...,x_n$ and that f is at least continuous in the rectangle defined by the lower and upper bounds on the variables, or is composed of continuous functions.
- $g_i(x)$: Set of m real-valued constraint functions defining the feasible region of the problem. They are assumed to be continuous with respect to the variables $x_1,...,x_n$ at least in the rectangle definied by the bounds on the variables.
- x_l, x_u: Two n-dimensional vectors defining lower and upper bounds for the variables.

EMP is also capable to solve linear and nonlinear systems determined by equality and inequality conditions, respectively. In this case, only the constraints are declared by the user and EMP inserts the objective function

$$f(x) = x^T x$$

so that a feasible solution with minimal Euclidean norm is calculated. Note that x^T denotes the transpose of the vector x.

To facilitate input and output of problem functions and to exploit special mathematical structures by the choice of a suitable algorithm, some options are available for providing the functions f and $g_1,...,g_m$.

a) **Objective function:**

Several options are available for formulating the objective function and for facilitating its input:

- Linear function, i.e.

$$f(x) = c^T x$$

with an n-dimensional vector c. Only the coefficients of c need to be determined.

- Linear least squares function, i.e.

$$f(x) = \frac{1}{2}||Cx - d||$$

where $||.||$ denotes the Euclidean norm. C is an l by n matrix and d a vector of length l. Only C and d need to be defined in this case.

- Quadratic function, i.e.

$$f(x) = \frac{1}{2}x^T Cx + d^T x$$

where C is an n by n matrix, and d a vector of length n. Only C and d must be defined.

- L_1-data fitting function, i.e.

$$f(x) = |h_1(x)| + \ldots + |h_l(x)|$$

The individual functions $h_1,...,h_l$ are assumed to be continuously differentiable. Alternatively each function can be considered as a result of a parameter estimation experiment subject to a model function $H(t, x)$, so that

$$h_i(x) = w_i(H(t_i, x) - y_i)$$

for $i = 1,...,l$, where w_i denotes the weight, t_i the independent model data, e.g. observation time, and y_i the dependent or observed data of the i-th experiment, $i = 1,...,l$. Besides of these data, only the model function $H(t, x)$ needs to be declared, which depends on a real variable t and a vector x of the n independent variables. H should be continuously differentiable.

- L_2-data fitting or nonlinear least squares function, i.e.

$$f(x) = h_1(x)^2 + \ldots + h_l(x)^2$$

The l observation functions $h_1,...,h_l$ are continuously differentiable and are declared individually instead of the composed function f. As above each h_i can be replaced by a parameter estimation experiment, i.e. by a term of the form $w_i(H(t_i, x) - y_i)$.

- Maximum-norm data fitting, i.e.

$$f(x) = \max\{|h_1(x)|, \ldots, |h_l(x)|\}$$

where all individual functions are continuously differentiable. Again each function can be considered as the result of a parameter estimation experiment subject to a model function $H(t, x)$.

- Maximum of functions, i.e.

$$f(x) = \max\{h_1(x), ..., h_l(x)\}$$

The individual functions h_1,...,h_l are continuously differentiable and could be realizations of a parameter estimation experiment subject to a model function $H(t, x)$.

- Vector of functions, i.e.

$$f(x) = (h_1(x), \ldots, h_l(x))^T$$

Each individual function must be continuously differentiable. In an interactive way, the user will be asked to define the way how the multicriteria decision is to be performed.

- Sum of functions, i.e.

$$f(x) = h_1(x) + \ldots + h_l(x)$$

As above, only the functions h_l,...,h_l are to be defined by the user and these functions should be continuously differentiable.

- Sum of simple functions, i.e.

$$f(x) = H(1, x) + \ldots + H(l, x)$$

Here it is assumed that each individual function $H(i, x)$, $i = 1$,...,l, possesses the same mathematical structure and depends only on an index i and the vector x of the decision variables. Again the function $H(i, x)$ is to be continuously differentiable.

- General function, i.e. it is supposed that no specific structure is available that could be exploited.

b) Constraints:
The restrictions are either assumed to be linear or of a general nonlinear type:

- No constraints, i.e. m is equal to zero.
- Linear constraints, i.e.

$$g_i(x) = x^T a_i + b_i$$

The vector a_i is the i-th row of an m by n matrix A and b_i the i-th coefficient of a vector b, $i = 1$,...,m. Only the data for A and b are requested by EMP.

- General constraints, i.e. at least one of the constraints is nonlinear. It is possible in practice, that all restrictions possess the same structure and depend at most on an index 'i' for the i-th constraint, i.e. that

$$g_i(x) = G(i, x)$$

In this case only some FORTRAN statements for defining $G(i, x)$ must be provided by a user.

The mathematical programming algorithms require the evaluation of gradients of all problem functions. If they cannot be formulated automatically by EMP, i.e. if the problem functions are neither linear nor quadratic, then the user has three options. In the first case, he requires the numerical evaluation by scaled forward differences, and no additional input is necessary. In the second case, he prefers to evaluate them analytically by a sequence of suitable FORTRAN statements. Moreover it is possible to let gradients be evaluated automatically, if the nonlinear functions can be described in analytical form that fits into a certain interpreter language.

In general it can be recommended to use the numerical approximation option. Analytical derivatives should be determined only if difference quotients produce significant round-off errors or if the additionally required n function evaluations are too expensive compared with one gradient evaluation.

3. Numerical Optimization Algorithms

The following FORTRAN algorithms are available to solve any of the mathematical programming problems of the type described in the previous section. Detailed user documentations are contained in EMP and can be displayed interactively.

NLPQL (Schittkowski (1985/86)):

NLPQL realizes a sequential quadratic programming (SQP-) method for solving the general nonlinear programming problem with continuously differentiable objective and constraint functions. The algorithm formulates a sequence of quadratic programming problems by linearizing the constraints and approximating the Lagrange function quadratically. By solving these subproblems, a search direction for the variables and the multipliers is obtained. Subsequently a line search is performed along that direction, to get a new iterate, i.e. a new guess for the variables and multipliers. The merit function to calculate the steplength parameter, is an augmented Lagrangian or an L_1-exact penalty function alternatively. Then a new approximation matrix for the Hessian of the Lagrange function is updated by the BFGS-quasi-Newton formula.

NLPQLA (Schittkowski (1990c)):

The code is an executable program where not only the problem data, but also nonlinear problem functions are read in from an input file. The corresponding language is close to FORTRAN and described in Schittkowski and Liepelt (1990) in detail. A summary is included in this documentation. After parsing and preprocessing the nonlinear functions, NLPQL is executed to solve the problem. Gradients are evaluated automatically.

Because of the interpretation of functions, the code is somewhat slower than the corresponding code generated by EMP, when the user supplies analytical gradients. However one avoids the compilation and linking phase and, in particular, the analytical generation of gradients 'by hand'. Since the gradients are evaluated exactly, the results are a little bit more precise than those obtained by numerical differentiation.

NLPQLB (Schittkowski (1990b)):

NLPQLB is an extension of NLPQLD in the sense that also problems with very many constraints can be solved, i.e. problems which cannot be solved by NLPQLD directly because of too large storage requirements for the two-dimensional matrix of the linearized constraints. Problems of this type arise e.g. when solving problems with restrictions depending on certain parameters from an infinite set, where discretization is used.

E04VDF (NAG: Gill e.al. (1983a)):

The underlying mathematical idea is very similar to that of NLPQL, i.e. E04VDF realizes a sequential quadratic programming method. In contrast to NLPQL, the Hessian of an augmented Lagrangian is approximated instead of the Lagrangian itself, and a 'hot' start is possible for the quadratic programming subproblem, to get an initial guess for the first basis. It is allowed to define linear constraints separately and all constraints possess upper and lower bounds.

ELL (Schittkowski (1986a)):

In this case, it will be tried to solve the nonlinear programming problem by a variant of the ellipsoid-method, which was proposed by Shor (1977) for solving convex mathematical programming problems. Starting with an ellipsoid containing the rectangle defined by lower and upper bounds on the variables, a sequence of ellipsoids is constructed with volumes decreasing linearly to zero. Any new ellipsoid is uniquely determined by the requirement, that it should contain one half of the previous one with minimal volume. The cutting half-space is determined by the gradient of a special penalty function. Iterates are the centers of the ellipsoids.

Basically, an ellipsoid method is only capable to solve unconstrained problems. Constraints and bounds for the variables are taken into account by an L_1-penalty function. The corresponding penalty factor must be defined by the user.

The convergence speed of the ellipsoid method is at most linear and depends on the number of variables. Since multipliers are not approximated, a precise stopping condition cannot be given in the constrained case. However it is possible to predetermine the number of iterations to achieve a relative reduction of the volumes with respect to the starting ellipsoid.

M1FC1 (Lemarechal, Strodiot, Bihain (1981)):

The algorithm solves unconstrained nonlinear programming problems either with a smooth or nonsmooth objective function. Constraints are taken into account by formulating an L_1-penalty function, where the corresponding penalty parameter must be determined by the user. If a gradient of the objective function or a constraint is to be calculated analytically at a non-differentiable point, then at least a subgradient must be available.

Proceeding now from an unconstrained optimization problem, the algorithm collects a certain user provided number of previously computed gradients to formulate a bundle, i.e. an interior approximation of the ϵ-subdifferential. A minimum-norm feasible point of the bundle is calculated then to get a search direction. Subsequently a line search is performed to obtain a new iterate.

BT (Schramm (1989)):

The BT-algorithm is very similar to M1FC1 in the sense that also non-smooth problems can be solved. BT realizes a combination of bundle and trust region approach. Constraints are taken into account by adding a L_1-penalty function to the objective function.

UNT (Törn, Zilinskas (1989)):

The algorithm is based on a statistical model of the objective function which is estimated using all previous function values. Constraints are handled by adding a L_1-penalty function to the objective. The code is designed to find the global optimum of a single valued function on a feasible region defined by upper and lower bounds. Local solutions found during the iteration process, are reported. The algorithm does not require any gradient information, i.e. is also capable to solve non-smooth or even non-continuous problems.

It must assumed that the number of global isolated minima is not toobig, i.e. is in the order of ten. For smooth and well-defined problems, the usage of gradient-type algorithms, e.g. of the SQP-methods, is recommended. The number of function evaluations and the internal working time for some auxiliary computations might be too large in this case. On the other hand, the code is quite robust e.g. when solving problems with noise.

GLOPT (Törn, Zilinskas (1989)):

GLOPT realizes a random search algorithm to find the global minimum of an arbitrary objective function subject to upper and lower bounds on the variables. Clustering is performed to isolate local minima which are reported. The L_1-penalty function with a user-provided penalty parameter is used to take additional constraints into account.

ZXMWD (IMSL: Fletcher (1972)):

Problems with box constraints are transformed into unconstrained problems by using trigonometric functions. General nonlinear constraints are taken into account by an L_2-penalty function. The unconstrained problem is then solved by a quasi-Newton method of Fletcher (1972). Smooth problem functions are required.

Besides of the penalty parameter, the user is asked to specify a certain number of starting points which are generated randomly. Then about four iterations are performed by the quasi-Newton method and the five results with the lowest function values are then taken to continue the iteration. Thus the code can be used in particular when it is supposed that the problem possesses various local minima.

MCO (Schittkowski (1986b)):

The multicriteria problem mentioned in the previous section, is transformed into a nonlinear programming problem with one differentiable objective function, which is then solved by NLPQL. Three different attempts are available to obtain the transformed problem:

(1) Sum of weighted functions
(2) Sum of weighted functions with additional bounds on objective functions
(3) Selecting one function, suppressing the other ones

The corresponding weights are defined interactively when executing the FORTRAN-code, and can be modified during the same session. A list of efficient points calculated during an interactive session, is kept in memory for further processing.

DFNLP (Schittkowski (1986c)):

The program DFNLP solves constrained data fitting problems in L_1, L_2 and maximum norm and, in addition, min-max problems by transforming them into a suitable nonlinear programming problem. This problem is then solved by algorithm NLPQL. For least-squares problems, typical features of special purpose implemetations are retained, in particular the usage of Gauss-Newton type search directions.

DFNLPA (Schittkowski (1990d)):

Similar to NLPQLA, the executable program requires the input of the nonlinear problem functions symbolically on a special file, which is preprocessed. Then DFNLP is called with the same options as described above.

DFELL (Schittkowski (1986d)):

DFELL realizes an ellipsoid algorithm for solving L_1, L_2, maximum norm and min-max problems directly without transforming them to a constrained nonlinear programming problem as done in DFNLP. Constraints are taken into account by formulating an L_2-penalty function. After some arrangements of data, the code ELL is executed to solve the problem.

DFM1FC1 (Lemarechal, Strodiot, Bihain (1981)):

Very similar to DFELL, the least squares problem is transformed into an unconstrained problem and then solved by M1FC1.

NLSNIP (Lindström (1983)):

The algorithm solves nonlinear least squares problems subject to nonlinear equality and inequality constraints. The Gauss-Newton method is modified to handle constraints by an active set strategy. By solving the resulting linear least squares problem with linear equality constraints, a search direction is obtained. Using a penalty function subject to a norm that must be specified by the user, a line search is performed to get a new iterate. To stabilize the algorithm, a subspace minimization option is included in particular for large residual problems. Alternatively it is possible to provide second derivatives and the algorithm switches to Newton's method automatically, if necessary, i.e. if the Gauss-Newton search direction does not lead to a sufficient success.

E04FDF (NAG: Gill, Murray (1978)):

The algorithm solves unconstrained least squares problems by a modified Gauss-Newton method and uses only function evaluations. Gradients are approximated numerically. Constraints and bounds are not taken into account, and are simply omitted when solving a problem.

E04GCF (NAG: Gill, Murray (1978)):

The algorithm solves unconstrained least squares problems by a modified Gauss-Newton method and requires also gradient evaluations. A quasi-Newton method is used to approximate part of the Hessian of the objective function.

E04GEF (NAG: Gill, Murray (1978)):

The algorithm solves unconstrained least squares problems by a modified Gauss-Newton method and requires also gradient evaluations. A difference formula is used to approximate part of the Hessian of the objective function.

ZXSSQ (IMSL: Brown, Dennis (1972)):

The unconstrained least squares problem is solved by a modification of the Levenberg-Marquardt algorithm. Gradients are evaluated numerically. Some options are available to modify the Marquardt parameter before starting the algorithm. Constraints are not taken into account.

DN2GB (Dennis, Gay, Welsh (1981a, 1981b)):

The algorithm solves least squares problems with simple bound constraints by a modified Newton method and requires also gradient evaluations. A difference formula is used to approximate part of the Hessian of the objective function. Convergence is achieved by exploiting a trust region approach. If necessary, the algorithm reduces to a Gauss-Newton or Levenberg-Marquardt method. Constraints different from bounds are not taken into account.

DFEXTR (Törn, Zilinskas (1989)):

The algorithm is capable to solve least squares problems subject to upper and lower bounds on the variables, where three different norms are available to define the objective function. Constraints are added by a L_1-penalty term. The search is performed using successively connected random line searches combined with line searches on randomly generated lines. The one-dimensional minimization algorithm is based on a statistical model similar to the UNT-code for general purpose optimization. Thus the algorithm is able to search for the global minimum of the problem without requiring any gradient information.

QL (Schittkowski (1986e), Powell (1983)):

The mathematical method was proposed by Goldfarb and Idnani (1983) and can be characterized as a dual approach. Starting from a Cholesky-decomposition of the objective function matrix, the minimum of the unconstrained problem is found immediately. Successively all violated constraints are incorporated into a 'working set' defining a certain subspace, where the minimum of the objective function is recalculated. It might be necessary to drop constraints from the working set, until the optimal solution is reached.

E04NAF (NAG: Gill e.al. (1983b)):

The program solves quadratic programming problems by the primal method of Gill e.al. (1983b), and realizes an active set strategy. The objective function matrix must be symmetric, but is allowed to be indefinite.

LP (Schittkowski (1986f)):

EMP is not designed to solve large and sparse linear programming problems or linear programming problems with a special structure. A specific modelling language as known from linear programming applications, is therefore not available. The input of sparse matrices is facilitated in the way that the user is allowed to to insert only the non-zero entries of matrices and vectors, or to define the matrix values by one arithmetic expression. In the latter case, the elements may be calculated somewhere else, so that only values of a two-dimensional array can be transferred. The linear program is solved by the simplex method.

E04MBF (NAG: Gill e.al. (1983b)):

This code is based on the quadratic programming method E04NAF and uses the primal method included there. Linear constraints must be defined with two-sided bounds.

ZX3LP (IMSL):

The code realizes a simplex algorithm. A transformation of the given problem is required, since the code accepts only lower zero bounds for the variables.

4. The User Interface of EMP

All actions of EMP are controlled by commands. They are displayed in form of a menue, where the initial of the desired function must be typed by the user. From the viewpoint of a user, they should be considered as self-contained programs, i.e. they can be used independently from each other. If problem data are generated or altered, the corresponding data will be saved in the internal data base. Whenever EMP executes an operating system command, e.g. for compiling and linking a FORTRAN program, a separate subprocess is generated and executed.

Once a command is specified, EMP asks the user to answer further questions e.g. in the form

** Analytical derivatives (Y/N):*

In the above example, a user has to type either 'Y' for yes or 'N' for no. It is always assumed that the less probable answer is 'Y', so that in this case a 'Y' has to be typed exactly and any other input is interpreted as 'N'. But whenever a user does not know the precise meaning of the brief information given, he is allowed to press '?'. He obtains then more detailed information before he has to answer the question again. In the same situation it might happen that a user wants to cancel the present execution of a command, e.g. if he notices a severe previous input error. By typing the sign '<' he will return immediately to main menue.

Most data must be defined in form of windows. Some of them are displayed subsequently in form of examples. Each window contains some information how to move the cursor, to delete characters and lines and how to leave it. Again a help window is displayed by typing '?' or, equivalently, 'F1' in the MS-DOS version.

In an interactive way, the user will be informed how to construct a new mathematical optimization problem. After input of the problem name and, optionally, some additional

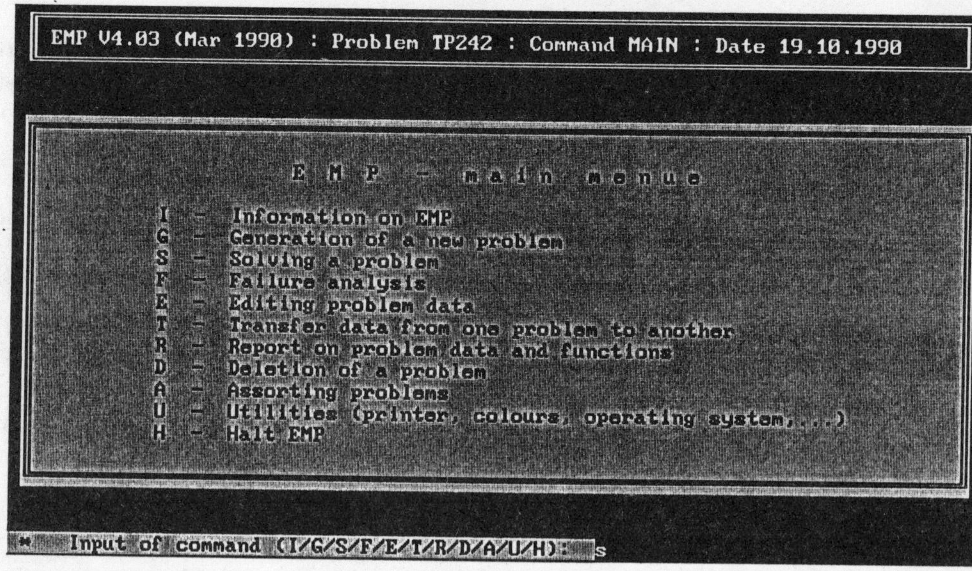

Figure 1: Main-menue of EMP

information on the practical background, the type of the problem and its functions must be specified. Then some dimensioning parameters are required, e.g. number of variables and constraints. User provided declaration statements, constant data, or parameter estimation data follow whenever required for constructing the actual problem under consideration.

Besides the input of statements defining function values, it is possible to define additional FORTRAN statements which will be inserted either into the main program or the subroutines evaluating the problem functions and gradients. Declaration statements e.g. for dimensioning auxiliary arrays or commons may be defined by the user and are inserted by EMP at the correct locations. Other additional statements can be prepared by the user and are placed directly after assigning actual iteration values to the variables, which can therefore be modified or used to prepare some initial data before calling the optimization algorithm or calculating the function and gradient values, respectively. Further statements can be inserted into the main program after executing the optimization subroutine, e.g. to process the achieved results. In this case, the user provided variable and function names contain the computed numerical values. Moreover the user may add some arbitrary FORTRAN subroutines or functions, which will be appended to the generated source code.

Except for the quadratic or linear programming problems, it is necessary to provide initial estimates for the variables and to declare upper and lower bounds. If all initial values and bounds are identical or depend at most on an integer 'i', then the input of these data can be reduced to only one line by typing a suitable arithmetic expression depending on an 'i'.

The evaluation of the problem functions depends on their specific type defined earlier. If a function is linear or quadratic for example, then only the corresponding matrices or vectors must be defined. In the general case, an arbitrary number of FORTRAN statements

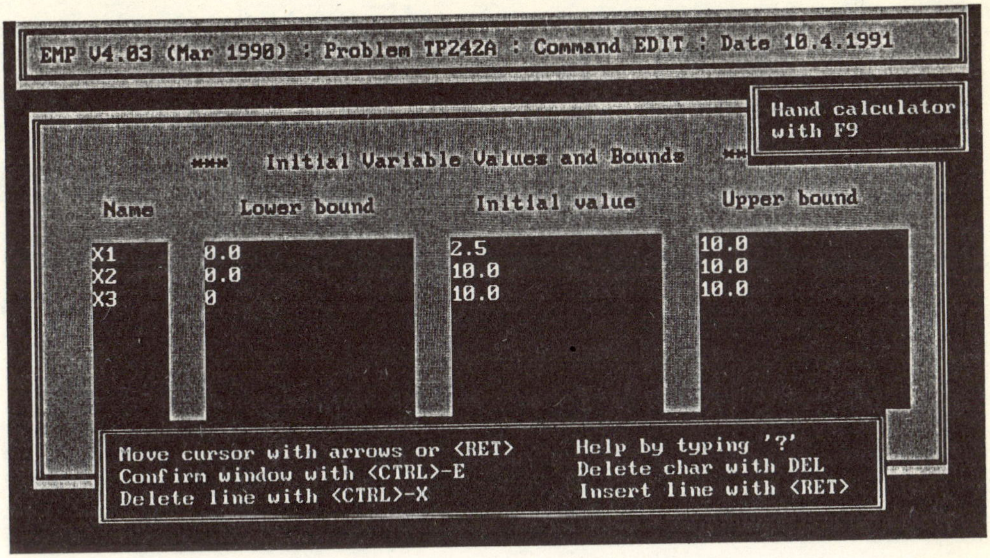

Figure 2: Input of optimization variables

must be typed by the user for addressing a numerical value to a function, i.e. for assigning a numerical value to a function name.

Note that the similar windows are also used to define additional statements discussed above.

The last action to generate a new problem is the request to determine those file names of object codes, which contain additional subroutines and which are to be linked with the FORTRAN code generated by EMP, and the corresponding solution algorithms. In case of symbolic function input and automatic differentiation, any information supplied here cannot be exploited.

5. Heuristic Proposal of an Optimization Algorithm

This commands starts the numerical solution of a problem that was previously constructed as described in the previous section. After input of the problem name, a user has the option to require the display of all available codes that could solve his optimization problem. The list contains a certainty factor for each proposed program which indicates a very rough approximation of a measure for the numerical performance of an algorithm. A value of 100 is the maximum attainable degree of belief, whereas a value of 0 indicates a very

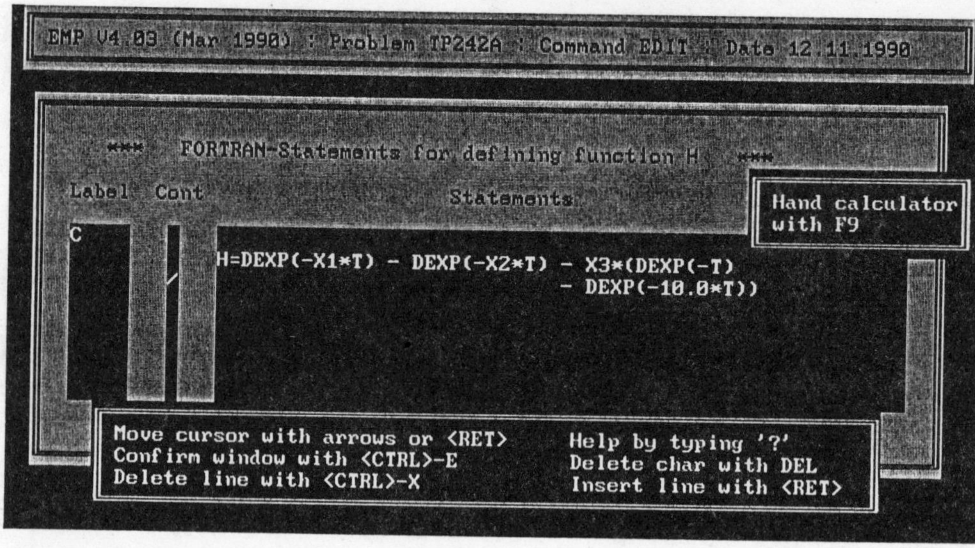

Figure 3: Input of objective function

poor performance of the algorithm on previous runs. The numerical values of the certainty factors are defined and updated in three different ways:

a) Initially every code obtains a certain permanent default value of the system author which is based on his own subjective experience.

b) Whenever a code could solve a problem succcessfully, so that the stopping criteria are satisfied subject to the provided tolerances, the corresponding permanent certainty factor of the code is increased. If, on the other hand, a failure is reported, then the permanent certainty factor is decreased. The factor is not altered at all if the iteration was inter- rupted due to the fact that the maximum number of iterations was attained.

c) When starting the solution of a problem, a local certainty factor is defined which gets the value of the permanent one, and all previous numerical solution attempts are investigated. If the problem could not be solved by a specific algorithm, then the local certainty factor is decreased significantly, and enlarged otherwise.

The local certainty factors are displayed to support the selection of a suitable code. It is hoped that the choice of these factors reflects the influence of special model structures and that EMP is capable to learn, i.e. to propose better and better solution methods in dependance on the problem to be solved.

Moreover the user is asked whether he wants to select a code 'by hand', where he may exploit the experience reflected by the certainty factors, or whether he prefers to initiate a rule-based code selection by the system. In this case, some additional questions must be answered and the outcome is the display of a list of codes in the order of their certainty.

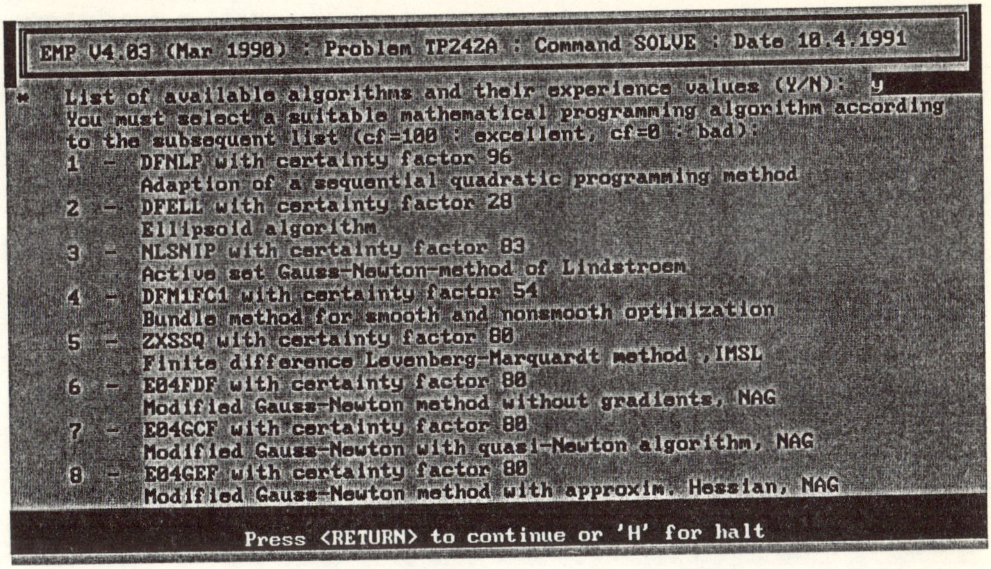

Figure 4: List of algorithms and certainty factors

The evaluation of the certainty factors is based on the given experience factors described above, some problem data like number of variables or constraints, numerical differentiation etc., and on the answers of the user. More precisely the following data and information are imbedded in the decision process:

- structure of the model (e.g. least squares)
- number of variables
- number of constraints
- type of constraints (e.g. linear, bounds)
- calculation type of (sub-)gradients (e.g. numerically)
- smooth problem functions
- noise in evaluating problem functions
- expected number active constraints
- ill-conditioned problem
- approximation of global solution
- location of starting point
- expensive function evaluations

It is selfevident that a user may reject the algorithm which got the largest certainty value, and choose another one. The described evaluation of heuristic knowledge is available only for the general nonlinear programming or the nonlinear least squares model, since only in these situations, a larger number of different codes is available to solve the problem.

More details on the underlying decision process and some test cases are described in Schittkowski (1990a). They outline, how an algorithm proposed by EMP, does work numerically compared with others that got a lower certainty factor.

Subsequently some additional decisions must be made by a user, e.g. the choice of a

```
EMP V4.03 (Mar 1990) : Problem TP78 : Command SOLVE : Date 10.4.1991

*  Smooth problem (Y/D/N):  y
*  Starting point close to a solution (Y/D/N):  n

*** EMP proposes the following algorithms together with evaluated
    certainty factors reflecting the degree of believe in the conclusion:

 CF   Code      Information

 99   DFNLPA    Adaption of a sequential quadratic programming method
 96   DFNLP     Adaption of a sequential quadratic programming method
 88   NLSNIP    Active set Gauss-Newton-method of Lindstroem
 87   DN2GB     Gay's method (Newton, quasi-Newton, Gauss-Newton)
 86   E04FDF    Modified Gauss-Newton method without gradients, NAG
 86   E04GCF    Modified Gauss-Newton with quasi-Newton algorithm, NAG
 86   ZXSSQ     Finite difference Levenberg-Marquardt method ,IMSL
 58   DFM1FC1   Bundle method for smooth and nonsmooth optimization
 42   DFELL     Ellipsoid algorithm
 28   DFEXT     Random line search algorithm

*  Accepting proposed algorithm (Y/N):  Y
```

Figure 5: Proposal of algorithms

suitable output flag. It is possible that a previously computed and eventually inaccurate approximation of the solution is available. Then the user is asked whether he wants to accept this guess as a starting point for the actual run or not. If some additional output from the underlying mathematical programming algorithm is required, then the information is displayed on the terminal in original form, in particular without individual user-provided names for functions or variables.

The generated FORTRAN code is written on a text file with the name 'EMPCODE.FOR' or 'empcode.f', respectively. The code consists of a main program and, if the problem functions are nonlinear, two subroutines for evaluating problem functions and corresponding gradients in a form required by the selected optimization code. EMP compiles this program, links it with a chosen nonlinear programming algorithm and eventually some user files, and executes the resulting program.

If the codes NLPQLA or DFNLPA are to be executed, then two input files are created which contain problem data and nonlinear functions in symbolic form. Since no compilation and linking is required, the programs are executed directly without delay.

All numerical results, performance data and termination reasons are stored in the underlying data base and are available for further processing. Afterwards the main-menue of EMP is displayed again and the user could choose additional actions, e.g. to investigate the obtained results. Note that after leaving the system, the last generated FORTRAN program is still available and could also be used furtheron independently from EMP. It is possible to direct the output of an optimization program to an existing file on request.

6. Heuristic Failure Analysis

Quite often, a problem can not be solved successfully in the way that the stopping criteria are satisfied within some given tolerances. Possible reasons are incorrect problem formulation e.g. leading to infeasible domains, errors in data input, programming errors for analytically defined gradients or inefficiency of the chosen algorithm.

All algorithms incorporated in EMP, report error situations by certain flags that are displayed in the optimization history table among other performance data. A value of '0' indicates a successful return as defined above, a value of '1' that the maximum number of iterations was attained, and a value greater than '1' a specific error situation depending on the algorithm chosen. To find out the meaning of the displayed numerical figure, the command 'FAILURE ANALYSIS' can be executed. In general, the corresponding information is taken from the user guides of the corresponding programs.

In some cases, e.g. if the code NLPQL or any other one based on NLPQL is chosen, some heuristic knowledge is available on possible origins of the failure. This knowledge is represented in form of rules with certainty factors and by executing the reasoning process, some possible reasons for the failure can be displayed in the order of their significance. Moreover these reasons are exploited again by rules to propose some alternative remedies. The user could investigate these recommendations and follow one of them whenever it seems to be profitable. An additional option is the possibility to require some explanations for understanding the reasoning process.

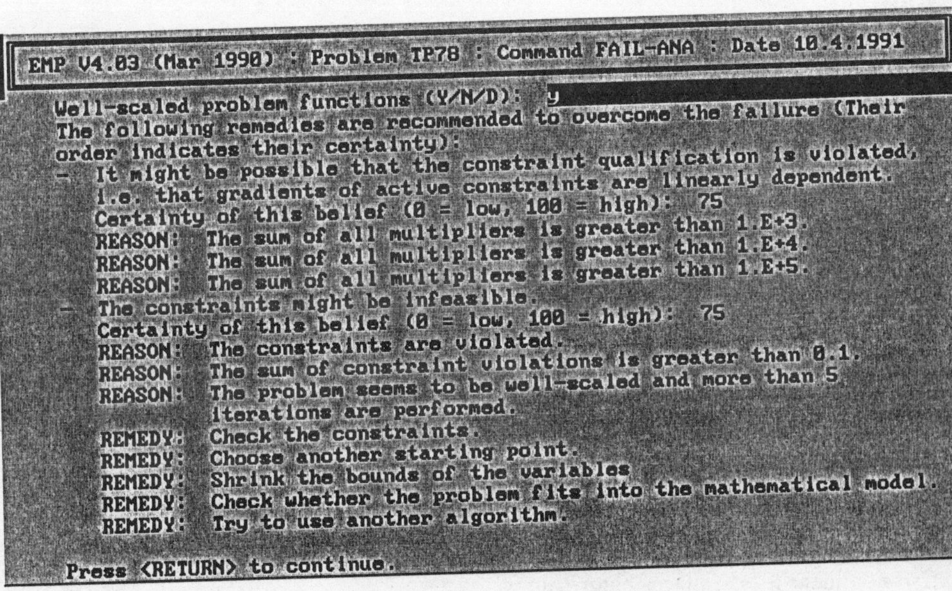

Figure 6: Failure analysis

A typical rule might be of the form

IF MUL>1.E+5
THEN RSNCQU WITH 30

reading as

'If the multiplier values are very large,
then there is some evidence that the constraint
qualification might be violated.'

The above rule asserts that a certain consequent is emphasized with a given degree of uncertainty, which could also be supported by other rules. Moreover there are other rules to conclude a possible remedy, e.g.

IF RSNCQU WITH 50 TO 100
THEN REMNEWIN WITH 95

reading as

'If the violated constraint qualification might be
a possible reason for false termination,
then it is recommended to use a new starting value
with a high certainty.'

Consequents must consist of so-called actions, i.e. an arbitrary and eventually empty sequence of SUSY commands, where antecedents are either logical expressions or again actions which have to be verified up to a certain range of uncertainty in order to be taken into account. More detailed information on the rule system is found in the SUSY documentation, cf. Schittkowski (1987).

References:

BROWN K.M., DENNIS J.E. (1972): Derivative free analogous of the Levenberg-Marquardt and Gauss-Newton algorithms for nonlinear least squares approximations
Numerische Mathematik, Vol.18, 289-297

DENNIS JR. D.M., GAY D.M., WELSCH R.E. (1981A): An adaptive nonlinear least-squares algorithm
ACM Transactions on Mathematical Software, Vol.7, 348-368

DENNIS JR. D.M., GAY D.M., WELSCH R.E. (1981B): Algorithm 573. NL2SOL - An adaptive nonlinear least-squares algorithm
ACM Transactions on Mathematical Software, Vol.7, 369-383

FLETCHER R. (1972): Fortran subroutines for minimization by quasi-Newton methods
Report R7125, AERE, Harwell, England

GILL P.E., MURRAY W. (1978): Algorithms for the solution of the non-linear least-squares problem
CIAM Journal on Numerical Analysis, Vol.15, 977-992

GILL P.E., MURRAY W., SAUNDERS M.A., WRIGHT M.H. (1983A): User's guide for SOL/NPSOL: a FORTRAN package for nonlinear programming
Report SOL 83-12, Department of Operations Research, Stanford University, Stanford, USA

GILL P.E., MURRAY W., SAUNDERS M.A., WRIGHT M.A. (1983B): User's guide for SOL/QPSOL: A FORTRAN package for quadratic programming
Report SOL SOL 83-7, Dept. of Operations Research, Stanford University, USA

GOLDFARB D., IDNANI A. (1983): A numerically stable dual method for solving strictly convex quadratic programs
Mathematical Programming, Vol.27, 1-33

GRIEWANK A. (1989): On automatic differentiation
in: Mathematical Programming: Recent Developments and Applications, ed. M. Iri, K. Tanabe, Kluwer Academic Publishers, Boston

LEMARECHAL C., STRODIOT J.-J., BIHAIN A. (1981): On a bundle algorithm for nonsmooth optimization
in: Mangasarian, Meyer, Robinson eds.: Nonlinear Programming, Academic Press

LIEPELT M., SCHITTKOWSKI K. (1990): PCOMP: A FORTRAN code for automatic differentiation
Report, Mathematisches Institut, Universitẗ Bayreuth, D-8580 Bayreuth

LINDSTRÖM P. (1983): Algorithms for nonlinear least squares particularly problems with constraints
Report UMINF-106.83, Institute of Information Processing, University of Umea, Sweden

POWELL M.J.D. (1983): On the quadratic programming algorithm of Goldfarb and Idnani
Report DAMTP 1983/Na 19, University of Cambridge, Great Britain

SCHITTKOWSKI K. (1985): Solving constrained nonlinear least squares problems by a general purpose SQP-method
in: Trends in Mathematical Optimization, K.-H. Hoffmann, J.-B. Hiriart-Urruty, C. Lemarechal, J. Zowe eds., International Series of Numerical Mathematics, Vol.84, Birkhäuser

SCHITTKOWSKI K. (1985/86): NLPQL: A FORTRAN subroutine solving constrained nonlinear programming problems
Annals of Operations Research, Vol. 5, 485-500

SCHITTKOWSKI K. (1986A): ELL: A FORTRAN implementation of an ellipsoid algorithm for nonlinear programming: User's guide
Report, Mathematisches Institut, Universität Bayreuth, FRG D-8580 Bayreuth

SCHITTKOWSKI K. (1986B): MCO: A FORTRAN implementation of an interactive multicriteria optimization method, user's guide
Report, Mathematisches Institut, Universität Bayreuth, D-8580 Bayreuth

SCHITTKOWSKI K. (1986C): DFNLP: A FORTRAN implementation of an SQP-algorithm for constrained nonlinear data fitting and min-max problems, user's guide
Report, Mathematisches Institut, Universität Bayreuth, D-8580 Bayreuth

SCHITTKOWSKI K. (1986D): DFELL: A FORTRAN implementation of an ellipsoid algorithm for nonlinear data fitting, user's guide
Report, Mathematisches Institut, Universität Bayreuth, D-8580 Bayreuth

SCHITTKOWSKI K. (1986E): QL: A FORTRAN implementation of a dual algorithm for quadratic programming, user's guide
Report, Mathematisches Institut, Universität Bayreuth, D-8580 Bayreuth

SCHITTKOWSKI K. (1986F): LP: A FORTRAN implementation of the simplex algorithm for linear programming, user's guide
Report, Mathematisches Institut, Universität Bayreuth, D-8580 Bayreuth

SCHITTKOWSKI K. (1987): Die Systementwicklungssprache SUSY
Report, Mathematisches Institut, Universität Bayreuth, D-8580 Bayreuth F.R.

SCHITTKOWSKI K. (1990A): Heuristic reasoning in mathematical programming
DFG-SP 'Anwendungsbezogene Optimierung und Steuerung', Report. No.209, Mathematisches Institut, Universität Bayreuth, D-8580 Bayreuth

SCHITTKOWSKI K. (1990B): Solving nonlinear programming problems with very many constraints
Report, Mathematisches Institut, Universität Bayreuth, D-8580 Bayreuth

SCHITTKOWSKI K. (1990C): NLPQLA: A nonlinear programming code with symbolic function input and automatic differentiation, user's guide
Report, Mathematisches Institut, Universität Bayreuth, D-8580 Bayreuth

SCHITTKOWSKI K. (1990D): DFNLPA: A nonlinear least squares code with symbolic function input and automatic differentiation, user's guide
Report, Mathematisches Institut, Universität Bayreuth, D-8580 Bayreuth

SCHRAMM H. (1989): Eine Kombination von Bundle- und Trust-Region-Verfahren zur Lösung nichtdifferenzierbarer Optimierungsprobleme
Dissertation, Mathematisches Institut, Universität Bayreuth

SHOR N.Z. (1977): Cut-off method with space extension in convex programming
Cybernetics, Vol.12, 94-96

TÖRN A., ZILINSKAS A. (1989): Global optimization
Lecture Notes in Computer Science, Vol. 350, Springer

MODELLING SYSTEMS WITH EXSPECT [1]

K.M. van Hee, L.J. Somers and M. Voorhoeve
Department of Mathematics and Computing Science
Eindhoven University of Technology

ABSTRACT

We describe a formal framework for modeling and prototyping complex systems, notably decision support systems. Our framework consists of a meta-model for discrete event systems, a language based upon this meta-model and a software environment for editing and validating system descriptions. The possibilities for using our framework for modelling and simulation are indicated and illustrated by a CIM example.

1. INTRODUCTION

Most automated systems that are built nowadays can be regarded as information systems, i.e. systems that collect, maintain and produce information about some other system called target system. A decision support system (DSS) is an information system focused at decisions that affect the target system. It can evaluate the effects of proposed decisions and generate decisions satisfying user-given criteria.

The term decision is used here for the unit of information sent to the target system. Its impact depends upon the granularity of the control process. A decision might be a simple control action (that influences the target system for a short period of time) or a set of such actions (e.g. a production plan for a batch of jobs), but it can also be a function that assigns actions to observed behaviour of the target system. In the latter case, a single decision may control the target system for an arbitrarily long period of time.

Designing a classical information system means automating an existing well-defined manual system. When designing a DSS, though, it is unwise to automate the existing (heuristic) decision processes entirely; care has to be taken in deciding which decision tasks can be automated. Many DSS projects in the past have failed by assigning too many tasks to the machine. The decision situation often proved more complicated than foreseen by the designers, rendering the automated procedures inadequate (cf. [Hee 89a]).

We describe a framework for the formal description and simulation of a wide variety of systems, called discrete event systems. These are characterized as a succession of states. This class of systems contains information systems as well as physical systems (e.g. robots).

Our framework plays a role in the requirements engineering phase of DSS design. Here, designers and decision makers (future DSS users) together try to establish the functionality of the DSS. The use of prototypes for this purpose is recommended. Experiments with the prototype can be

[1] Research participating in ESPRIT 2 project PROOFS

conducted, showing the strong and weak points of the prototype. With little turnaround time, the prototype can be adapted, until the users are satisfied with the functionality offered.

Prototypes of the DSS only are not always sufficient, though. The prototype experiments should be conducted under realistic but controllable circumstances. So the relevant parts of the target system should be simulated. Both tasks, prototyping of the DSS and simulation of the target system, can be performed by our framework, provided both the target system and the DSS can be modeled as a discrete event systems. The model of the target system should reflect its performance characteristics (namely the effects of decisions made by or through the DSS), while the model of the DSS should reflect its functionality.

Our framework thus integrates many activities (specification, prototyping and simulation) and aspects (data models, process models and process interaction) of DSS construction; moreover, it does so in a natural way close to intuition. It is possible to construct libraries of reusable components (model banks) to speed up the construction of DSS prototypes and target system simulation models. However, this paper stresses the way in which models are described and not how they are maintained and used (model management systems).

Our paper is organised as follows. In section 2, we introduce our framework. In section 3, we define its model, summarizing some properties. In section 4, we introduce its language.

In section 5, we describe a CIM example. The decision problem in this case is to provide a schedule for the execution of a given set of orders. In [Hee 91b] the DSS itself has been described; here we tackle the target system simulation and give the actual specification of a conveyor belt unit. This shows the compactness of specifications within the framework. We believe that the use of an integrated framework like ExSpect will improve the development of complex systems.

2. OVERVIEW OF THE FRAMEWORK

Some discrete event systems can be modeled as an automaton. Automata are characterized by a state space, input-output alphabet and transition function. Upon receiving input, the state of an automaton is modified and output is produced by applying the transition function to the old state and the received input. An expedient of this approach is Z (cf. [Hayes 87]); a high-level mathematical language is used to describe transition functions.

Automata are however static entities; it is of course possible to describe e.g. parallelism or temporal behaviour, but this has to be done explicitly. Our framework is essentialy dynamic; we describe a system as a network of automata that are communicating internally and with the outside world. Modeling systems as dynamic networks is very old; there exist a multitude of data flow diagramming techniques (e.g. [Yourdon 89]), although these techniques have no formal semantics.

We thus are led to distinguish the following three aspects of a discrete event system (reception of input and production of output are modeled as state transformations)

- the state spaces of components,
- the state transformations of components,
- the interaction structure.

Our model embodies these aspects; it is related to (coloured) Petri nets (CP nets, cf. [Jensen 87], for other Petri net variants cf. [Reisig 85]). Like in CP nets, triggers (tokens) have a colour and reside in typed channels (places). Processors (transitions) continuously consume and produce triggers. Unlike in CP nets, a colour has two components: a time stamp and a value. The consumption of triggers by a processor depends only upon their time stamps (lower time stamps have a higher priority) and is *globally* determined. The production of triggers depends only upon their values. This separation of concerns gives more clarity and better execution performance than in CP nets (where one can specify conditions upon the colours for token consumption), without sacrificing modeling power. We call our model the DES model and a system specified by it a DES. We can use Petri net theory to verify structural properties of systems modeled in our framework (cf. [Genrich 81]). Our model has at least the same power as DEVS [Concepcion 88].

Our language ExSpect is executable and thus allows prototyping and experimentation. It encourages the reuse of specified components and posesses an interface for the incorporation of external software. It has a functional, a dynamic and a structural part. The functional part is used to define types and functions: a many-sorted algebra. The type system consists of primitive types and type constructors to define new types. A sugared lambda calculus is used to define new functions from a set of primitive ones. The dynamic part of ExSpect uses types and functions to specify processors and channels and it defines their interaction structure. Finally, the structural part of ExSpect supports its use for large projects by modularization.

The state of a DES is the configuration of triggers in the channels. The state space of a channel is characterized by its type: the set of all multisets (bags) over this type. We thus specify state spaces by types, state transformations by functions and interaction structures by networks of processors and channels. A special kind of channels is called *stores*. These channels contain one and only one trigger. A processor that consumes a trigger from it must replace it immediately. This way of modeling corresponds to SADT [Marca 88].

We have developed a software tool to support the specification process. It consists of a graphical editor, a type checker that verifies the type correctness and an interpreter that simulates the specified system. The interpreter is connected to an asynchronous end-user interface. Decision makers, supported by the DSS prototype, can take part in simulating the target system and see the effects of their decisions.

Based on ExSpect, a logistic management game ("flight simulator") has been developed specifically for the training of decision makers [Flapper 90].

3. MODEL OF DISCRETE EVENT SYSTEMS

A DES consists of two kinds of components: *processors* and *channels* (transitions and places). To each channel corresponds a type (a set). A processor is connected to one or more input channels and zero or more output channels. To each association of an input channel to a processor a weight is attached (most weights equal 1). Channels are shared by processors. Channels contain *triggers* (tokens). A trigger has a *value* that belongs to the type of its channel and a real-valued *time stamp*. There may be more triggers in the same channel with the same value and time stamp. So a channel actually contains a bag of triggers.

At any moment a *transition* may occur, i.e. a change in the configuration of triggers in the channels (the *state*). (We attach a different meaning to the term transition than Petri net theory). Transitions occur instantaneously and are *executed* by processors. A processor p may execute if it is able to consume the right number of triggers from each of its input channels. This number must be equal to the weight of the input channel for p. The execution of a processor implies the consumption of the triggers from its input channels and the production of triggers in its output channels. The number and value of the produced triggers is a function of the values of the consumed triggers. An *event* is an assignment of triggers to a processor p such that p can execute. The *event time* of an event is the maximum of the time stamps of the triggers to be consumed. The *transition time* of a system in a certain state is the minimum of the possible event times. Being in a certain state, a system will select an event of which the event time equals the transition time and execute it, causing a state transition. The time stamps of produced triggers will be at least equal to the event time. It is thus clear that the transition times of successive events will be non-descending.

Formally, a DES is represented by the following components.

- A set P of processors,
- a set C of channels c, each with a set $V(c)$ of possible trigger values,
- a function I assigning to each processor a bag (weighted set) of input channels,
- a function O assigning to each processor a set of output channels,
- a set T of possible time stamps,
- for each processor p in P, a function f_p, satisfying the requirements below.

The domain of a function f_p is a set S of bags B of channel-trigger pairs. For any B in S, the number of pairs in B with channel c is equal to the weigth of c in $I(p)$. If all weights in $I(p)$ are 1, $I(p)$ becomes an ordinary set and S a set of functions B from channels in $I(p)$ to triggers (since each channel c occurs only once in a B).
The range of f_p is a bag of channel-trigger pairs such that the channels are in $O(p)$. Note that there is no weight restriction here; the number of triggers produced on each output channel is not fixed. This is the reason why $O(p)$ is a set and $I(p)$ a bag.
An invariant (pre- and post) condition for the functions f_p is that any trigger coupled to channel c has a value in the set $V(c)$. A postcondition is that the time stamp of any output trigger must be at least equal to the maximal time stamp of the input triggers.

We can derive from the above components a *transition system*, i.e. a state space $\mathcal{S}$ and a relation $\mathcal{R}$ giving for each state in $\mathcal{S}$ the set of possible next states (the *transition relation*). This is done as follows. $\mathcal{S}$ is the set of all bags of channel-trigger pairs $\langle c, t\rangle$, with t in $V(c)$. For any s in $\mathcal{S}$, we compute the possible events, i.e. subbags B of $\mathcal{S}$ and a processor p such that $f_p(B)$ is defined. We may say that p can execute or fire, caused by B. The event time of such an event is the maximal time stamp of the triggers in B. We construct the set $\mathcal{E}$ of possible events with minimal event time (the transition time). A next state is then computed by selecting a B, p pair from $\mathcal{E}$, subtracting B from $\mathcal{S}$ and adding $f_p(B)$ to the outcome.

The above formalization of the DES-framework has been elaborated in [Hee 89b]. It is even sligthly complicated further, since an event can consist of the simultaneous firing of more processors, thus allowing paralellism. However, a state transition caused by the such an event can be reached also by a sequence of single-processor transitions (serializability).

To represent a DES we use a diagram technique like for Petri nets. A diagram is isomorphic to an ordered graph containing the network of processors and channels (the first four components above). To such a diagram we must add a *type* for each channel and a *function* to each processor. Networks can be defined separately and used as a subnetwork in a larger network. It is thus possible to use a decomposition hierarchy (cf. [Huber 89]). A high-level DES diagram is very similar to a data flow diagram (cf. [Yourdon 89]).

In ExSpect, the computation of values of triggers is separated from the computation of their time stamps. The time stamps are computed by a delay depending on the values of the consumed triggers. This delay is added to the event time to obtain the time stamps of the produced triggers. When no delay is specified, the value 0 is taken. By not specifying delays, we have a timeless model; events are then ordered only by causality: triggers can be consumed only after production.

4. LANGUAGE OVERVIEW

As we remarked in the previous section, a DES diagram must be complemented by attaching types to channels and functions to processors. The definition of types and functions can be done in the functional part of our language ExSpect. Processors, channels and (sub)systems can be defined in the dynamic part of our language, graphically or by means of text.

Types are defined by means of type expressions, consisting of basic types and type operators. Functions are defined by means of expressions, built from basic constants and functions. We shall treat in this order basic types, type expressions, type definitions, expressions and function definitions. Then we move to the dynamic part and treat processor and system definitions. Channels are defined within a system. We do not treat modules; they are similar to modules in modern programming languages and affect the scope of definitions.

The basic types are `void`, `bool`, `num`, `real` and `str`. These correspond to the empty set, the booleans, the rationals, the floating point numbers and the strings, respectively. The basic type operators are *finite powerset* (denoted by a `$` prefix) and *cartesian product* (denoted by a `><` infix). If A and B are type expressions, then `$`A denotes the set of finite subsets of A and A `><` B denotes the set of pairs of objects, the first in A, the second in B. The type operator *mapping* (denoted by a `->` infix) is derived from set and cart. The type expression A `->` B denotes the set of mappings from A to B; a mapping is a finite set of pairs with different first components. Precedence is indicated by brackets.

The type definitions are represented as follows:

`type` *id* `from` *te*,

where *id* is an identifier and *te* a type expression. The following example illustrates some type definitions.

```
type coord from real><real;
type loc from coord->str;
```

A store of type `loc` can be regarded as a file containing the names of cities and their coordinates (longitude and latitude). The ExSpect type system is hierarchical; a type "inherits" all functions that can be applied to its supertypes.

Our set of basic functions includes all well-known set-theoretical, logical and numerical constants and functions. Actually only a few of them are truly basic; the others can be derived from them. Many of these functions are "sugared" to their customary symbolic infix or "circumfix" notations. For instance, the application of a mapping (to an element as well as to a set) is indicated by a dot infix. All binary function applications can be denoted in infix form. Expressions are built by constants, variables, function application and mapping construction. A mapping construction is an expression of the form

[*id* : *setexpr* | *expr*],

where *id* is an identifier, *setexpr* an expression denoting a set and *expr* an expression (probably containing *id* as parameter). Its meaning is the mapping $\lambda\, id \in setexpr \,:\, expr$.

Constant and function definitions are represented respectively as follows:

id := *expr* : *te*,

id [id_1 : te_1 , ... , id_n : te_n] := *expr* : *te*,

where the *ids* are identifiers, the *tes* type expressions and *expr* an expression. We give some examples.

```
min [x:real, y:real] := if x > y then x else y fi: real;
min [x:$real] := if rest(x)={} then pick(x)
                 else min(rest(x)) min pick(x) fi: real;
min [x: T->real] := min(rng(x)): real;
upd [x: T->S, y: T, z: S] :=
  [t: y ins dom(x)| if t=y then z else x.t fi]: T->S;
upd [x: T->S, y: T->S] :=
  [t: dom(x) union dom(y)|
    if t eltof dom(y) then y.t else x.t fi]: T->S;
```

The functions above are examples of basic functions defined in terms of still more primitive ones, c.q. `pi1`, `pi2`, (projections), `{}`, `ins`, `pick`, `rest`, `union` (resp. the empty set, insertion, picking an element from a set, the set without the picked element, set union), `dom` and `rng` (domain and range of mappings). `$[t:A|P]` is our notation for the subset of A where P holds. Some definitions are recursive and some *polymorphic*. A polymorphic definition uses *type variables* (`T`, `S`). Note the multiple definitions (overloading); they are allowed if no clashes occur. The `min` functions compute the minimum of two numbers, a set of numbers or a numerical mapping. The upd functions overwrite a mapping either by a specific value at a specific location or by a second mapping.

A library of mathematical functions has thus been constructed, which allows one to use the conventional mathematical notation to write expressions in. The main differences are that ExSpect does not allow quantification over infinite domains (in order to preserve executability) and that it requires ASCII characters only. We give some expressions in ExSpect with the "translation" in conventional mathematics.

ExSpect	Math
`$[t:A|P]`	$\{t \in A \mid P\}$
`all[t:A|P]`	$\forall t \in A : P$
`sum[t:A|E]`	$\Sigma t \in A : E$

Processor definitions have a header and contents. The header contains the processor name and its parameters, (channels and stores, sometimes values). The contents consists of concurrent (conditional) assignments of expressions to output channels and stores. A system is an aggregate of processors, channels and stores. Its definition header is similar to a processor header and the contents name the internal processors, subsystems, (initialized) channels and stores and describe the graph interconnecting them. Examples of processor and system definitions are given in the next section.

Definitions can be followed by a *where-part*, a list of definitions the scope of which is limited to the definition it follows. Where-parts can be nested; they belong to the structural component of ExSpect.

Future developments of the language include the integration with a semantic data model [Hee 91a] and (non-executable) Z-like high-level specifications.

5. EXAMPLE

Description:

This example is inspired by the 'KWEST' miniature factory built at the FAW in Ulm [FAW 90]. The factory consists of a number of processing and storage units, and a transport system connecting them. The main emphasis lies within the transport system.

The transport system consists of a large number of fixed and turnable conveyor belt units and some robot arms. Objects are taken from storage, undergo a series of operations by the processing units and then are stored again.

The conveyor belt units are connected, so that the objects have various routes through the factory. The following figure gives an impression.

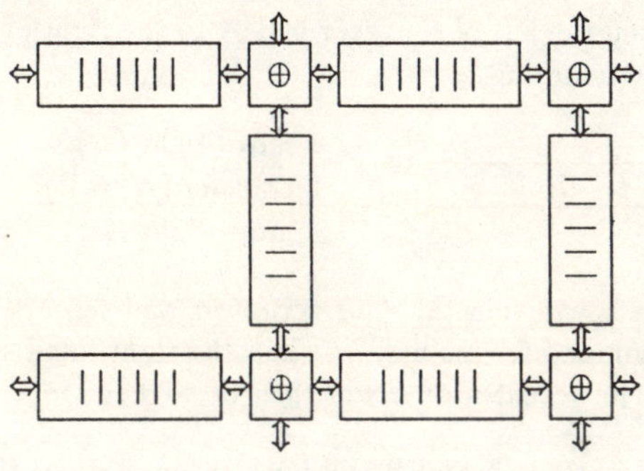

A scheduler decides what route the objects have to follow through the factory and in what order they have to be processed. The control module monitors the goings-on in the factory and implements the decisions of the scheduler. The interface between the actual factory and the controller consists of actuators and sensors.

The sensors detect e.g. the presence of an object at a specific location, or tell that an object has been grasped or released. The actuators cause the processing and transport units to start or stop performing a certain action.

For instance a fixed conveyor belt unit has an actuator to set it moving to the left or right or stop it. It has a sensor on either side; so it detects when an object has just entered the unit and when it is about to leave it.

The purpose of the miniature factory is to try out various scheduling and control algorithms. The factory has been built in hardware (Fischer-Technik), so many problems one encounters in reality (e.g. objects getting stuck or falling) are seen here too.

We describe here the design of the controller, and give hints to the way the simulation of the factory can be done in ExSpect.

Design of controller:

The controller has a schedule of tasks to be executed. It sends actuator signals and receives sensor signals. It is advisable to split the controller in a conceptual and a physical part. The conceptual part gives commands telling to perform some action (or step) and receives answers telling that some step has been performed successfully. The physical part performs the conversion between steps, units and actuator/sensor signals. Graphically this is represented as follows.

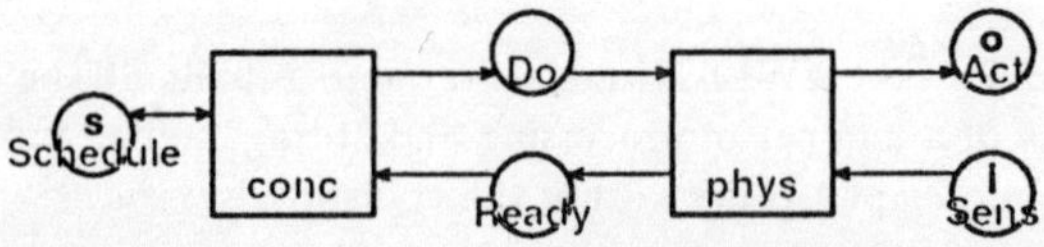

The same actuator or sensor signals can mean completely different things in a different context. So the physical part has its own stores that retain the context. Also, it takes care that no unit performs two steps at a time. It has its own queue of steps waiting to be performed.

A step corresponds with a set of active units, one or two actuator signals, a sensor signal indicating its end, and one or two actuator signals to be performed after its ending. For instance the transport of an object from the left of conveyor belt A to the right of conveyor belt B in the configuration below takes the following steps.

1 move right (A)
2 transfer (A to B)
3 move right (B)

The physical part possesses a conversion table for actuators and sensors. Starting step 1 above will result in an actuator command for moving A; when the right-hand sensor of A fires, it will report the step as finished. The actuator of A will then be told to stop.

The second step will then be started: A and B will both set in motion; the step will be finished when the left-hand sensor of B fires; A and B will be stopped. The third step will be started, telling B to move until its right-hand sensor fires.

Of course all this stopping and immediately restarting of conveyor belts is not very nice. The physical part should stop such a device with some delay; a restart within the delay period simply cancels the stop command.

By the division of the controller in two parts, we have achieved that we can model a schedule as a partially ordered structure of steps. Some steps have to precede other ones, but large parts of the schedule can be executed in parallel. The conceptual part can start a step as soon as its predecessors have finished.

Simulation:

Simulating the physical part plus the factory is also simple; for each step a malfunction probability has to be given and a probability distribution for its execution time. When a step is started, drawing a random number decides whether a malfunction is reported (which the user has to fix interactively) or whether a delay is drawn from the distribution; after this delay the step is reported as finished. Of course this simulation does not cover all possible error situations but for trying out scheduling strategies it suffices most of the time.

Simulating only the factory is a somewhat harder task. One way is to take the conceptual simulation and invert the conversion for the physical part of the control, but this does no add anything new. The best way is to simulate the real factory as it is built.

For each type of unit a special-purpose subsystem must be defined. These subsystems are installed, connected to the control module (via control channels) and to each other (via physical channels) if they can transfer objects to each other.

So for instance a conveyor belt unit has a sensor output, an actuator input and a physical input and a physical output pin at either end. It has a state indicating whether it is moving and in what direction and whether and where objects are present. A user channel is present for reporting errors.

When an actuator signal comes in, the belt starts or stops moving as prescribed. When an object is transferred at either end, the state is examined to determine whether the belt is moving in the right direction (if not, an error is reported). The next event (e.g. sensor firing) is forecast.

Every time the belts speed is altered, the position of the object is recorded. Forecast events will be ignored after a speed change and (if the belt keeps moving) a new event is forecast. When an event occurs, also a new event is forecast.

This definition describes a "continuous" belt. Since ExSpect is designed to describe discrete event systems, some elements of the belt definition may look tricky. Of course it is also possible to define a simpler "discrete" belt approximating the continuous one.

Implementation:

We give the ExSpect definition for the conveyor belt. A transport system consisting of a small number of conveyor belts has actually been simulated.

The architecture of a conveyor belt consists of a store for the last recorded position and one for the time of this recording. There are processors for the reception of an object at either end, for accepting actuator commands (speed changes), for event forecasting and for examining and (if correctly forecast) execution of forecast events. These last two processors are triggered by internal channels.

The architecture is graphically depicted by our editor as follows. For reasons of readability, all stores have been grouped together in a single store called 'STATE'.

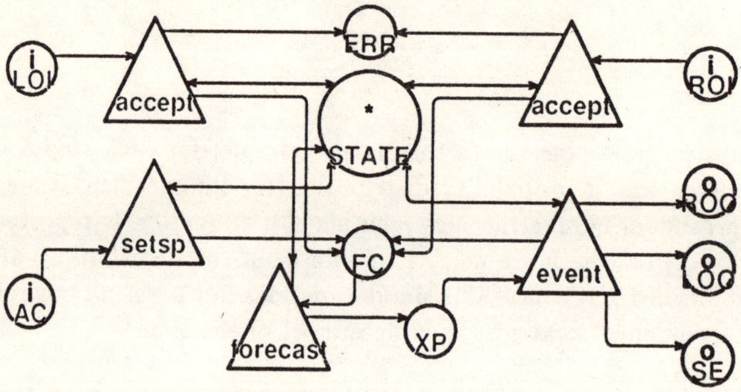

In textual format, the full definition is as follows. The same definition should be reused throughout, so a parameter 'ME' for identification is added.

```
-- imported from domain specific library
type obj in help1; -- objects to be transported
o: obj in help1;

-- imported from 1-dimensional physical library: position, speed, direction
type pos from real; -- position
nopos: pos in help2; -- indicates absence of object on belt
near [x: pos, y: pos] : bool in help2; -- x = y modulo float error
type speed from real;
newpos [x: pos, y: real, z: speed]: pos in help2;
  -- position of object starting at x with speed z after y time units
type dir in help2; -- direction
left: dir in help2;
right: dir in help2;
ok [x: dir, y: speed] : bool in help2; -- speed accords with direction

-- belt-specific constants; to be scaled
export sevpos := {<<0.0,''>>,<<0.1,'L'>>,<<0.9,'R'>>,<<1.0,''>>}: pos -> str;
  -- event triggering positions with sensor message; to be scaled
evpos := dom(sevpos): $pos;
ep [x: dir] := if x=left then min(evpos) else max(evpos) fi: pos;
export acsp := {<<'-',-1.0>>,<<'H',0.0>>,<<'+',1.0>>}: str -> speed;
  -- possible speeds with actuator commands

-- belt definition
export sys belt
  [in LOI: obj, ROI: obj, AC: str, out LOO: obj, ROO: obj, SE: str,
   val ME: str] :=
store CURSP: speed init 0.0,
store OLDP: pos init nopos,
store OLDT: real init -1.0,
store time: real in system,
channel FC: $void,
channel XP: pos,
```

```
channel ERR: str in user,
accept (in LOI, out FC, ERR, store CURSP, OLDP, OLDT, time, val ME, left),
accept (in ROI, out FC, ERR, store CURSP, OLDP, OLDT, time, val ME, right),
setsp (in AC, out FC, store CURSP, OLDP, OLDT, time),
forecast (in FC, out XP, store CURSP, OLDP),
event (in XP, out FC, LOO, ROO, SE, store CURSP, OLDP, OLDT, time, val ME);

-- belt processors
proc accept -- accepts object from either end (indicated by d)
  [in OI: obj, out FC: $void, ERR: str,
   store SP: speed, P: pos, T: real, time: real,
   val ME: str, d: dir] :=
if P = nopos and ok(d,SP) then T <- time, P <- ep(d), FC <- {}
else ERR <- ME cat 'not ready' fi;

proc setsp -- implements actuator commands
  [in AC: str, out FC: $void, store SP: speed, P: pos, T: real, time: real]
:=
if SP != acsp.AC and P != nopos
then P <- newpos(P,time-T,SP), T <- time, FC <- {} fi,
SP <- acsp.AC;

proc forecast -- forecasts new event: sensor or object output
  [in FC: $void, out XP: pos, store SP: speed, P: pos] :=
if SP != 0.0 then XP <- next delay (next-P)/SP fi
where
next := if SP > 0.0 then min($[t: evpos| t>P])
                    else max($[t: evpos| t<P]) fi: pos;
end;

proc event -- checks and executes forecast events
  [in XP: pos, out FC: $void, LOO: obj, ROO: obj, SE: str,
   store SP: speed, P: pos, T: real, time: real, val ME: str] :=
if XP near newpos(P,time-T,SP)
then if XP=ep(left)
     then ROO <- o, P <- nopos
     else if XP=ep(right)
          then LOO <- o, P <- nopos
          else SE <- ME cat sevpos.XP, P <- XP, T <- time, FC <- {}
fi   fi   fi;
```

The above definition is of a deterministic, ideal belt. A possible extension would be to introduce random disturbances in the belts motion and failure possibilities.

LITERATURE

Concepcion 88: A.I. Concepcion, B.P. Zeigler,
DEVS formalism: a framework for hierarchical model development,
IEEE Trans. Softw. Eng. 14 (1988) pp.228-241.

FAW 90: FAW Ulm, Annual Report '90, FAW Ulm 1990.

Flapper 90: S.D.P. Flapper, C. Noorlander,
A Flight Simulator for Logistic Managers and Planners,
Proc. 1990 Eur. Simulation Multiconference, Neuremberg, Germany, 1990.

Genrich 81: H.J. Genrich, K. Lautenbach,
System Modelling with high-level Petri Nets,
Theor. Comp. Sci. 13, (1981), pp.109-136.

Hayes 87: I. Hayes, Specification case studies, Prentice Hall 1987.

Hee 89a: K.M. van Hee, A. Lapinski, OR and AI approaches to decision support,
Decision Support Systems 4 (1989), pp.447-459.

Hee 89b: K.M. van Hee, L.J.A.M. Somers, M. Voorhoeve,
Executable specifications for distributed information systems,
in: E.D. Falkenberg, P. Lindgreen (eds.),
Information System Concepts: an In-Depth Analysis, North-Holland 1989.

Hee 91a: K.M. van Hee, P.A.C. Verkoulen,
Integration of a Data Model and Petri Nets,
in: Proceedings 12-th Conference on Petri Nets, to appear.

Hee 91b: K.M. van Hee, L.J.A.M. Somers, M. Voorhoeve,
A modeling environment for decision support systems,
Decision Support Systems 7 (1991), to appear.

Huber 89: P. Huber, K. Jensen, R.M. Shapiro, Hierarchies in Coloured Petri Nets,
in: Proceedings 10th Conference on Petri Nets, Bonn 1989.

Jensen 87: K. Jensen, Coloured Petri Nets,
in: G. Rosenberg(ed.), Petri Nets: central models and their properties,
Springer 1987 (LNCS 188), pp.248-299.

Marca 88: D.A. Marca, C.L. McGowan,
SADT: structured analysis and design technique, McGraw-Hill 1988.

Reisig 85: W. Reisig, Petri Nets, EATCS Monographs on Theoretical Computer Science,
Springer 1985.

Yourdon 89: E. Yourdon, Modern Structured Analysis, Prentice-Hall 1989.

Adress of the authors:
Eindhoven University of Technology
Den Dolech 2, P.O. Box 513
5600MB Eindhoven, The Netherlands

Experiences in Decision Support Systems

Peter J. VERBEEK
L+T Informatica
Luchthavenweg 54
P.O. Box 57010
5605 AA Eindhoven
The Netherlands

September 4, 1991

Abstract

The phenomenon of Decision Support Systems has only just emerged. Theory has hardly been founded and even practical guidelines are not yet available. In this paper a framework to structure the design of the product 'Decision Support System' is presented. This framework describes the functions that a DSS should offer to a planner, and explains why these functions are required. How the framework can be implemented is illustrated by the description of a Decision Support System built for a strategic manpower planning problem of airline pilots. Furthermore ideas on the design process are presented.

1 Introduction

Decision Support Systems

Only very recently the concept of Decision Support Systems (DSS) emerged (Keen (1981), Fisher (1986), Keen (1986), Sprague (1987)). It seems that there is a growing need for applications of DSS's (Van Hee (1984)). However, a theoretical basis for the characterization, design and development of DSS has hardly been established yet. On the other hand practical guidelines for when a DSS is appropriate, what it should offer and how a DSS should be developed, are not readily available either. Most practitioners do not have a development methodology suitable for the development of a DSS.

We present a framework to structure the functional design of the product 'Decision Support System'. The design *process* or *development* of a DSS will be adressed at the end of this paper. How the framework for the functional design presented can be implemented, is illustrated by a case study. OR algorithms will not be discussed here, nor will a full functional description of the system be given. The paper focusses on a practical framework for the design of a DSS. In the case study a system was designed to support strategic manpower planning of airline pilots at Royal Dutch Airlines (KLM).

Pilot Manpower Planning

Because of the rapid growth in the airline industry most airlines face an increasing need for qualified and experienced pilots. The strategic manpower planning problem essentially is the question of when to schedule transition training for pilots from one group of pilots to another and when to hire new pilots so as to minimize surplusses and shortages of pilots and training costs. The availability of pilots can be a crucial constraint in the ability to arrive at the most attractive flight schedule. Hence it may seriously influence the marketing planning of an airline. Because the airline market is extremely volatile (Hofton (1983), Espahbodi & Espahbodi (1984)) the ability to react quickly on a changing market becomes a requirement to survive. This requires flexibility in operations as well as a fast planning process. Therefore, an effective and efficient strategic manpower planning of pilots is of vital importance to an airline.

In section 2 several basic questions on DSS are presented; *why* they are needed, *when* they are appropriate and *what* they should offer. In section 3 the problem situation of the KLM case is described. In section 4 it is indicated why a DSS was an appropriate way of support for this case. In section 5 it is described *how* the framework presented in section 2, was used to build a DSS to support the KLM planning. In section 6 we describe the ideas on the design process of a DSS, that we developed based on the development experiences with DSS within KLM.

2 A View on DSS

There are many definitions of DSS. They range from very broad definitions to narrower ones. Broad ones say they are computer based tools used to support decision making (Keen (1986)) so that LOTUS 1-2-3 can be considered a DSS. A narrower one is for example the definition given by Sprague (1987) who considers a model-base as a vital element in a DSS. Our definition of a DSS is the one of Anthonisse et al. (1988), who prefer the term Interactive Planning System for their view on DSS.

Traditionally a DSS is described by defining its components; a data-base, a model-base and intermediate software that allows the user to handle the available data and models, (Turban (1988)). Instead of using the *components* of a DSS as a framework to structure the design of a DSS this paper will focus on the *functions* that a DSS should offer.

DSS: When and Why ?

Anthonisse et al. (1988) describe the characteristics they have in mind about the planner and the problem he has to solve:

> *"We assume that the user is a trained professional, knowledgable about his subject area but not necessarily familiar with the techniques of operations research and computer science. The planning situation he is facing is complex in at least two respects. First, the the objectives and constraints are numerous and difficult to quantify. That is, it is impossible to construct a model that precisely captures the real-life situation. Secondly, the process required to achieve an acceptable plan cannot be completely specified in advance. Even after the plan has been developed, it may be difficult to say which of the steps taken were directly relevant to the construction of the final plan".*

In fact they answer the question *When to develop a DSS ?*. They do not explicitly motivate *why* they have *these* characteristics in mind. We see these characteristics plus the existence of a *regularly reoccurring* planning situation as the initial conditions to make the development of a DSS worthwile. It will be pointed out why these conditions are needed to ensure that a DSS will be appropriate.

- *Regularity*
  Regularity in the planning situation is needed because otherwise it is not economical, both in terms of development time and money, to develop a DSS.

- *Skilled Planners*
  One view is that if this condition is not fulfilled one should develop an

"Automated Decision System" instead of a DSS or, usually better, replace the planners by skilled ones. On the other hand, one can also give the DSS capabilities that make it useful as a training instrument, (supposing that sufficient essential knowledge can be aquired and made available to users by the system).

- *Complexity*
  If a clear "recipe" of actions were available, describing the way to create an acceptable plan, it is sufficient to develop just an automatic plan generator following this recipe. The condition of goals and constraints to be numerous implies that it is unlikely that an optimal solution -or even a good one- is found without the support of (OR) models. On the other hand, the condition that goals and constraints are difficult to quantify implies that human judgement and experience are needed to achieve an acceptable plan.
  Complexity can be defined in a lot of ways. In addition to the two aspects mentioned, it could be that the problem has stochastic elements or that it includes NP-hard subproblems.

Functions of a DSS

In many complex decision situations formalized solution strategies (models) are a great tool to help solving decision problems. Among these one can think of the use of techniques from the fields of Operations Research/Management Science (optimization, descriptive models and simulation, statistics and forecasting, multiple criteria decision problems) as well as Artificial Intelligence (Knowledge- or Rule-based systems).

If it is already hard to *enumerate* all the relevant goals (criteria) and restrictions that an effective supporting tool must contain more than just formalized solution strategies is needed. We believe that a skilled professional planner has certain qualities that cannot be replaced by formalized solution strategies. He can use his creativity to find new solution strategies or adapt the trade-off between several criteria in changing circumstances. To create his plan he will use facts, judgements, experiences and expectations that an analyst would never be able to capture in an automated system. (Note: sometimes the planner himself acts as the analyst!). If only an automatic plan-generator is offered *many solutions cannot be reached* because a formal solution strategy is used. In addition in most decision situations it is not acceptable that the *responsibility* for the decision strategy is taken over by a machine. Responsibility means more than just the power to accept or reject a solution. Therefore, it can be concluded that a DSS should aim at an optimal combination of the qualities of both formalized solution strategies and a human problem solver.

According to the ideas described above, we used the following framework for the design of a DSS, grouped into four functions that should be offered:

- *Manipulation of a Plan*
  The system should at least support the traditional solution strategy of the planner i.e. he must always be able to build a plan taking *all* decisions *himself.* In this way the planner can use his own judgements and experiences to find his way to a solution. In the same spirit he should always be able to change any plan regardless how it was created.
  Because the planner should be able to play an important role in the solution strategy the man-machine communication should be optimal. This implies that effort must be devoted to spot functionalities convenient for the planner.

- *Representation of a Plan*
  To be able to perform meaningful manipulations of a plan it is important to provide the planner with representations of the current state of a plan. The representations should be such that they provide insights to the planner and stimulate his creativity. Especially graphical representations can be helpful because "A picture can say more than a thousand words" (this saying is especially true for numbers! (Bell (1985), Benbasat & Dexter (1985)).

- *Evaluation of a Plan*
  To support the planner on his path to reach an acceptable solution it is obvious that we need to provide him with a set of possibilities to evaluate the quality of the plan in its current state. The quality is defined by a score on the relevant criteria. Spotting these criteria requires careful analysis of aspects that determine the value of a certain plan to the planner.
  We think that evaluation functions are very important in a DSS for two reasons:

  1. *Multicriteria Decision Situations*
     As OR practitioners we often ask ourselves the question: What is the best possible plan ? Unfortunately in most planning situations *many* goals or criteria for a best plan can be defined. Sometimes we are lucky in the sense that we can aggregate the criteria in a meaningful way by defining an appropriate cost function. In many situations however, a multicriteria decision problem is not effectively supported by automating the trade-offs made by a human decision maker in an aggregated "cost" function. (Note: In many practical cases the assumptions needed to make weighting appropriate are too strong, (Hobbs (1985), Roy (1971)).
  2. *Limitations of Modelling*
     Many years of OR practice have learned that it is at least rather optimistic to believe that all relevant constraints and goals can be incorporated in one plan-generating algorithm, (Ackoff (1960), Shepardson (1985)). In addition it can sometimes be very difficult to

incorporate a new kind of constraint, variable or goal in such an algorithm. The score on a criterion as well as the degree of violation of constraints can often be evaluated easily.

Therefore we should provide the planner with several insightful representations of the score of a plan on the relevant citeria. The evaluation of a plan on several criteria also allows the planner to make a final choice between alternative plans based directly on his own preferences.

- *Generation of a Plan*
  The qualities of formalized solution strategies can be exploited in the automatic generation of a plan according to an algoritm. This may concern a complete plan in which all decisions are made, but it may also include strategies for subproblems that can be very useful in supporting the planner on his path to a solution. One may also consider the function to complete an incomplete plan, e.g. the planner makes some crucial decisions himself and uses some algorithm to complete the plan. So, in fact there can be a whole spectrum in between the extremes of a purely "manual" strategy and a purely "automatic" strategy.
  Very often formalized solution strategies cannot cope with all aspects of the problem that the planner can make explicit to the analyst. Therefore it is likely that in many cases several strategies or models are appropriate, covering different aspects of the problem.

3 Case Description

3.1 The Manpower Planning Problem

General
In this section the pilot manpower process at KLM will be described. The planning process is triggered by the staff Bureau of Planning & Research that provides new fleet plans for the future. The strategic planning involves scenario analyses with a planning horizon of ten years long. In manpower planning we usually work with a number of (disjunctive) groups of personnel. In the KLM case groups are called seats and they are identified by a combination of a certain type of aircraft and a function in the cockpit (e.g. a Captain B747). Some aircraft types have three pilot cockpit functions; captains, first officers and second officers, but most do not have a second officer function. In each seat a number of pilots is available -Supply- and there is a certain Demand for pilots to execute the flight schedule and other tasks.

Supply
Pilots can only contribute to the supply of one seat. Pilots can work full-time or part-time. In general pilots retire at the age of 56, but early retirements

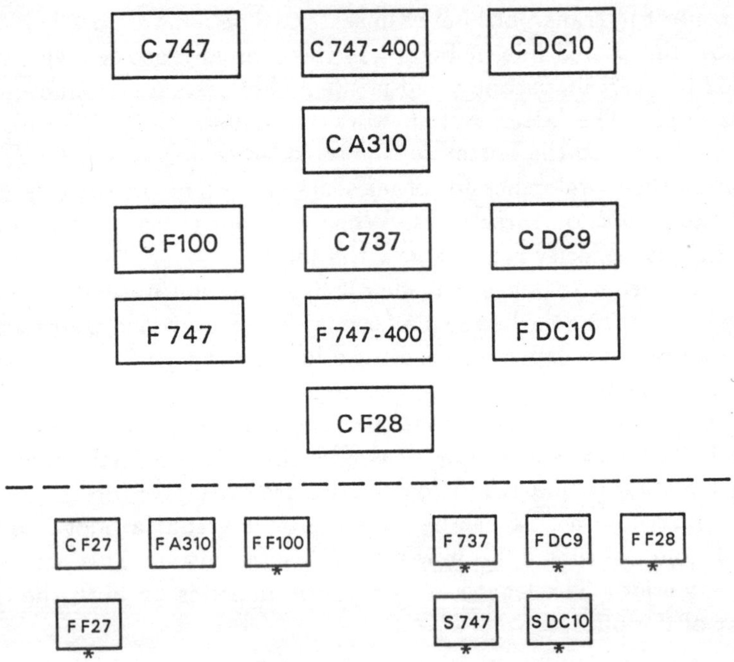

Figure 1: Seat Ranking

are allowed as well as a later retirement (up to 58). The supply is occasionally reduced by attrition.

Demand

The demand for pilots consists of requirements for production (performing the flight schedule) and other requirements. These other requirements include desk duties, recurrent training, instruction, vacation, sickness, and "crew-management" courses. The demand can be grouped into several categories. The *size* of demand is a constant plus a percentage of the number of pilots available in a given seat.

Some of the requirements -for instance vacation- are not a priori assigned to a given period; a decision is taken by the planner on how to spread these requirements over a specified set of time periods. In the sequel these decisions will be referred to as the allocation of "flexible" demand. At KLM some requirements must be allocated in the summer season, some in the winter season and some within a year.

Transitions

The seats can be ranked by decreasing salary as shown in Figure 1. New hires from outside the company are only allowed in the lowest seats (marked with * in Figure 1).

With respect to transitions between seats two systems are used: in the lowest seats (below the dotted line in Figure 1) the company decides which pilot will be assigned to a certain vacancy, and in the higher seats a system of preferential bidding is used. The latter system works as follows. All pilots entering the company are added to the bottom of the so called seniority list. Once a year all pilots express their preference for other seats on a form. In the sequel this will be referred to as *bids* on these seats. When a vacancy occurs, the bidding pilot with the highest seniority ranking gets the job.

Most pilots seem to make a trade-off between waiting longer for a bigger promotion or accepting earlier a smaller one. Their decisions are based on their own preferences, their expectations on the future supply of vacancies and their estimate of the actions of their competitors.

A concern for the planners is that the time that the pilots spend in a certain seat should not be too short. One reason is that the required experience is at stake and the other is that transition courses are expensive (up to 125,000 USD a course). Therefore a rule has been agreed saying that a pilot has to stay a minimum amount of time in his new seat after a transition. This period is called the Binding Period. The length of this period depends on both the "old" and "new" seat of the pilot.

Transition Training

When a transition is needed a pilot has to attend a course program of about three months in order to qualify him for the new job. The course program that has to be attended depends on both the old and new seat of a pilot. During a transition course the pilots are in general not available for production. However, pilots trained to become a captain are productive as first officers during a part of their training. During the training the pilots also need a certain amount of instructor and simulator time. These two resources, however, have limited capacities. The restriction on simulator time for example, implies that it is not possible to have more than a fixed number of pilots in training simultanuously for any seat of the same type of aircraft. The instructors are regular pilots qualified as instructor and must be substracted from the available amount of manpower. For any course an instructor can be either a captain or a first officer. The number of available instructors is not a constraint for the strategic planning.

Results of the Planning Process

The result of a planning session consists of a series of decisions:

- the number of transitions between seats and the period at which they are scheduled
- the number of new pilots hired for each period
- the amount of instruction tasks assigned to a seat for a certain period
- the amount of flexible demand allocated to each period for each seat

These decisions are taken so as to minimize surplusses and shortages of pilots and training cost. For most airlines the prevention of shortages is by far the most important.

The Reaction Lag
Because of the preferential bidding system and the fact that in general pilots want to move upwards in the hierarchy, it may take as much as seven transitions to replace a retiring pilot in a top seat and keep all other seats at a constant level. If no surplus of pilots is available along this "chain", this means a reaction time-lag of almost two years.

3.2 History in Support

The problem of strategic manpower planning of pilots is almost as old as the airline industry. The first publications of OR contributions appear in the early sixtics when the Airline Group of IFORS was founded. The interest in this particular problem has been rising recently (Gershkoff (1989)). This is probably due to the rapid growth of the airline market and the fact that most airlines see their ambitious growth plans frustrated by the lack of qualified pilots in the right place and time. At the same time the recognition of DSS and the awareness of the differences with a classical OR approach is emerging among airline OR practitioners (Johanson (1982), Pean & Odier (1987), Chevrinais & Thibault (1988) & Zarate (1989) and the references mentioned by Etschmaier & Mathaisel (1985)).

The literature on manpower planning describes almost exclusively the so called Push and Pull models. Push models are based on Markov theory and suppose static transition probabilities between groups of personnel. Pull models are based on a desirable level of supply and probabilities that describe the choice between delivering groups. Both types of models are not suitable for this problem, the main reason being that the transition probabilities are not stable and hard to predict (Van der Kuilen (1989)). The source of the instability stems from the small size of the groups and the fact that the transition process depends on the behaviour of individual pilots.

The available literature concerning applications on this problem is reviewed briefly in Verbeek (1988). Probably for competitive arguments, most of the papers do not explicitly give a formulation of the models that were developed. Mixed Integer models based on groups of pilots (i.e. non individual) were implemented at United Airlines and American Airlines. These models are solved by a LP code and some rounding procedures. To produce a realistic plan the transition patterns have to be "realistic" which can be very different from "optimal". Therefore a group-based MIP formulation must contain restrictions specifying a division between delivering seats, e.g. for seat x 30 % will come from seat y etc. So this type of models also have the main disadvantage of the Push and Pull models.

Another observation is that the tools that have been built for this problem up to now are all in the classical tradition, in the sense that they merely attempt to automate decisions rather than support them.

4 Why does KLM need a DSS ?

The tools that the planners currently have available to support their planning process did not satisfy their needs. As a consequence they wanted a new tool. The goals to be achieved by a new tool are described in the next section. The conditions that suggest the development of a DSS, as described in section 2, are fulfilled:

1. The strategic manpower planning problem for pilots is indeed a regularly reoccurring planning situation. At KLM, planning activities in this area go back to 1961.
2. The strategic manpower planning problem for pilots is a complex problem:
    - Thousands of variables, parameters and constraints have to be taken into account.
    - Some constraints are "soft" in the sense that they might be violated a "little bit". However, the planners are not able to quantify a priori the "little bit".
    - Some of the relations between the variables and parameters cannot be expressed in a nice mathematical form.
    - With some approximations we formulated several models to describe the problem (Verbeek & Kolen (1988), Verbeek (1988) and Van der Kuilen (1989)). These models gave us insight in the complexity of the actual problem.
    - More than one criterion is important in defining a most preferred plan.
3. The planners are skilled professionals at their domain. They have a vast knowledge of the problem and years of experience in producing plans.

5 Description of the Strategic Manpower Planning System

The Decision Support System for the strategic manpower planning problem of KLM pilots was called CAPTAINS. CAPTAINS is organized in three parts:

- a data preparation part

- (interactive) planning support
- a reporting part

In this section first some general information will be given and briefly the preparation part will be described. After that a description of the actual planning support is given. The reporting part of the system will not be discussed in this paper.

5.1 General Description

Goals

Two goals were defined for the development of CAPTAINS:

1. *Improvements in effectivity*
   Effectivity of a plan is defined here as how good a given plan "scores" on certain defined goals (these are in fact the criteria on which a plan is judged compared to others).
   - The goal is to generate better plans with a combination of ***support*** from automated algorithms plus an appropriate level of ***interaction*** with the planner.
   - A fast planning process allows several plans to be created for one scenario. By evaluation and selection a higher degree of effectivity is expected.
2. *Improvements in efficiency*
   Efficiency of a planning process is defined here as the effort that is needed to produce an acceptable plan. This may be measured in troughput time and employee costs. The goal is to speed up the planning process as much as possible to increase flexibility. The planning process should be fast enough to respond to questions of the management in such a time- span that the options for action are reduced as little as possible.

User Interface

The user-interface of CAPTAINS is basically menu driven. The planner selects items in a menu by pointing at them with a mouse. These menus can either be the well known list of items with a box around it or any distinct part of the screen ("special menus"). These special menus are conveniently indicated by color, brightness or lines. The several different screens have no compulsory order. For each screen it was determined which screens should be reachable directly from that screen, leaving as much freedom for the planning strategy as possible.

Scenarios and Plans

CAPTAINS has a data preparation part and a planning part. In general, a *plan* can be defined as a series of decisions. In this case a plan is defined as a series of oriented transitions between pairs of seats allocated to a time period, a series of flexible demands allocated to a time period for each seat, and a series of instruction requirements allocated to a seat and time period. In the data preparation part all relevant data are prepared for the actual planning. Such a set of basic data will be referred to as a *scenario*.

Planning Preparation

In the preparation phase the planner may create, copy, modify or delete scenarios. In this phase all database functions reside as well as functions to select a given (or new) scenario and (possibly) an existing plan for the planning phase. In the preparation phase it is possible to add, delete, change, inspect or print the data. A scenario consists of a description of the seats and seat-related data, a description of the possible transitions and their training programs, the production requirements, parameters to compute the additional requirements, individual personnel data, general personnel data, parameters required for plan generating models and data required for evaluations.

5.2 The Planning Phase

The planning phase will de described along the four functions of a Decision Support System; Representation, Manipulation, Evaluation and Generation.

Representation of a Plan and Working Style

When the choice "Planning" has been made in a higher menu the *General Year Screen* appears which shows a matrix with colored boxes. The colored boxes indicate the balance between supply and demand for all seats for each of the 10 planning years. A box will be red in case of a "serious" shortage, green in case of a "serious" surplus and a neutral color when the balance is in between. The screen has a menu-bar containing the options *Parameters* which allows the planner to change his definition of a serious shortage or surplus and a *Calculate* option to generate automatically a whole plan. It is possible to "zoom in" on the situation in each seat for twelve months of a selected year. If one of the colored boxes in the matrix is selected, the *Basic Seat Screen* appears for the selected year and seat (see Figure 3). In the Basic Seat Screen the situation of one seat is shown for twelve months. The balance between supply and demand is given in a bar-graph using the same colors as in the General Year Screen. Below the graph a table with information on several variables is given. A second table provides information on the decision variables. These decisions can be manipulated directly from this screen as described in the next section. The option Calculate in the menu-bar contains the options *Return* and *Parameters* as before, *Calculate* which contains a set of "partial" generators here (as opposed to the generation of a complete plan). The menu-bar also offers the *Evaluate* option. Because of the fact that a transition between seats implies that the situation in two seats

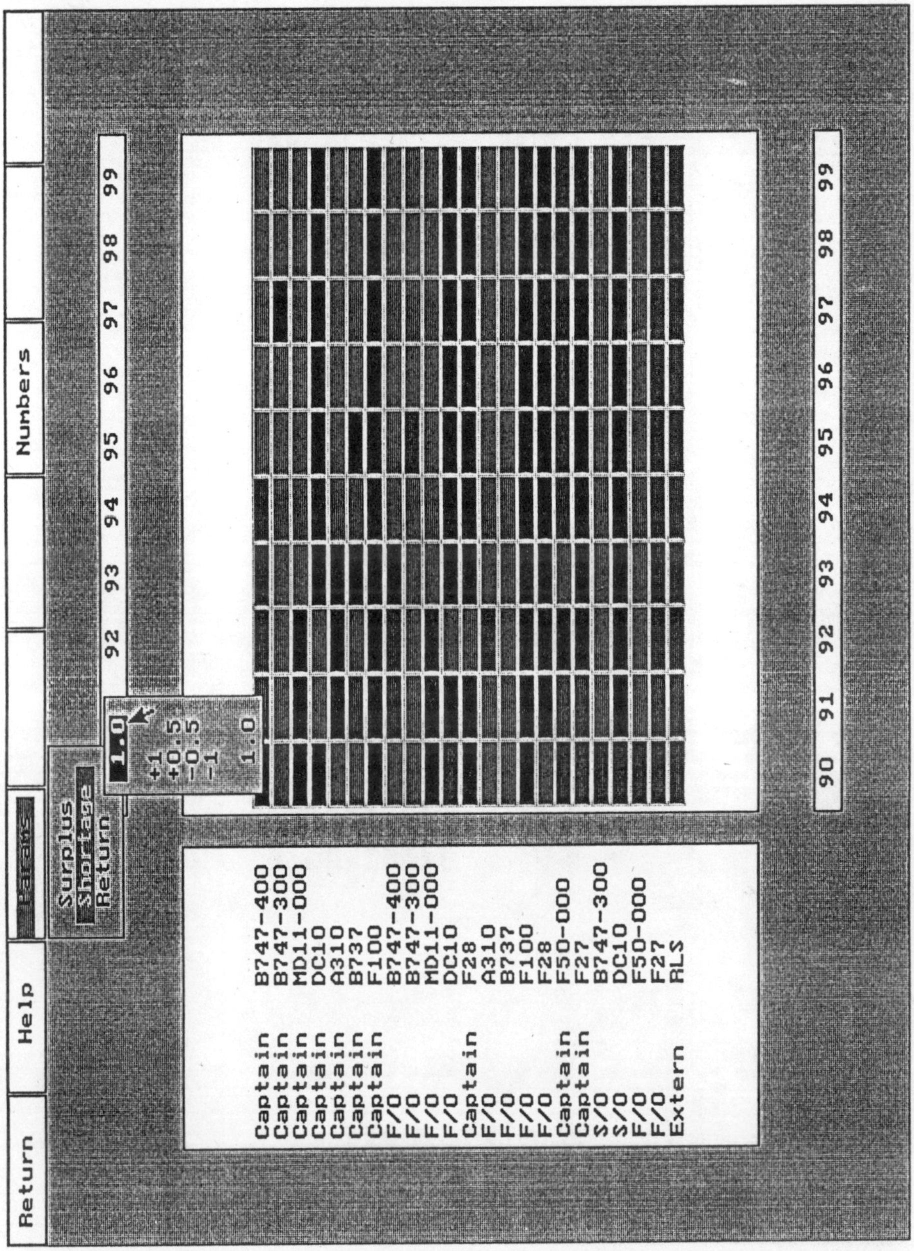

Figure 2: The General Year Screen

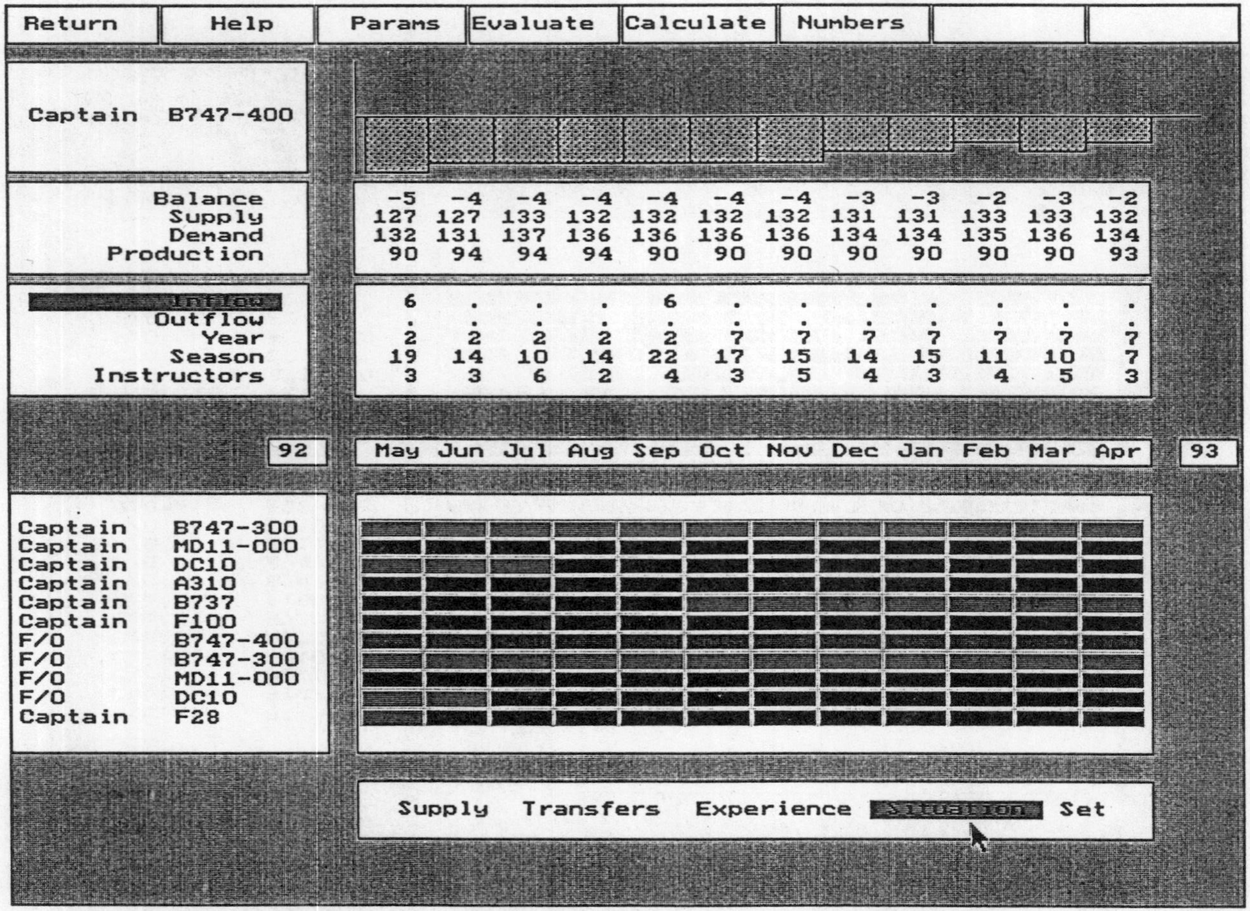

Figure 3: The Basic Seat Screen

will change, it is possible to get a second Basic Seat Screen at the same time. (Note: this is also convenient because several considerations apply to a captain and a first officer seat of one aircraft type).

Manipulation of a Plan

General
Any given plan, finished or not, can be manipulated by making new decisions or removing existing ones. Decisions that can be manipulated are the values of all decision variables shown in the Basic Seat Screen: transitions (*Inflow* or *Outflow*), allocation of flexible demand per year (*Year*) and per season (*Season*) and the allocation of instructors (*Instructors*).

Inflow
When the planner selects Inflow the Basic Seat Screen will move to the upper screen area and at the lower screen area a list of seats (sources) appears. If an Inflow-value for a specific period was selected, a list of possible "delivering" seats for transitions towards the selected seat appears. The *Time Dependent Seat List* provides information on these seats. The information is given for the month in which a pilot would have to leave his old seat. The information consists of the balance between supply and demand, the size of the seat, the experience level, the number of leavers, and the number of leavers that went to the selected inflow seat. Based on the information provided the planner can choose a delivering seat. If a seat name is selected this implies that a source for a possible transition has been chosen and the Basic Seat Screen for this seat appears. When two seats are shown on the screen and an Inflow-value is selected in the upper seat a small "Action Menu" appears, to add or delete a number of transitions from the lower to the upper seat, (see Figure 5).

When the planner selects the word Inflow from the Basic Seat Screen at the upper screen area the *Time-Independent-Seat- List* appears in the lower screen area. This is also a list of possible sources for transitions towards the selected seat providing information on them. The difference with the Time- Dependent list is that the information is given for twelve months instead of one. Only one of the five aspects mentioned above is shown because of space limitations. The others can be selected by a menu-bar. This list can provide a more dynamic view on a certain aspect.

Again, if a seat name is selected this implies that a source for a possible transition has been selected and the Basic Seat Screen for this seat is shown in the lower screen area. When an Inflow- value is selected the small action menu appears as described above.

Outflow
Outflow works very similar to Inflow according to the principle of consistency.

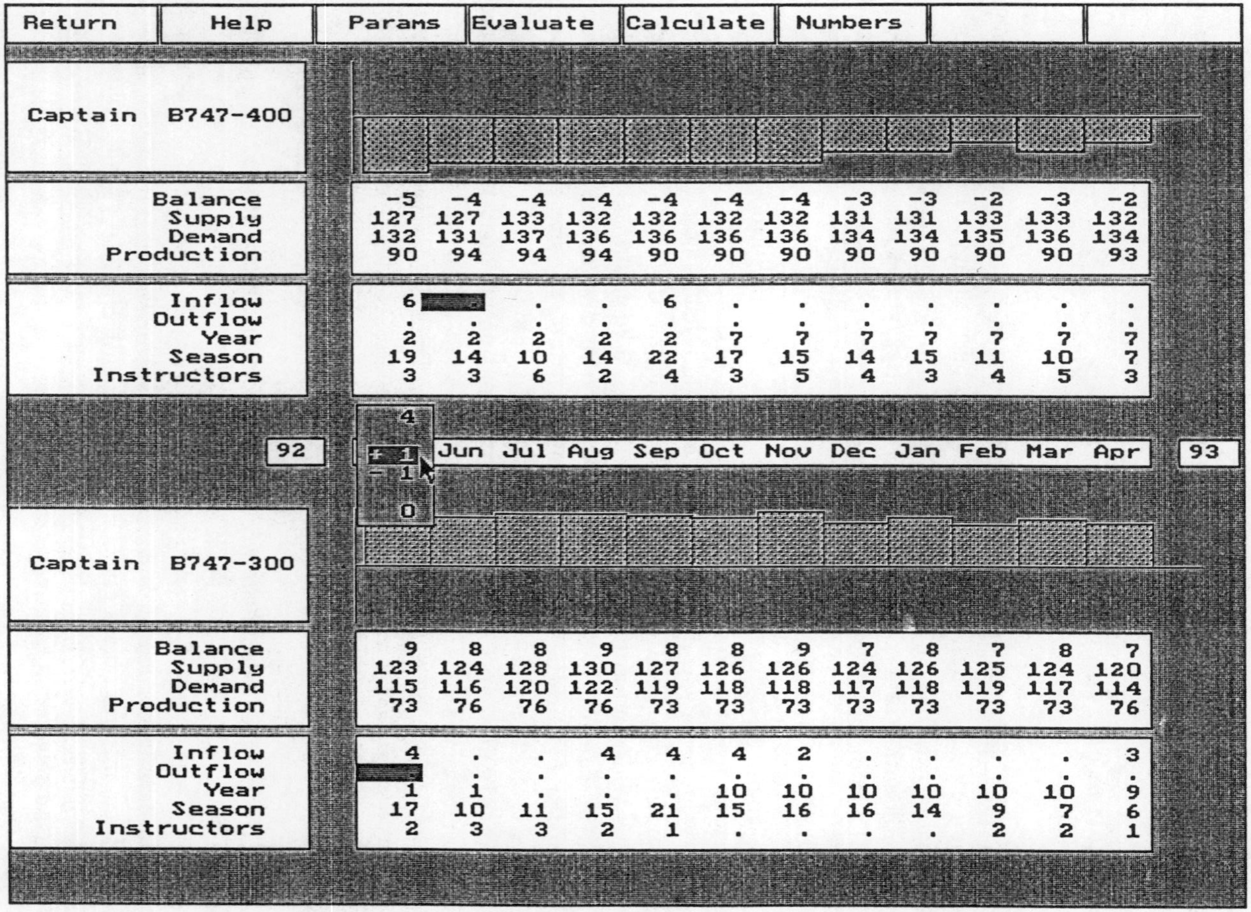

Figure 4: Scheduling a Transition

When Outflow is selected in the upper screen area the Basic Seat Screen for this seat moves to the lower screen area (and vice versa for selecting Inflow in the lower screen area).

Year/Season

By selecting the Year (or Season) option this line gets an "active" color and the planner has to select two time periods to get an action menu to allocate flexible demand between those two periods.

Instructors

By selecting Instructors, the Basic Seat Screens for the captains seat and first officer seat of the current aircraft type will be shown in the upper and the lower screen area respectively. Like the Year option, an action menu will appear when a period is selected.

Generation of a Plan

By selecting the Calculate option the planner gets a menu in which several algorithms to solve (sub)problems are presented. Before discussing the generation of a whole plan first describe several subproblems are described. For some of the (sub)problems mathematical programming can be used. In the first version of CAPTAINS however, only heuristics have been implemented.

Flexible Demand

A certain amount of flexible demand has to be allocated for each seat within each year and season. The Flexible demand option in the Calculate menu reallocates the flexible demand in a seat automatically. The problem of how to allocate the flexible demand so as to minimize the cost of shortages and surplusses can be formulated as follows:

MINIMIZE:

$$\sum_{t=1}^{12} C_m * M(t) + C_p * P(t)$$

SUBJECT TO:

$$B(t) - P(t) + M(t) + F_s(t) + F_y(t) = 0 \quad \text{for } t = 1..12 \tag{1}$$

$$\sum_{t=1}^{5} F_s(t) = A_s \tag{2}$$

$$\sum_{t=6}^{12} F_s(t) = A_w \tag{3}$$

$$\sum_{t=1}^{12} F_y(t) = A_y \tag{4}$$

$$P(t), M(t), F_s(t), F_y(t) \in Z_0+ \tag{5}$$

where B(t) is a constant indicating the original balance between supply and demand, P(t) idicates a surplus, M(t) a shortage, $F_s(t)$ the allocated seasonal demand and $F_y(t)$ the allocated yearly demand. The constants A_s, A_w and A_y specify the amount to be allocated in the summer season, winter season and year respectively. The constants C_m and C_p give the cost per unit shortage or surplus. In practice the planner also prefers a smooth allocation over time. This subproblem can be solved as a minimum cost network flow problem.

Fill Inflow
If shortages occur in a certain seat and year, the planner may want to avoid them by adding transitions automatically according to a Fill Inflow algorithm. Adding transitions means that the need for vacancies has to be determined as well as the seats where the candidates come from. Given the allocation of the flexible demand, the determination of the need for vacancies can be modelled as follows:

MINIMIZE:

$$\sum_{t=1}^{12} C_m * M(t) + C_p * P(t)$$

SUBJECT TO:

$$B(t) - P(t) + M(t) - I(t) = 0 \qquad for\ \ t = 1..12 \tag{6}$$

$$I(t) \leq CAP(t) \tag{7}$$

$$P(t), M(t) \in Z_0+ \tag{8}$$

$$I(t) \in N \tag{9}$$

where I(t) is the number of transitions towards the seat and CAP(t) is the inflow capacity. This subproblem can be solved as a minimum cost network flow problem. However, when a transition is added the balance in the delivering and receiving seat will change. So it is clear that the determination of the number of vacancies and the allocation of flexible demand are related. Combining these two subproblems in one formulation leaves us with a mixed integer problem, where the matrix is not totally unimodular (Verbeek (1988)). In CAPTAINS the combined problem is solved by a heuristic. The planner has the option whether or not to work with a restricted capacity. For the determination of the delivering seats a simple decision rule is used. This rule is based on the size of the possible delivering seats and their relative position in the hierarchy.

Instructors
The allocation of the instruction tasks to the captains or first officer seat can also be done automatically. This subproblem can be modelled as follows:
MINIMIZE:

$$\sum_{s=1}^{2}\sum_{t=1}^{12} C_m * M(s,t) + C_p * P(s,t)$$

SUBJECT TO:

$$B(s,t) - P(s,t) + M(s,t) - INS(s,t) = 0 \qquad (10)$$
$$for\ t = 1..12\ ,\ \ s = 1..2$$

$$\sum_{s=1}^{2} INS(s,t) = AMINS(t) \qquad (11)$$
$$for\ t = 1..12$$

$$\sum_{t=1}^{12} INS(1,t) - f * \sum_{t=1}^{12} INS(2,t) = 0 \qquad (12)$$

$$P(t), M(t), INS(t) \in Z_0+ \qquad (13)$$

where INS(s,t) is the amount of instruction tasks in seat s at time t, AMINS(t) is the amount of instruction tasks for period t and f is a factor that specifies a division of instruction tasks between the two seats for a year. This subproblem can be solved with a LP algorithm.

A whole plan
We formulated a mixed integer model based on individuals, (Verbeek (1987)) but the size was too big to be solved with any commercial software (Note: currently 19 seats, 120 months and 900 pilots). Because of the enormous influence of the bidding system we developed a heuristic approach based on simulation of pilot behaviour and "local" optimization (Verbeek (1988)). With local we mean solving one-seat subproblems. Because it is based on individuals it is easy to handle individual candidate selection criteria such as experience. Interactions with the model are possible by letting the planner define (a part of) the vacancies or transitions himself. This heuristic has been implemented in Version 1 of CAPTAINS.

We also developed a Network Flow formulation to give the planners the opportunity to analyze the alternative possibilities and cost when the bidding system may be violated, (Verbeek & Kolen (1988)). This model will be incorporated in Version 2 of the system.

Evaluation of a Plan

If the Evaluation option is chosen a menu appears in which a list of possible evaluations is shown. Some evaluations concern one seat for one year but scrolling to other time periods or seats is possible. The evaluation screens can also be printed. Graphical as well as alpha-numeric representations (tables) are used whatever seemed the most convenient *to* and *for* the planner.

Among the evaluations offered are the following:

- Mutation Matrix
  This is a table for all seats in which the values of the following variables are shown per year: Gross Supply at the start of the year, Retirements, Attrition, Transitions Out and Transitions In.

- Transition Matrix
  This is a matrix that gives all transitions in one year grouped per "From-To" combination as well as row and column totals.

- Seat Survey Table
  This is a table that gives the values of all parts of the supply and demand as well as their totals and the balance for twelve months of one seat.

- Flexible Demand Graph
  This option gives for one seat three bar-charts above each other with a common time axis of twelve months. The upper chart gives the amount of seasonal flexible demand allocated, the middle one the allocation of the yearly flexible demand and the lower gives the balance between supply and demand. The planner can evaluate whether the allocation of a specific flexible demand is not too extreme and also whether it is effective with respect to the balance between supply and demand.

- Experience Development Graph
  This is a graph in which the number of experienced pilots is plotted over time as a percentage of the total number of pilots in a seat. In the graph a line is shown for each seat of one aircraft. If the experience drops below the critical level defined by the planner the relevant part of the line is shown in red.

- Training Capacity Graph
  This is a bar-graph in which the amount of simulator capacity required is plotted against the available capacity over time. The graph shows the capacity for one aircraft. If more capacity is required than available the relevant part of the graph is shown in red.
  Optionally the planner can get each bar of the graph splitted up into capacity needed for the captains, first officer and second officer seat shown in slightly different colors.

6 Development Process

It has been argued by several authors that established methods for developing Information Systems in general are inadequate for developing DSS. We tried to develop ideas on this design process by carrying out several DSS projects. In Verbeek (1991) we give a full description of the development process of the CAPTAINS system, as well as an evaluation of the development process. In Verbeek (1991) the same is done for another system. Based on experiences with these two systems we developed the following ideas about the design process of DSS. The following list must be seen only as a collection of ideas, not (yet) as an attempt to describe an approach of developing DSS. To achieve that goal we should first collect more case study material, then develop a design method and then test it against a sufficient number of cases.

The list below is grouped into ideas on project initiation, project organization, project management, working method, conditions and resources and communication.

1. **Project Initiation**
   - *recognition of DSS*
     We believe that DSS is different from an 'ordinary' MIS and that certain situations are supported more effectively by a DSS. Therefore, it is very important for the developers to recognize the special character of the situation that they are asked to support. Early recognition is also important because in developing a DSS, a special development methodology is required.
   - *risk*
     DSS projects belong to the category 'high risk-high payoff'. The project must be organized accordingly.
2. **Project Organization**
   - *structure and responsibilities*
     From the developer's side as well as the user's side there must be very clear responsibilities for making decisions. It is crucial that this decision making structure functions smoothly and has enough commitment from higher management. The project leader(s) must control project quality with respect to planning (efficiency and effectivity) as well as communication, and must be responsible for taking the actions needed. Often, the user's organization has problems to make enough time available for system development since regular tasks must be fulfilled. If it is not possible to reserve enough time (and it should not be underestimated!), an external user project leader should be added to the

user organization. This functionary is directly responsible for quality control of the project from the user's side.

- *user involvement*

  A DSS project should be carried out with considerable user involvement, but in general they should not be the actual designers. In this way, the responsibility for the quality of the design is clear.

- *developers team*

  It is very important that the developers team:

  * includes all required skills for a project
  * has clear individual responsibilities
  * functions as a whole: the participants must have enough knowledge of each other's specialties to have a good idea what can be achieved together
  * has continuity
  * has experience in developing DSS.

3. Project Management

- *trade-off*

  A project planning tries to estimate delivery time and resources needed for a specified product quality. It often is a contract between user organization and developer organization. It is important to note that there often is a trade-off between delivery time, resources required and product quality. The responsible project leader(s) should be conscious of this trade-off in case deviations from the planning emerge.

- *development methodology*

  The development methodology should be based on the principle of incremental growth of a system. Since the first version of the system should be a *usable version*, actual use of this first version is important! Prototyping in the sense of 'throw away' systems may be used for several parts of the system where extreme uncertainty exists. After a first version has been delivered, new versions can be agreed upon. These versions must have a fixed time span (not too long with respect to the user wishes). Together with the users an agreement must be reached on priorities, given the resource requirements for 'the list of possible additions' computed by the developers.

4. Working Method

- *common philosophy*

  It is very important that developers and users share a common 'philosophy' on DSS as a product, as well as on the design process.

- *user requirements*
  The future user often does not have a clear idea, or no idea at all, what his future tool should be like. This is because usually he has no knowledge of technical and functional possibilities with information systems. The user should be given at least some knowledge of functional possibilities with information systems. A way of doing this is to let him study a number of systems that (a) resemble his own planning/decision situation, and (b) exhibit an interesting man-machine interface and/or functions. Working with graphic illustrations of the planner's future tool, will have better chances of receiving sufficient attention than written functional descriptions.
- *domain knowledge*
  Usually, the developers have no domain knowledge when they start working on a project. It is crucial that they obtain this knowledge, but especially for DSS this can be a difficult task. The developers as well as the users should take into account that this can be a time consuming activity, and much rechecking is required.
- *idealized design*
  Users and designers should constantly keep the 'ideal design' in mind. This attitude stimulates having new ideas for a better design and makes them more conscious of the quality that is produced. New ideas and requirements that are agreed not to be an element of the next version of the system (because of project planning reasons), should be well documented and should serve as a basis for a future version of the system.
- *phases and scope*
  First, a global exploration of the problem area is needed. We call this a 'Definition Study' (cf. Turner et al. (1987)). When a specific direction for supporting the problem area has been chosen, a number of (DSS) projects may have been defined. For each of these projects a 'Project Plan' has to be developed. This plan should be based on a detailed process description. The plan should specify the project organization, the goals to be achieved by the project, the required functionality in global terms, the expected resources required and delivery date. It serves as a contract between user and developer.
  Where the definition study must have a broad scope, the concrete project plan must have a limited scope. Especially, since a first usable version of the system must be available fast, it may be wise to put off connections with other systems to (a) later version(s) of the DSS.

- *process description*
  The definition study includes a description of the information flows involved. An element of the documentation of the definition study must be a detailed process description of the planning *activities* of the planner. This includes activities that are not actual observable information flows.
- *when to start designing*
  One argument for starting to design as early as possible is that usually, a significant learning process for both user and designer emerges during the design. Also, when there is a high risk involved (for example, for the development of algorithms) and delivery time is important, one should start designing as early as possible. An argument for waiting with designing is that designers can collect more domain knowledge. A compromise is to start designing as soon as the developers 'feel' they have a clear view of an 'invariant' basis: the *key decisions and basic data.*
- *design framework*
  The description of a DSS in terms of scenarios and plans, and the functions that a DSS should fulfill (see section 2) provide a very useful framework for designing a DSS. Giving special attention to each of these elements assures that the most essential parts of the system are covered.
- *data entry and retrieval*
  The effort needed to design and build the Preparation component of a DSS should not be underestimated.
  (In our two cases it was severely underestimated, although the developers had experience with more administrative oriented systems!)
- *design documentation*
  There should be a good documentation of the design and the design process. For each development group meeting, minutes should be kept and dispersed directly after a meeting. The functional design of a DSS is often changed, therefore the documentation system should allow for changes with a minimum of effort. Also the reasons for changes should be documented (which is especially helpful in preventing 'cycling' in specifications).
- *models and algorithms*
  The design of (OR) models and algorithms must be documented. Especially in the case when the algorithm designer and programmer are not the same person, high standards for documentation are required. Even when they are the same person, it is important with respect to possible discontinuity in the design team.

When there is a separate programmer, he should be able to express a broader view than just programming the instructions in the functional design. If this is the case, he can act as a valuable sparring partner to the algorithm designer (especially with respect to implementation aspects).

- *product delivery*
  The delivery of a (new version of a) system should be carefully prepared by providing good training to the user and good service afterwards. The ideal situation is that the person providing service is located within the same building and continuously available.

5. Conditions and Resources

- *continuity*
  Continuity on the developer's side often is a problem. Preferably this should be guaranteed in advance as a part of the user-developer contract.
- *availability*
  On the user's side availability often is a problem. This should be guaranteed in advance as a part of the user-developer contract.
- *technical platform*
  The developers must have a clear overview of the technical possibilities, and advantages and disadvantages of the available tools and techniques. Without this, there is a risk of a wrong choice of technology and a risk of time loss due to aquiring the necessary knowledge.

6. Communication

- *importance*
  We see the development of a DSS as a social process, where the quality of the interaction between the people involved determines the quality of the eventual product and service delivered more than many other factors involved (e.g. the development methodology chosen). For DSS good communication is especially important because the domain knowledge is more complex than for more administrative oriented systems.
- *location*
  Geographical location can be an important factor in the quality of communication. Especially in the design and delivery phase, it can be very helpful to locate the developers at the users site. At the users' site, it is important to have meetings not disturbed by the current state of affairs. (Often, one or more planners have a responsibility that cannot be delegated and constantly receive new information and have to react on it.)

- *monitoring*
  Part of the project leader's tasks is to monitor the quality of communication and whether expectations on the user's side and the developer's side still match.
  At some points, it can be helpful to organize long brainstorm or discussion sessions to stimulate the establishment of a *strong shared* vision for the future.

7 Conclusions

What has been done

The contribution of this paper has three aspects:

- a framework to structure the design of a Decision Support System has been presented. How these ideas can be implemented is illustrated by CAPTAINS. It is my hope that this paper can act as a good example for OR practitioners and that it can contribute to the general discussion of the following questions:
  * when is a DSS appropriate ?
  * what should a DSS offer ?
  * how to implement a DSS ?
- a collection of ideas on the DSS *development process* is presented. Hopefully this will eventually lead to useful checklists for DSS designers.
- a novel approach to the strategic pilot manpower planning problem has been provided, with the potential of a competitive advantage in the airline industry.

The CAPTAINS system is fully operational for some time now, (Note: the first version has been released 10th of august 1989, and actual operational use started in May 1990) we are confident that it contributes to significant improvements in the quality of the planning by reaching both goals mentioned in section 5. This confidence is based on the planners' first reactions. Since the start the planners were enthousiastic about the representation, evaluation and generation functions, but at first they did not seem recognize the advantages of the manipulation function. Probably the latter judgement was caused by the fact that they have never worked with a system that provides more interaction than changing the input. Working with CAPTAINS for some time however, changed their opinion. In Verbeek (1991) an evaluation is given of the degree of appreciation by the users. Although there were some drawbacks too, the general opinion was very positive.

What was learned

Through CAPTAINS we learned how vital all four described functions of a DSS are for a successful implementation. In this approach it is important to recognize the priorities of the planner with respect to the four functions mentioned, and to determine development priorities together. The most important succes factor however, seems to be a close cooperation with the planner and the will and ability to concentrate contineously on the question " *What is needed by and convenient for the planner ?*".

Concerning the development process of a DSS we described our ideas in the previous section.

Future Research

It has been argued by several authors that established methods for developing Information Systems in general are inadequate for developing DSS. This is confirmed by our own experience. Eventually, we want to establish a successful development method for building DSS. Because we have chosen a case study approach, we are conscious that the conclusions we obtained from our case studies can strictly speaking only be claimed to hold for the *specific cases* studied. However, we do agree with Johansson (1980) when he says:

> *I don't like the idea of asserting that every decision situation is unique, and that therefore no generalizations are possible. A better and more optimistic view to my mind is the credo that even though some details are always different, there are communalities across sufficiently many cases ... so that some genral findings can shown to apply. ... I am forced to admit however that this is only a hypothesis of mine rather than an empirical finding that can be genralized.*

We see the process of establishing a successful development method for building DSS as follows:

1. first, *a collection* of case study experiences must be built up, large enough to avoid the problem of limited external validity;
2. based on the collection of case studies, a structured working method can be proposed on how to develop DSS; and
3. finally, the method must be tested by performing field tests.

Of course, this must be seen as an iterative process. Probably different approaches will be suited for different situations (e.g. group support versus personal support, or building tailored applications versus more general 'shells').

To make such an approach feasible, case studies must be broadly documented so that researchers with different research interests may use the material. Furthermore, because it is not feasible to cover all possible (future) research interests in publications, it is important that research networks give researchers the possibility to get access to additional information later on, e.g. for acquiring non-documented information or for allowing longitudinal studies. We think that networks such as the *Dutch Decision Support Research Group* and the *EURO Working Group on DSS* have an important role to play in trying to realize this ideal.

Concerning the discussion on the fundamental questions in DSS there is a need for more integration in the current research. It is important that researchers from the OR, the MIS and the AI community discuss *together* their development methodologies under the umbrella of DSS. In addition more attention has to be paid to the question of when to apply what, both in the functions an Information System should offer and the techniques that are applied.

Acknowledgements
The author is indebted to the other members of the CAPTAINS development team for sharing their experiences and creative ideas.

References

[1] Ackoff, R.L. (1960). "Unsuccessful Case Studies and Why", *Operations Research*, 8.

[2] Anthonisse, J.M. & J.K. Lenstra & M.W.P. Savelsbergh, (1988). "Behind the Screen: DSS from an OR Point of View", *Decision Support Systems*, Vol. 4.

[3] Benbasat, I. & A.S. Dexter, (1985)."An Experimental Evaluation of Graphical and Color Enhanced Presentation", *Management Science.*

[4] Bell, P.C. (1985). "Visual Interactive Modelling in Operational Research: Successes and Opportunities", *Journal of the Operational Research Society*, Vol. 36, No. 11.

[5] Chevrinais, H. & H. Thibault (1988). "GERONIMO: An Interactive Model for Smoothing a Crew Management Workload Curve", *Proceedings of the 28th Annual Symposium of the Airline Group of IFORS*, Cape Cod, USA.

[6] Espahbodi H. & R. Espahbodi (1984). "Predicting Failure in the Airline Industry with Financial Models", *Transportation Research A*, Vol. 18A, No. 5/6.

[7] Etschmaier, M.M. & D.F.X. Mathaisel (1985). "Airline Scheduling: An Overview", *Transportation Science*, 19.

[8] Gershkoff, I., (1989). "Opening Speech", *Symposium of the AGIFORS Crew Management Study Group of the Airline Group of IFORS*, Minneapolis.

[9] Van Hee, K.M. (1984). "Trends in Information Systems for Management", *Working paper, Technical University of Eindhoven*, Eindhoven, the Netherlands.

[10] Hobbs, B.F. (1985). "Experiments in MCDM and what we can learn from them", in: Y.Y. Haimes & V. Chankong, "*Decsion Making with Multiple Objectives*", Springer Verlag.

[11] Hofton, A.H. (1984). "Forecasting in Air Transport - a Critical Review of the Techniques Available", *Paper No. 1073 Department of Air Transport, College of Aeronautics Cranfield*, presented at the Symposium on "Planning Airline Fleet Composition", at RAcS, january 1983.

[12] Johansson, J.K. (1980). "Case studies, generalizations, and degrees of freedom in managerial research: possibilities and pitfalls", discussion paper, Institute of International Business, Stockholm School of Ecenomics, Stockholm, May 1980.

[13] Johanson, C. (1982). "Graphic Crew Pairing Design", paper presented at the *The International Airlines Operations Planning Symposium*, Montreal.

[14] Keen, P.G.W. (1981). "Decision Support Systems- Lessons for the 80's", *DSS-81 Transactions* (June).

[15] Keen, P.G.W. (1986). "Decision Support Systems: the next Decade", in: E.R. Mc Lean & H.G. Sol (eds.) "*Decision Support Systems: a Decade in Perspective*", North Holland, Amsterdam.

[16] Pean, M. & E. Odier (1987). "CHEOPS and MOHICAN, two Interactive Models on Microcomputer", *Proceedings of the 27th Annual AGIFORS Symposium*, Sydney.

[17] Roy, B. (1971). "Problems and Methods with Multiple Objective Functions", *Mathematical Programming*, 1.

[18] Shepardson, F. (1985). "Modelling the Bus Crew Scheduling Problem", *Computer Scheduling of Public Transport*, 2.

[19] Sprague, R.H. Jr. (1987). "DSS in Context", *Decision Support Systems*, Vol. 3, No. 3.

[20] Turban, E. (1988). "*Decision Support Systems and Expert Systems*", Mc Millan Publishing Company Inc., New York.

[21] Turner, W.S. et al. (1987), "SDM: System Development Methodology", North Holland/PANDATA, Amsterdam/Rijswijk, completely revised version.

[22] Van der Kuilen, N. (1989), "Approaches based on Transition Probabilities for the Pilot Manpower Planning Problem", (dutch), *Master Thesis OR, Faculty of Economics*, Erasmus University, Rotterdam.

[23] Verbeek P.J. (1987). "Mixed Integer Formulations based on Individual Pilots", *Personal Notes Memores4*.

[24] Verbeek, P.J. & A.W.J. Kolen (1988). "A Network Flow Model for Pilot Manpower Planning at KLM", *Proceedings of the AGIFORS CMSG*, Copenhagen.

[25] Verbeek, P.J. (1988). "A Heuristic Concept Based on Seniority to Support Pilot Manpower Planning", *Proceedings of the 28th Annual AGIFORS Symposium*, Cape Cod, USA.

[26] Verbeek, P.J. (1991). "Learning About Decision Support Systems, two cases on Manpower Planning in an Airline", Phd. Thesis Erasmus University Rotterdam, Rotterdam, May 1991, also published with Thesis Publishers, Amsterdam.

[27] Zarate, P. (1989). "An Interactive Support for the Elaboration of Specifications in DSS", paper presented at the *Sixth EURO Summer Institute*, Madeira, Portugal.

THE USE OF ADAPTIVITY AND SIMULATION IN PLANNING SUPPORT SYSTEMS

Alexander Verbraeck and Richard de Jong
Delft University of Technology
Department of Information Systems
P.O. Box 356
2600 AJ Delft, The Netherlands

ABSTRACT

1. Introduction

Planning is a difficult task, as well for human beings as for computers. In this paper we focus on one aspect of planning activities called *short term planning* or *sequencing and scheduling*. Sometimes, the term *operational planning* is also used. Here, we see sequencing and scheduling as a part of operational planning.

In a large number of organizations, scheduling is still done manually, with results that are far from optimal. Providing the planner with suitable computer hardware and software has proved to be a difficult task. Smith *et al.* (1986) describe it as follows for production scheduling "Perhaps the single most significant obstacle to improved factory performance is the complexity associated with constructing and maintaining good production schedules. ... Existing computer–based techniques for production scheduling are capable of incorporating only a small fraction of this scheduling knowledge and, as a result, typically produce schedules that bear little resemblance to the actual state of the factory".

Due to the fast industrialization and the growing internationalization, new machines and techniques are being introduced on the production floor in a rapid pace. Other aspects of the organizations are changing very fast as well. The growing complexity of machinery and factories, the increasing demand for "Just In Time" production and delivery, the objective of small inventories, and the fast changes in production processes and order mix make that scheduling is becoming a very difficult task.

At the Department of Information Systems of Delft University of Technology, two research projects are dealing with the development of scheduling support systems that can operate in a dynamic environment. The first project deals with the construction of a production planning environment that uses a simulation model of the production process to gain insight into the dynamic aspects of the schedule, and two feed–back cycles to update the scheduling rules and the simulation model parameters. In the second project, a vehicle routing and scheduling support system is being developed. To ensure punctual departures and arrivals, a "trip data analyzer" and a "trip execution simulator" are used in a feedback connection between trip execution and trip planning. Both systems will be described in the following sections.

2. A Support Environment for Production Scheduling

Implementing a system for production scheduling is not an easy task. A number of problems arise when building such a system:

- The information systems expert has only a limited insight in the production processes that are to be scheduled by the planner. Important functions or decision objects are easily forgotten.
- It is very difficult for the information systems expert to guess whether the planner uses the "right" or optimal methods. It is also difficult to predict whether other methods will give better results or not.
- The decision rules of the planner are very hard to get. A lot of planners can only answer most questions on a low abstraction level using examples of their daily work instead of the structures the IS–designer is interested in.
- Designing the user interface for a planning system is a very difficult problem. How do we guarantee that the interface gives the planner enough insight into the plan and the planning process.
- Most planners who are planning manually work with large plan–boards. Compared to that, a computer screen can only contain a small amount of information.
- In most cases there are communication problems between the information systems designer and the planner: The planner finds it difficult to present his problems and data on the abstraction level the information engineer asks for. The information engineer has troubles with the generalization of the remarks and exceptions the planner confronts him with.
- Current CASE–tools and schemes do not offer enough power and flexibility to help to describe a dynamic and complex planning process.

Therefore, we suggest a number of steps for designing and building a production planning system:

1. Analyze the tasks of the planner;
2. Analyze and enclose the relevant part of the production;
3. Build a simulation model of the production. Take care of verification and validation of the model. Show the model (if possible with animation) to the planner;
4. Build the production planning system using a number of pre–formed modules;
5. Use the system with continuous adaptation of the decision models and the simulation model. Even when you start with an empty rule–base the system will "learn" from the feedback of the planner and the production.

In a case at a tin–can company, the tasks of a production planner have been analyzed using a task description technique as described by Bots (1989). The proposed information system is suited for the support of most relevant tasks of the production planner. When building a scheduling system, it is necessary to make a choice between processing by hand and processing by the computer on each task of the production planner. Some tasks need computing power, and these can be more easily carried out by the computer, other tasks require creativity or insight in new and unknown concepts, and can better be done by hand. Of course, support of manual processes by the information system is always possible.

The suggested architecture for the environment consists of various parts (see figure 1).

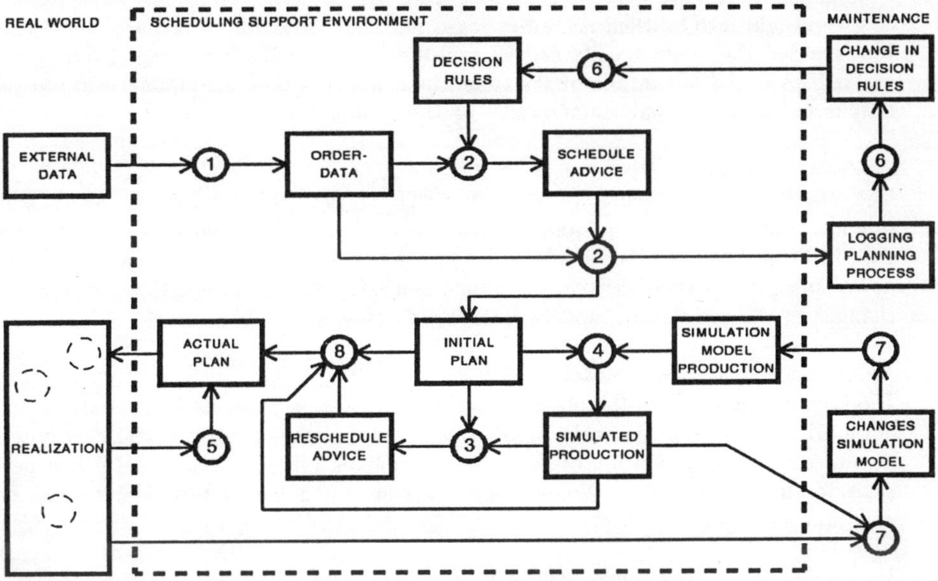

Figure 1. Architecture of the Scheduling Support Environment

The following eight modules are the most important components of the system (Verbraeck, 1990).

1. *Administrative support*
The planner has a number of administrative tasks: order handling, report generation, keeping track of customers and products. Support of these functions provides the input for the rest of the system automatically.

2. *Scheduling support*
A production planner has to make a schedule for the following period. First, an initial distribution of resources for a part of the orders is made. In a manual system the planner attaches and moves small cards along a plan–wall. The planner has limited insight into length, overlap or tuning of different orders. The system uses decision rules to present a planning advice to the planner and a simulation model of the production to calculate bottlenecks in possible places of the orders.

3. *Rescheduling support*
When all orders have been planned, the first version of the plan is ready. It is just a preliminary version of the plan, and not the optimal version. Once all orders have been scheduled, the planner can begin rescheduling until some of the criteria have been met (minimum time for readjusting machines, full use of expensive resources, etc.). It is possible to freeze different versions of the plan. If after rescheduling, the plan is worse than the previous version, the original variant can be used again.

4. *Simulation feedback*
The simulation model gives direct feedback to the user. Realistic disturbances of the production process are introduced. Sensitivity analysis is one of the techniques used

to give insight into bottlenecks, adjusting times and utilization of resources. The runs that created the worst results can be reproduced for analyzing. When building the system, an initial advantage of the simulation model is that the planner can use the output to validate a particular model of the production.

5. *Analysis of feedback from the production*
   One of the starting-points of this approach is that the production department provides feedback to the planner in order that the original plan can be compared with it. Production results are applied in two ways. Firstly they are used to keep the actual plan up to date. Secondly, comparison of plan and production can lead to changes in the simulation model of the production.

6. *Maintenance of decision models*
   The suggestions given to the planner by the system are compared with the decisions. Both differences and similarities are saved with all relevant decision attributes. Periodically an accumulation of decision situations is analyzed and the effect of new decision rules is measured. When using the simulation model this analysis can be done automatically.

7. *Maintenance of simulation model*
   The simulation model of the production is being validated continuously: all feed-back from the production is used to adjust the parameters in the model. This can be done either automatically or by hand. Changes in production methods are shown to the planner indirectly by simulating a new plan.

8. *Control of the production department*
   The plan is produced in such a way that the production department can use it. If necessary, comments can be added to the plan.

When all orders for a certain time-period are scheduled, an initial plan is created. As the initial plan is in fact a simulation of the expected production, a number of simulation runs are executed to check the feasibility of the plan and to identify bottlenecks. The planner can reschedule orders using the simulation output. After some iterations a final plan will be ready. The final schedule will be presented to the production for realization. Feed-back from the production is used to keep the plan up to date. When necessary, rescheduling can take place after severe disturbances.
Comparison of simulated production plan and actual production following the same plan, can lead to changes in the parameters of the simulation model. For some parameters, like lead time, number and length of disturbances and actual time of processing, it is possible to provide changes automatically.

3. A Vehicle Routing and Scheduling Support System

In spite of the importance of strict time windows in vehicle routing and scheduling, little attention is paid to punctuality of departures and arrivals. In most vehicle routing and scheduling problems, time windows demarcate an interval in which a customer has to be visited. If the time window may not be violated, it will be called *strict*. There are some trip planning systems that are able to handle strict time windows. However, the fact that the trip *plan* meets the requirements does not automatically hold for trip *execution* as well.

The trip planning problem has a number of important characteristics:

1. The planner has administrative tasks. Before, during, and after the actual planning task, a large number of administrative tasks are being performed. These tasks ensure that the data to make and change the schedule is available in time, and that information that is gathered during scheduling, trip execution, and comparison between plan and realization is reported to others within the organization. A trip planning system should support these administrative tasks to guarantee that the information system has the necessary information on time.

2. The planner has detailed knowledge about the problem domain. In most cases, the planner uses experience and a lot of not–formalizable rules to create the plan. This detailed knowledge cannot be elicited completely. Therefore, the planning system should be interactive.

3. The problem domain structure changes over time. New roads, congestion changes, and other loading or unloading sequences require an adjustment of planning strategies and of the trip execution model. Both the planning rules and the problem domain model should be easy to adapt.

4. The problem domain contains many stochastic elements. Driving style, busy roads, waiting times, etc. all attribute to uncertainties in trip execution, and to the possibility that strict time windows are violated. The consequences of the stochastic nature of reality on trip execution should be made explicit in the planning process.

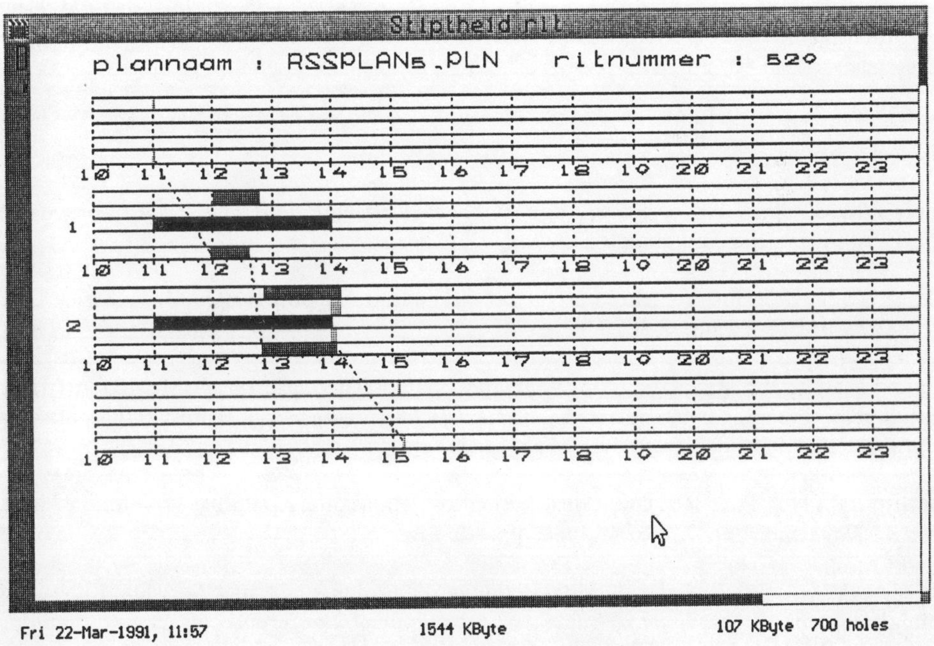

Figure 2. Output from the trip execution simulator.

Using the above characteristics of the planning process, and the adaptive feedback concepts of Passino and Antsaklis (1989), a trip planning and trip execution environment has been developed. In *adaptive feedback*, execution results are analyzed afterwards, and using the analysis outcomes, adaptations to the planning environment are made. The adaptations can lead to changes of the objectives of the planner or to changes of the trip execution model.

The support environment that has been developed contains a *trip data analyzer* and a *trip execution simulator*. Both tools are part of the adaptive feedback connection between trip execution and trip planning. The trip plan is generated by an *interactive trip planner*. An example of the output from the trip execution simulator is shown in figure 2. The components of the system are described in more detail in de Jong and Sol (1990).

4. Conclusions

One of the largest problems a planner is facing, is the lack of insight in the effects of decisions on schedule efficiency. First results of these research projects show, that in comparison with manual planning, insight is increased when using simulation techniques to evaluate a schedule. The dynamic aspects of the schedule, like for instance the effects of stochastic influences, can be clarified using simulation output.

We expect that the adaptive components of the system will solve part of the other planning problems planning like changes in model parameters, in model structure, and in the requirements of management. Current research is focusing on gathering information on the effectiveness of both adaptation cycles in the scheduling support systems.

5. References

Bots, P.W.G., *An Environment to Support Problem Solving*, PhD Thesis, Delft University of Technology, the Netherlands, 1989.

Jong, R. de, H.G. Sol, Vehicle Routing and Scheduling Support: Coping with Strict Time Windows. In: *Proceedings ICIS* 1990.

Passino, K.M., P.J. Antsaklis, A System and Control Theoretic Perspective on Artificial Intelligence Planning Systems. In: *Applied Artificial Intelligence* 3, Hemisphere Publishing Corporation, 1989, pp. 1–32.

Smith, S.F., M.S. Fox, P.S. Ow, Constructing and Maintaining Detailed Production Plans. In: *AI Magazine*, Vol. 7, No. 4, 1986, pp. 45–61.

Verbraeck, A., Adaptive Production Planning Environments Using Decision Rules and Simulation. In: *Proceedings of the First International Conference on Expert Planning Systems*, Brighton, U.K., 27–29 June, 1990, IEE Conference Publication Number 322, London, 1990, pp. 147–151.

SCHEDULING WITH TIME WINDOWS AND SOLUTION SET RESTRICTION

Wolfgang S. Wittig
Technische Hochschule Leipzig, Fachbereich Mathematik und Informatik
Karl-Liebknecht-Str. 132, PF 66, O-7030 Leipzig

1. Introduction

Let us consider special assignment problems, where a set A of tasks (e.g. transport tasks) and a set B of recources (e.g. vehicles, trucks or trains) are given. The tasks will be realized in such a way that for each task A_i a vehicle B_j from the set B is choosen. This defines a homomorphism from A into B :

$$A = \{A_1, A_2, \ldots, A_p\}, \quad B = \{B_1, B_2, \ldots, B_q\}, \quad A \dashrightarrow B.$$

For some problem classes like scheduling problems, routing problems, travelling salesman problems, job-shop problems and configuration problems the basic task can be formulated as an assignment problem with additional constraints and conventions. Each homomorphism A ---> B which satifies these constraints is called a solution or plan of the given problem.

The number of feasible solutions of the assignment problem is q^p if there are no other conditions or conventions restricting this number. In most practical problems the given constraints do not allow to determine the number of feasible solutions previously, and this number can vary between its extremal values, from 0 to q^p.
Optimal solutions of the given problem are defined with respect to goal functions. For the solution of the problem diverse exact or heuristic algorithms are used to determine several optimal or suboptimal plans.

Another problem which is dealt in the paper is to restrict the number of efficient solutions in multicriteria optimization. In case of Pareto optimality with more than 3 goals the number of non-dominated solutions may not be significantly smaller than the number of all feasible solutions. Some ideas are discussed to restrict the set of Pareto optimal solutions of a certain subset from which one can choose a solution to employ in an interactive way.

2. Scheduling as an Assignment Problem

In this paper distribution systems containing m dispatching points and n receiving points will be considered. The distances between dispatching and receiving points are given and also the transport times and returning times at all routes. The control aim is to determine a scheduling plan satisfying the demands of all given transport tasks and which is optimal with respect to the given goal functions.

A constructive algorithm for determination of solutions of the distribution system is to assign a truck to the first transport task, after that to assign this truck or another truck to the second transport task etc.. The trucks are enumerated in the sequence of their usage.

A solution is called feasible if it contains an assignment of exactly one truck to each task.

Without restrictions the number of possible assignments in such a distribution system with p transport tasks and q trucks is given by

$$s_{p,q} = \sum_{k=1}^{\min(p,q)} s_p(k) .$$

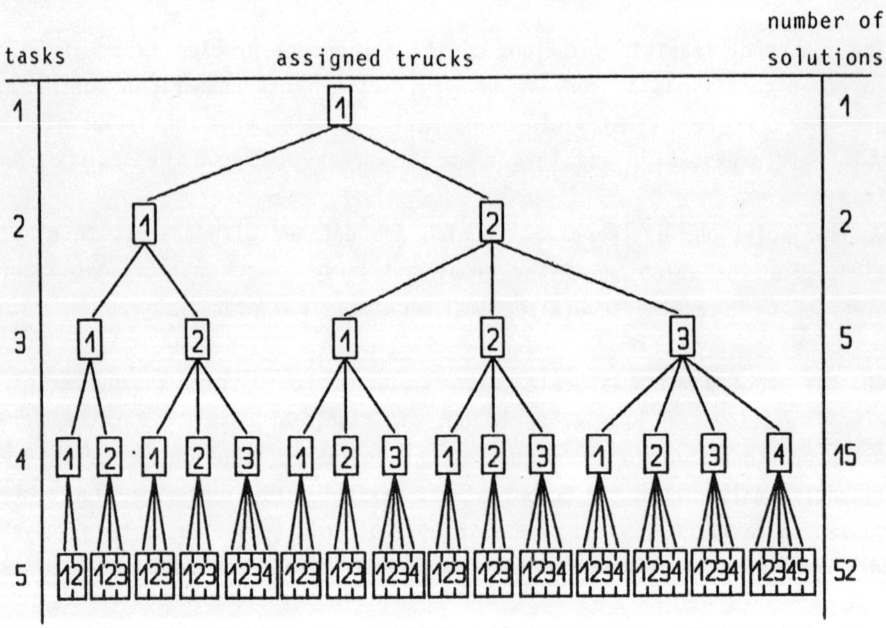

Fig. 1: Assignment tree for a system without further constraints

There $s_i(k)$ denotes the number of solutions containing the first i tasks where precisely k trucks are used, where

$$s_i(1) = s_i(i) = 1 \qquad i = 1, 2, 3, \ldots$$
$$s_i(k) = s_{i-1}(k-1) + k\, s_{i-1}(k)\ , \qquad 1 < k < i.$$

The assignment tree of a system with 5 tasks is shown in fig. 1, where the number of the truck assigned to the corresponding task is put in the squares. A table with the numbers of possible assignments is given in [2].

3. Scheduling with Time Windows, 1 Dispatching Point

Usually the receivers order transport tasks for a time period like a day or a week . The order information consists of

- the name or number of the receiver ordering this task,
- a list of products ordered,
- arrival time window $[c_i, d_i]$ or time point d_i,
- special information.

In this paper the ordered products are unimportant, and we assume that time points can be enlarged to time windows. Putting the tasks in order for a system with only 1 transport line it is sufficient to consider the end points of the arrival time windows.

In case of n receivers the transport time from the dispatching point to the receivers is given, and thus the departure time windows can be calculated. The sequence of the end points of the departure time windows is used to order the transport tasks, and in this way we get a list with the following entries:

$[a_i, b_i]$ departure time window of task i,
h_i transport time of task i to the receiver,
g_i transport plus returning time of task i.

In the solution tree a solution is branched to new ones by assigning the next task i. This can be done by using the constructive algorithm described above, but only those trucks can be assigned to a further task which are returned to the dispatching point in time. Otherwise the next truck gets this task as its first journey.

There are different strategies, for example:

(a) assign all trucks which are returned before time point b_i and furthermore the next truck which is unused till now (as long as possible),

(b) assign the truck which is returned earliest before time point a_i, otherwise assign this truck if it is returned before b_i, and a next truck which is unused till now (as long as possible),

(c) assign the truck which is returned earliest before time point b_i, otherwise assign a next truck which is unused till now.

Goals in such 1-n-systems (with 1 dispatcher, n receivers) may be, e.g.:

- minimization of the number of trucks required,
- maximization of the minimal time reserve,
- minimization of the sum of waiting times,
- minimization of the maximal number of tasks per truck.

The strategy (c) is only useful to optimize the first goal, and the strategy (b) can not be applied when goals like the fourth arise.

The solution tree for an example of a distribution system containing 5 tasks and 4 trucks with time windows is shown in fig. 2. For every solution the number of the truck assigned to the corresponding task and the values of two goals (number of trucks required, minimum of time reserve) are put in the squares. The information about a solution does not only consist of the goal values but also of information about the return time points of all trucks used, etc.

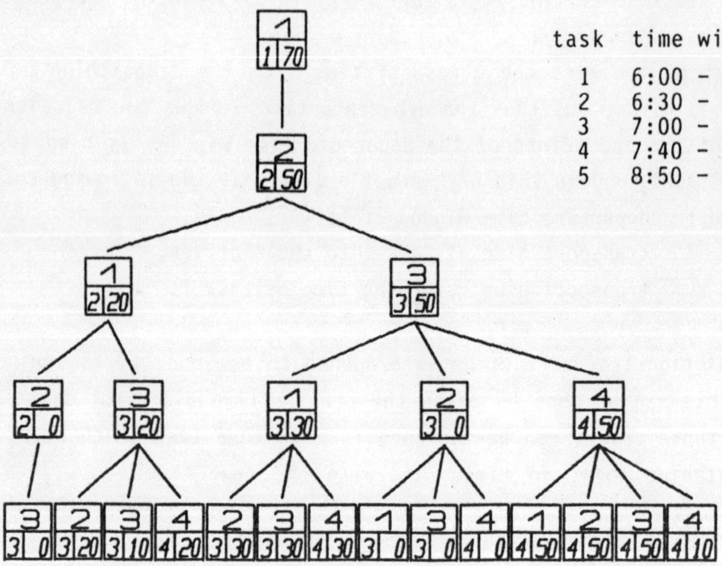

task	time window	g_i
1	6:00 - 7:10	120
2	6:30 - 7:20	120
3	7:00 - 8:20	120
4	7:40 - 8:30	120
5	8:50 - 9:50	120

Fig. 2: Assignment tree for a system with time windows

Some examples are solved with different numbers of tasks, various time windows and with different numbers of trucks by using the strategies (a), (b), (c). The numbers of calculated solutions (c.s., nodes of the assignment tree) and of feasible solutions (f.s., nodes in the last assignment level) are given in the following table.

example	tasks	trucks	(a): c.s.	f.s.	(b): c.s.	f.s.	(c): c.s.	f.s.
1	5	4	23	14	12	4	5	1
2	5	4	30	18	12	4	5	1
3	8	4	247	150	37	11	8	1
4	8	5	138	74	34	10	8	1
5	14	6	295	16	91	3	14	1
6	20	7	410	260	218	35	20	1
7	40	11			537	91	40	1

4. Scheduling with Time Windows, m Dispatching Points

Assignments for m-n-systems (with m dispatchers, n receivers) can be realized in a similar way.

In this case the order information consists of

- the name or number of the receiver ordering this task,
- a list of products ordered,
- the name or number of the dispatching point,
- arrival time window $[c_i, d_i]$,
- special information.

If the transport time from the given dispatching points to the receivers is known, the departure time windows $[a_i, b_i]$ can be calculated in a similar way as it is described above, but the return of the truck to the point of departure is not necessary.

If the transport tasks are sorted according to the end point of the departure time windows we will get a list with the following entries:

$[a_i, b_i]$ departure time window of task i,

h_i transport time from the dispatcher to the receiver.

The information about a solution which is important for branching consists of the arrival time points of each truck at the last receivers instead of the return time points to a dispatcher which have been used in section 3.

All possible return time points of a truck to the dispatcher of task i have to be calculated to decide which trucks may be assigned to the task i. The above outlined strategies and also other strategies may be used.

Additional goals in such m-n-systems may be, e.g.:

- minimization of the sum of transport and return distances,
- minimization of the maximal number of points visited per truck.

5. Scheduling with a Set of Given Drives

In distribution systems with transport by railway the scheduling has to be done for trains instead for trucks. Furthermore, a set of possible routes is given. For a special route the departure place and arrival place, and the departure and arrival time points are given [1].

A task may be transported from the dispatcher to the receiver by using only one of these routes, and further we demand that the arrival time point is within the arrival time window of the task. To realize the next task a train must also use one of the routes to return to the dispatching places of this task.

It is clear that a route can be used by one train only, but most many of the given routes are not applied.

To assign a train to a task at first the possible transport route from the dispatcher to the receiver of the task have to be determined and second all trains are to find which may return from their actual place to this dispatching place using one of the routes.

The most significant goals in this class of scheduling problems will be:

- minimization of the sum of transport and return distances,
- maximization of the minimal time reserve,

but some of the following goals may also be considered:

- minimization of the number of trains required,
- minimization of the sum of waiting times,
- minimization of the maximal number of visited points per train,
- minimization of the maximal number of tasks per train.

6. Scheduling with Knowledge Based Conditions

Additional constraints in scheduling may be, e.g.:

- restrictions of tasks arriving per day to a receiver,
- restrictions of tasks departing per day from a dispatcher,
- restrictions of realizable routes in a subset of routes,
- restrictions based on special task information.

Some kinds of such constraints in the case of railway oriented scheduling are considered in [1].
If no feasible solutions or only unsatisfactory plans are obtained it is possible to omit some of the constraints.

It follows that a scheduling model consists of the parts:

- constraints which have to be satisfied absolutly,
- goal functions to decide which plans are optimal or should be included into the set of efficient solutions,
- additional evaluation functions as a help for an interactive selection of plans from the set of efficient solutions,
- wishes as constraints or goals which are renunciable.

Depending on the evaluation and on the number of feasible solutions changes in the modelling are possible in that way, that a constraint becomes a goal or an evaluation function, a goal may be transformed to a constraint etc.
Actually, such changes are realized interactively, but in the future knowledge based systems for modelling will be performed which are controlled by goals and results.

7. Solution Set Restriction

The decision about the optimality of a plan is simple in the case of only one goal. In case of more than one goal function, usually a hierarchy of the goals, a linear combination of the goals or the principle of Pareto optimality are used.
All these possibilities are not satisfactory when users of the scheduling system would also like to know plans in the neighbourhood of optimal plans to get a set of suboptimal solutions, from which a user can choose a plan using additional criteria, too.

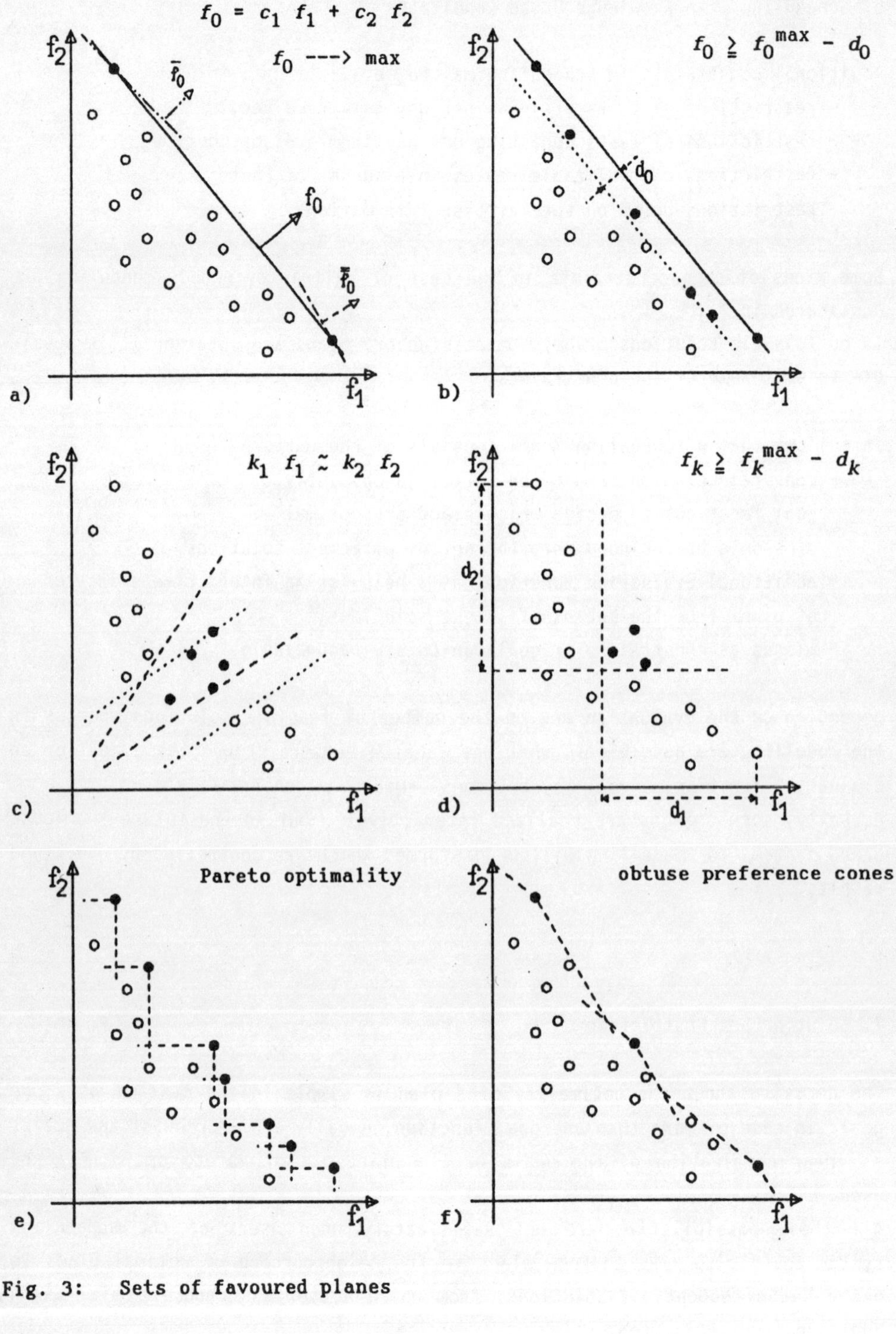

Fig. 3: Sets of favoured planes

In the case of a linear combination of the goal function such sets of suboptimal solutions may be the following:

- optimal solutions for weights which are changed by small pertubations (see fig. 3.a),
- solutions which are at most d_0 worse than the optimal solution (fig. 3.b).

Other sets of favoured plans may be found by

- given relations between the goals (fig. 3.c),
- solutions which are at most d_k worse than the optimal values f_k (fig. 3.d).

In multicriteria optimization such sets may be found using

- Pareto optimal solutions (fig. 3.e),
- Pareto optimal solutions in the case of obtuse preference cones (fig. 3.f).

In fig. 3 these possibilities are described for two goal functions.

If the so generalized set of favoured plans includes a lot of solutions (e.g. more than 20) it is necessary to reduce this number.
Using obtuse cones as a compromise between a linear combination of all goals and the Pareto optimality is one of several possibilities to reduce the solution set.

If the number of favoured solutions exceeds a given bound the user may decide interactively which solutions have to be dropped from the solution set. This way allows to change automatically the weights, the distances or the directions for the computation of suboptimal plans for each situation described in fig. 3. A short description of this reduction approach is given in [2].

The goal values as well as their graphical representation should be a help for the user in this decisiion process.
An example with 18 planes is given in the following table:

Nr.	1	2	3	4	5	6	7	8	9	10	11	12	13	14	15	16	17	18
f_1	10	20	20	30	45	70	35	35	100	25	65	120	90	90	25	55	75	65
f_2	115	135	75	80	40	55	105	60	25	50	70	15	10	35	95	60	30	45
f_3	90	125	95	85	55	65	15	45	45	45	60	60	90	75	75	60	105	75
A		+				+	+		+		+	+		+				
B		+	+	+		+	+		+		+	+	+	+	+		+	+

7 of these planes (39 %) are Pareto optimal if only the goals f_1 and f_2 are considered (row A, see also fig. 3), using the 3 goals f_2, f_3, f_1 72 % of the given planes are Pareto optimal (row B, see also fig. 4).

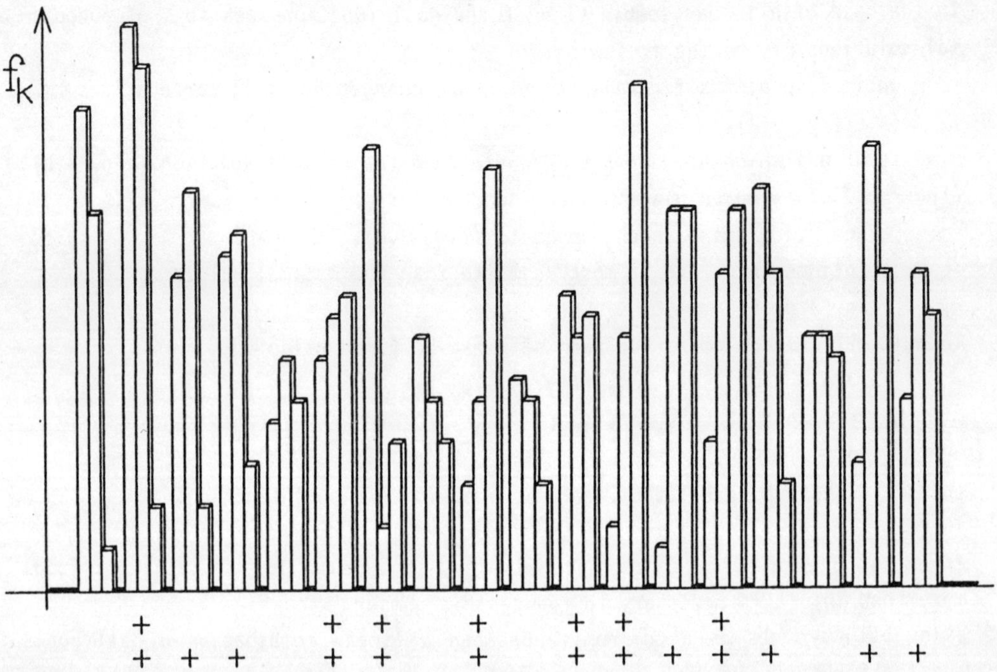

Fig. 4: Graphical representation of solutions, 3 goals

8. Controlled Deep Search

For reducing the number of planes to be calculated it is important to find rapidly some suboptimal solutions which allow to bound the assignment tree.

A deep search with backtracking controlled by a linear combination of goal functions and evaluation functions, too, is a first idea, which we discuss for the example shown in fig. 2.

The goal functions f_1 and f_2 which denote

f_1 ... number of trucks used,

f_2 ... minimum of reserve time

are considered.

To branch a solution node in the assignment tree strategy (a) is applied, and to bound the assignment tree the usual Pareto optimality based on f_1 and f_2 is used.

A preference sequence of the points to be branched may be performed, e.g., by

a) f_1 ---> minimum,

b) $f_1 - 0.1 f_2$ ---> minimum,

c) $f_1 - 0.04 f_2$ ---> minimum,

d) $f_1 - 0.04 f_2 - 2i$ ---> minimum,

where i is the number of tasks which have already got an assignment.

The resulting assignment trees using the preference functions a) and b) are shown in fig. 5, where the numbers denote the computing sequence. The assignment trees c) and d) differ from b) only in an exchange of two branches.

The points at the ends of the branching lines are characterized by following signs:

- ✱ Pareto optimal solutions
- ⊀ later dominated solutions
- – at once dominated solutions
- ⋉ bounded branches
- + solutions not to be computed

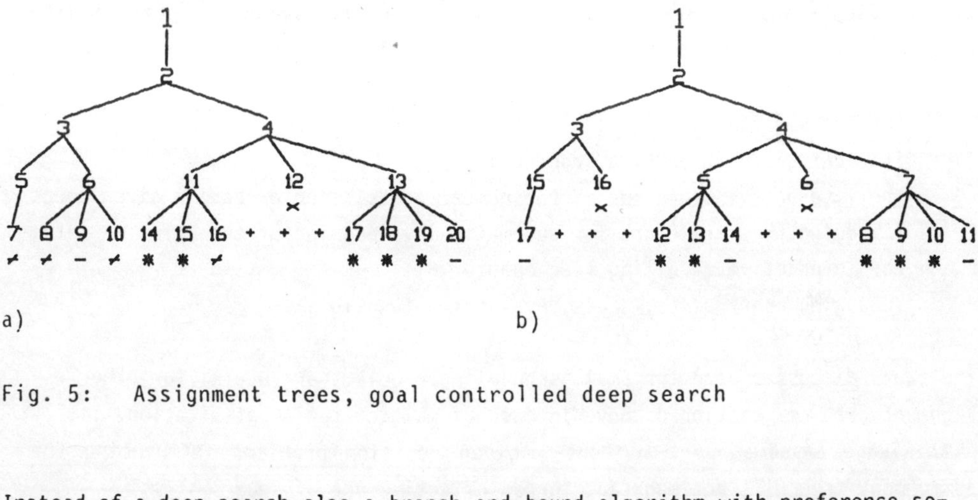

a) b)

Fig. 5: Assignment trees, goal controlled deep search

Instead of a deep search also a branch and bound algorithm with preference sequences is realizable where a deep search can be supported by including the assign level number i into the preference function as it was done in case d), and this idea seems to offer more flexibility.

In fig. 6 the resulting assignment trees for the preference functions a) and d) are shown. The assignment trees do not differ in the form but only in the branching numbers in comparison to fig. 5.
Significant differences will occur for larger examples.

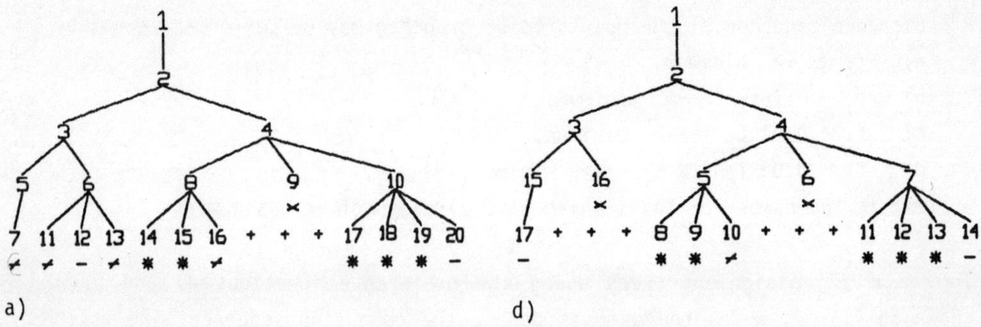

Fig. 6: Assignment trees, branch and bound algorithm

9. Conclusions

In the paper special assignment problems are considered. Using a goal controlled deep search or branch and bound algorithm for the construction of the assignment tree, the number of solutions to be calculated and the number of efficient solutions of the assignment problem depend on the following facts:

- the choosen combination of weights in the preference function (to control the branching sequence),
- the interactive decisions if the number of solution exceeds a given bound (changing the parameters for automatically reducing of the solution set),
- the interactive modelling (see chapter 6) (changing constraints, goals, evaluation functions).

The ideas discussed here for small scheduling problems are useful for other assignment problems mentioned above in case of multicriteria optimization, too. A knowledge based support for the 3 given decision problems influencing the assignment tree will be important for an effective use of such systems.

References:

[1] W.S.Wittig: A Decision Support System with Knowledge Based Components for Control of a Production Transportation Line in Civil Engineering. 14th IFIP Conference on System Modelling and Optimization, Preprints, Wissensch. Berichte TH Leipzig 1989/5, pp.114-115

[2] W.S.Wittig: Fahrplanerzeugung mit wissensbasierter Begrenzung der Lösungsmengen. Wissensch. Zeitschrift TH Leipzig 15 (1991) 1/2, pp.103-114

Lecture Notes in Control and Information Sciences

Edited by M. Thoma and A. Wyner

Lecture Notes in Control and Information Sciences

Edited by M. Thoma and A. Wyner

Vol. 156: R. P. Hämäläinen, H. K. Ehtamo (Eds.)
Differential Games –
Developments in Modelling and Computation
Proceedings of the Fourth International Symposium
on Differential Games and Applications
August 9-10, 1990, Helsinki University of Technology,
Finland
XIII, 292 pages. 1991

Vol. 157: R. P. Hämäläinen, H. K. Ehtamo (Eds.)
Dynamic Games in Economic Analysis
Proceedings of the Fourth International Symposium
on Differential Games and Applications
August 9-10, 1990, Helsinki University of Technology,
Finland
XIII, 311 pages. 1991

Vol. 158: K. Warwick, M. Kárný,
A. Halousková (Eds.)
Advanced Methods in Adaptive Control
for Industrial Applications
X, 331 pages. 1991

Vol. 159: X. Li, J. Yong (Eds.)
Control Theory of Distributed Parameter Systems
and Applications
Proceedings of the IFIP WG 7.2 Working Conference,
Shanghai, China, May 6–9, 1990
VIII, 219 pages. 1991

Vol. 160: P. V. Kokotović (Ed.)
Foundations of Adaptive Control
IX, 525 pages. 1991

Vol. 161: L. Gerencsér, P. E. Caines (Eds.)
Topics in Stochastic Systems:
Modelling, Estimation and Adaptive Control
IV, 401 pages, 1991

Vol. 162: C. Canudas de Wit (Ed.)
Advanced Robot Control
IX, 314 pages, 1991

Vol. 163: V. L. Mehrmann
The Autonomous Linear Quadratic
Control Problem
Theory and Numerical Solution
VI, 177 pages, 1991

Vol. 164: I. Lasiecka, R. Triggiani
Differential and Algebraic Riccati Equations
with Application to Boundary/Point
Control Problems: Continuous Theory
and Approximation Theory
XI, 160 pages, 1991

Vol. 165: G. Jacob, F. Lamnabhi-Lagarrigue (Eds.)
Algebraic Computing in Control
Proceedings of the First European Conference
Paris, March 13–15, 1991
IX, 385 pages. 1991

Vol. 166: L. L. M. van der Wegen
Local Disturbance Decoupling
with Stability for Nonlinear Systems
V, 135 pages, 1991

Vol. 167: M. Rao
Integrated System for Intelligent Control
VIII, 133 pages. 1992

Vol. 168: P. Dorato, L. Fortuna, G. Muscato
Robust Control for Unstructured Perturbations –
An Introduction
VI, 117 pages. 1992

Vol. 169: V. M. Kuntzevich, M. Lychak
Guaranteed Estimates, Adaptation
and Robustness in Control Systems
IV, 209 pages. 1992

Vol. 170: J. M. Skowronski, H. Flashner,
R. S. Guttalu (Eds.)
Mechanics and Control
Proceedings of the 4th Workshop
on Control Mechanics, January 21–23, 1991
University of Southern California, USA
IV, 301 pages. 1992

Vol. 171: P. Stefanidis, A. P. Papliński,
M. J. Gibbard
Numerical Operations with Polynomial Matrices
Application to Multi-Variable Dynamic
Compensator Design
VIII, 205 pages. 1992

Vol. 172: H. Tolle, E. Ersü
Neurocontrol
Learning Control Systems
Inspired by Neuronal Architectures
and Human Problem Solving Strategies
X, 211 pages. 1992

Vol. 173: W. Krabs
On Moment Theory and Controllability
of One-Dimensional Vibrating
Systems and Heating Processes
VII, 174 pages. 1992